T0323042

Democracy Under Siege?

Volumes of a Collaborative Research Programme
Among Election Study Teams from Around the World

Series editors: Hans-Dieter Klingemann and Ian McAllister

The Comparative Study of Electoral Systems (CSES) is a collaborative programme of research among election study teams from around the world. Participating countries include a common module of survey questions in their post-election studies. The resulting data are deposited along with voting, demographic, district, and macro variables. The studies are then merged into a single, free, public dataset for use in comparative study and cross-level analysis.

The set of volumes in this series is based on these CSES modules, and the volumes address the key theoretical issues and empirical debates in the study of elections and representative democracy. Some of the volumes will be organized around the theoretical issues raised by a particular module, while others will be thematic in their focus. Taken together, these volumes will provide a rigorous and ongoing contribution to understanding the expansion and consolidation of democracy in the twenty-first century.

COMPARATIVE STUDY *of* ELECTORAL SYSTEMS

Further information on CSES activities can be obtained from:

CSES Secretariat
Center for Political Studies
Institute for Social Research
The University of Michigan
426 Thompson Street
Ann Arbor, Michigan 481042321
USA

CSES web site: http://www.cses.org

Democracy Under Siege?

Parties, Voters, and Elections
After the Great Recession

Timothy Hellwig, Yesola Kweon, and Jack Vowles

OXFORD
UNIVERSITY PRESS

OXFORD
UNIVERSITY PRESS

Great Clarendon Street, Oxford, OX2 6DP,
United Kingdom

Oxford University Press is a department of the University of Oxford.
It furthers the University's objective of excellence in research, scholarship,
and education by publishing worldwide. Oxford is a registered trade mark of
Oxford University Press in the UK and in certain other countries

© Timothy Hellwig, Yesola Kweon, and Jack Vowles 2020

The moral rights of the authors have been asserted

First Edition published in 2020

Impression: 3

Published in the United States of America by Oxford University Press
198 Madison Avenue, New York, NY 10016, United States of America

British Library Cataloguing in Publication Data
Data available

Library of Congress Control Number: 2020937729

ISBN 978-0-19-884620-8

Printed and bound in Great Britain by
Clays Ltd, Elcograf S.p.A.

Links to third party websites are provided by Oxford in good faith and
for information only. Oxford disclaims any responsibility for the materials
contained in any third party website referenced in this work.

Series Editors' Preface

Democracy—its past, present and, most importantly, its future—is one of the foremost preoccupations of the twenty-first century. The rise of populism and the far right in Europe, the election of Donald Trump in the United States, and the Brexit debate in the United Kingdom, have all provided a greater incentive for scholars and practitioners to understand the dynamics of public opinion towards democracy and the processes that underpin it. This concern has never been more relevant, as the young participate less in elections, party attachments weaken in electorates, and political debate becomes more polarized.

It is this vital component of democracy—its public support—that the Comparative Study of Electoral Systems (CSES) project is designed to investigate. Beginning in 1994, the CSES has conducted large-scale surveys across a wide range of countries in order to understand mass political behaviour under varying institutional arrangements. This enables us to address some of the key questions about the process of democratization across the world. The unique capacity of the CSES to trace the interaction between mass political behaviour and institutional structures sets it apart from all of the other cross-national projects in political science.

This CSES Oxford book series presents the key findings from this major research project. The inaugural volume, edited by Hans-Dieter Klingemann, documented much of the project's historical background, the basic principles of data collection, and provided sample chapters showing many of the analytical possibilities of this unique data collection. This volume is based on the first module of survey questions in the CSES, completed in 2001, which examines the interaction of political institutions and political behaviour regarding attitudes towards the democratic regime, the political authorities, and the quality of the political process generally.

As with the first volume, the second one, edited by Russell J. Dalton and Christopher J. Anderson, addresses the fundamental question of whether the institutional structure of elections affects the nature of the public's choices. The first question looks at explanations for turnout, and how institutions structure the likelihood of voting. The second question discusses determinants of individual electoral behaviour and examines the role of institutions in shaping what kinds of political attitudes voters acquire.

The third volume in the series, by Russell J. Dalton, David Farrell, and Ian McAllister, describes and explains the role of political parties in election campaigns, in forming the electoral choice of voters and their role in government and opposition. The theoretical arguments relate to the logic of the responsible parties model. It is the first study to test these ideas using a comprehensive and comparative design. It demonstrates the importance of the left–right schema to enable political positioning, political communication, and political representation.

Representation and accountability are the focus of the fourth volume, edited by Jacques Thomassen. Inspired by Arend Lijphart's theory, the analyses contrast voting and elections in countries of majoritarian Westminster and consensus democracies. The volume asks the question: do consensus models of democracy serve the interests of their citizens better than majoritarian systems? The answer is that formal institutions such as the electoral system matter less than might be expected. What do matter are the characteristics of the party system, such as the level of polarization and the clarity of accountability.

The fifth volume, edited by Jack Vowles and Georgios Xezonakis, asks how globalization affects democratic mass politics, and in particular the political attitudes and behaviour of ordinary citizens and the policies of political parties—not just governments. This represents an important corrective for the extant research, which has so far dealt mostly with the public policy implications of globalization. The contributors to the volume show that the relentless march of globalization over the past two decades has created winners and losers, with the political impact of the latter group being dependent on the extent to which they are able to translate economic insecurity into political action.

The current volume, by Timothy Hellwig, Yesola Kweon, and Jack Vowles, examines the impact of the 2007–8 global financial crisis (GFC) on public opinion towards democracy. Using CSES data collected in OECD countries between 1996 and 2017, they argue that the GFC represents a fault-line in mass political behaviour and attitudes rather than, as some other scholars have argued, a temporary interruption to long-term trends. The authors argue that, rather than the conditions of the global economy dominating national politics, how political parties, leaders, and institutions responded to the crisis mattered.

Placing the response of political elites to the crisis within a theoretical framework based on social cleavages, Hellwig, Kweon, and Vowles view the policy responses of governments as crucial to how events impacted on the mass public. In particular, political elites have the potential to alter the policy discourse by emphasizing certain economic policies; this in turn influenced the form and direction of public opinion towards the crisis. This is very much a 'top–down' approach, through which not just policy choices, but also political institutions and party competition, helped to shape citizens' experiences of crisis and recovery.

This is an approach and argument that the CSES is perfectly designed to test. By measuring public opinion as well as political institutions cross-nationally, it can enable the institutional environment to be brought into the equation, enhancing our understanding of the complex relationship between individual choice and institutional context. Such analyses were impossible until the CSES was established. Now, with surveys collected between 1996 and 2017 using strictly comparable methodologies, a vital time component is added. All of this is used to great effect in the current volume.

All of the CSES data are freely available and can be downloaded from our website (http://www.cses.org).

Hans-Dieter Klingemann
Ian McAllister
Series Editors

Preface and Acknowledgements

This book is made possible by the confluence of three sets of circumstances. The first was the unfortunate downturn in the global political economy during 2008–10. The global financial crisis, and then Great Recession, provided the exogenous shock which motivated this inquiry into how parties and voters respond to rapid economic change. The second was the existence of a rich and unique data source in the Comparative Study of Electoral Systems (CSES). This book could not have been written without the CSES from which the most part of its data is drawn. Coincidentally, the CSES celebrated its twenty-fifth anniversary in 2019, the year in which this book was completed. The third aspect of the confluence was what turned to be the highly complementary nature of our collaboration.

A large part of Module 4 (2011–2016) of the CSES was designed to investigate the ongoing effects of the global financial crisis on political behaviour. Module 4 marked a change from previous practice: for the first time, proposals for the content of the module were solicited both from within and without the CSES Planning Committee. From within the Planning Committee, Jack Vowles led the initial Task Force that called for proposals, and himself submitted questions largely aimed at estimating individual-level risks and risk perceptions. From outside, Chris Wlezien and Stuart Soroka proposed questions to tap into thermostatic policy respones, and Michael Lewis Beck, Martial Foucault, and Richard Nadeau proposed instruments designed to estimate ownership of assets and 'positional' economic voting. The convergence of the ideas behind these submissions led to agreement in the Planning Committee and among collaborators in general that the 'main theme' of Module 4 would become 'distributional politics and social protection' (CSES 2011). Jack Vowles led the Task Force that put the final touches on this section of the Module.

Meanwhile, Jack was working on a project that led to the publication of *Globalization and Domestic Politics* (Vowles and Xezonakis 2016), published by Oxford University Press as part of the CSES book series to which this book also belongs. Tim Hellwig was one of the chapter authors and from about 2013 onwards Tim and Jack began discussing, and then working on, ideas for this book. The first advanced release of Module 4 was in May 2014. Our first paper drawing on the data was presented at the 2014 American Political Science Association conference in Washington, DC. Meanwhile Tim had been awarded a Visiting Fellowship through the Research School of Social Sciences at the Australian National University, and in February 2015 took a side trip to Wellington for us to begin work on the project in earnest. Later that year, Jack took up a visiting scholarship sponsored by Indiana University's Institute for Advanced Study, enabling collaboration in Bloomington over a week in September. We thank both the ANU and IU for their support. Meanwile, papers drawing on our early work were presented at the 2015 conferences of Elections, Public Opinion and Parties in the UK, and the Australian Society for Quantitative Political Science Conference. Jack visited Bloomington for another week in September 2016 for further round of collaborative work. In the summer of 2015, Yesola Kweon began work on the project, drawing on her own research on social cleavages, labour markets, and welfare states. After the completion of her Ph.D. in 2017, Jack and Tim invited her to join the team as a co-author. The resulting effort represents an equal collaboration among the thee authors. After the full release of the Module 4 dataset in May 2018, preparation of the book moved into the final stages.

Most of the chapters in this book were initially presented as papers at various APSA, EPOP, ASQPS, Midwest, and European Political Science Association conferences over the period 2016–19. The authors are grateful to the discussants and members of the audiences who gave us useful feedback, including Andre Blais, Michele Fenzl, Ed Fieldhouse, Rachel Gibson, Jane Green, Simon Jackman, Richard Johnston, Mike Lewis-Beck, Ian McAllister, Alex Pacek, Andrew Philips, Steve Quinlan, and Mary Stegmaier. The most recent paper to be presented in this form was at the Canadian Political Science Conference in June 2019. This conference provided the opportunity for all three authors to meet again in person and after the conference we put in three days of intensive work. We are most grateful to Professor Richard Johnston for arranging our use of a meeting room and facilities at UBC's Institute for European Studies. Torben Iversen, Philipp Rehm, and Stefanie Walter provided helpful guidance on measuring labour market indicators, and we are grateful to Marina Costa Lobo, Pedro Magalhães, Michael Marsh, and Rune Stubager for anwering our questions about different national election studies series. And we thank Sam Bigwood, Kallen Brunson, and Joseph Johnson for their research assistance.

Within the framework of the CSES, the authors are grateful to series editor and former Planning Committee Chair Ian McAllister and CSES Director of Studies Dave Howell for their support and encouragement of our project. CSES Project Manager Steve Quinlan also deserves our thanks for his production of the CSES integrated module dataset that made it much easier for us to use pooled CSES data for our time series analysis.

Next, the authors would like to thank each other for their collegiality, good humour, and deep engagement with and commitment to our joint enterprise. All chapters were initially drafted by one or other of us, but they have all been greatly amended by way of challenge, critique, and often intense debate. Our meetings in various locations were supplemented by frequent video conferences over the internet. During our meetings we have greatly enjoyed each other's company, and come out of the collaboration with deepened intellectual respect and friendship for each other.

Last but not least, we would like to thank our respective families—Tana, Claire, and Owen, Derek and Theo, and Anna—for their toleration of our distraction from family and personal life that a project of this nature inevitably entails.

This book emphasizes the importance of national recoveries for understanding the politics of economic crises. As we were finalizing this manuscript at the end of 2019, it looked as though most if not all of the world's economies had, at long last, recovered from the calamitous events of 2007–2009. We knew, however, that the 'Great' Recession would not be the last, and that insights from our analyses of elections before and after the GFC could inform future scholars and policymakers about electoral politics in the wake of large-scale economic downturns. The economic consequences of the novel coronavirus pandemic of 2020 means—unfortunately—that our opportunity to apply these lessons once again will arise far sooner than we had anticipated.

Timothy Hellwig
Yesola Kweon
Jack Vowles

Contents

List of Figures

List of Tables

Part I
The Crisis's Long Shadow on Democratic Politics

1

Continuity and Change

The Shock, the Recovery, and the Mass Politics of Economic Crises

As the crisis revealed, government by market forces was at best a fragile condition. As the global financial crisis imploded, it was the markets themselves that needed governing, by state action on a gigantic scale. And that meant that who governed and where they obtained their political support was not incidental. Elections and party politics did matter.

Tooze 2018, 578

The global financial crisis (GFC) began in 2007 and was signalled by the fall of Lehman Brothers in 2008. The subsequent 'great recession' generated an economic shock that continues to reverberate in Europe, North America, and around the world. Following on from the shock into financial markets, a second crisis of 'sovereign debt' engulfed many advanced industrial economies. Many governments bailed out banks, and others found themselves facing unsustainable increases in the interest needed to service their existing debts. Governments struggled to cope, several losing office at elections following. But after an initial economic stimulus, austerity politics emerged in many countries affected, offset in part by deficit spending but in the main by cuts in social expenditure (OECD 2019). Over the ensuing decade, variations in levels of market exposure and in government responses led to variations in the stability and performances of various national economies. Ten years on, the economic implications of the GFC and great recession for national economies remain to be seen. In some countries, outward signs of the economic effects the crisis persist; in Southern Europe, for instance, the recovery has been slow and uneven, with the rich gaining disproportionately from the recovery (LIS 2019). Elsewhere, the twin crises seem a thing of the past. The United States, for instance, boasts a strong growth rate and low jobless levels,

Democracy Under Siege? Parties, Voters, and Elections After the Great Recession. Timothy Hellwig, Yesola Kweon, and Jack Vowles, Oxford University Press (2020). © Timothy Hellwig, Yesola Kweon, and Jack Vowles. DOI: 10.1093/oso/9780198846208.001.0001

albeit fuelled in part by continued deficit spending and increasing sovereign debt that is at a historical peak, but apparently tolerated by financial markets.

While the economic implications have yet to be fully realized, the crises' lasting impact on politics equally deserve our attention. How has the global financial crisis shaped party politics, public opinion, and electoral behaviour in the rich democracies? Across these different settings, has the crisis effect been modest and temporary, or severe and prolonged? What, if anything, can politicians and policymakers do to buffer or redirect the crises effects on citizen beliefs and actions? More fundamentally, in terms of how voters decide, does GFC represent a fundamental break with the past or does post-crisis politics largely resemble that which came before? These questions are the focus of this book. Its analysis focuses on the thirty-five countries that belonged to the Organization for Economic Development and Co-operation (OECD) as of 2016. OECD members must demonstrate a commitment to democracy and a market economy, two requirements that define our country case selection criteria.

Despite many claims to the contrary, this book argues that the crisis has had strong, deep, and continuing effects on mass politics across the OECD democracies. We leverage data from some 150,000 individuals across over 100 nationally representative post-election sample surveys from the 1990s to 2017 to show that the drivers of individual attitudes and political behaviours have changed after the crisis years. Public responses to the crisis, however, are directed—or *managed*—by political elites. Our argument and evidence emphasize the role of politicians and policymakers as important actors capable of mediating—in a positive or adverse way—the crisis' impact on citizen politics. Far from signalling the triumph of global finance over national politics, we find, as historian Adam Tooze (2018) argues, that 'elections and party politics did matter'.

In this introductory chapter, we develop our theoretical framework for understanding the mass politics of the crisis events of 2007–10. We first situate the project in the current research on the larger question of electoral change, and then turn to extant scholarship on how the GFC has (or has not) contributed to electoral change. We then advance our argument. While informed by previous work on social cleavages, party (de)alignments and critical junctures, we claim that the policy decisions and positions taken by political elites shaped how the crisis situation played out in mass opinion and behaviour. Theoretically, our approach is distinguished from those which precede it by placing relatively greater emphasis on parties as strategic actors responding to high levels of uncertainty among the electorate. Empirically, our inquiry is made possible by a rich collection of individual-level post-election surveys from across the OECD ranging in total from the 1990s through 2017. Thanks to the coordinating role of the Comparative Study of Electoral Systems (CSES), these surveys include measures that enable us to test our political economy arguments at the individual level and across a range of contexts for the first time. Subsequent chapters test our claims with respect to voter perceptions, policy preferences, political participation, performance assessments, and, ultimately, voting choice. We conclude with a consideration of how the tumultuous period of 2007–9 has affected democratic attitudes more broadly.

1.1. Continuity and Change in Electoral Politics

Questions of continuity versus change in democratic societies has long sparked debate in the comparative political economy of advanced capitalism (Katzenstein 1978; Goldthorpe 1984; Gourevitch 1986; Kitschelt et al. 1999; Beramendi et al. 2015) and in the study of parties and elections (Dalton, Beck, and Flanagan 1984; Franklin et al. 1992; Hutter and Kriesi 2019). Anchoring debates in these literatures is the question of social change in the face of an external shock. This 'external shock' may take several forms but typically comes as part of what is arguably the destructive nature of global capitalism, be it the Great Depression, the OPEC-induced crisis of the 1970s, the Latin American debt crisis in the 1980s, the Asian financial crisis of the 1990s, or, most recently, the GFC. Such global events are bound to lead to policy reform, blame avoidance, and a general departure from 'politics as usual'. The question is whether the shock produces a political realignment or whether effects are only temporary, with the bases of party competition and voter choice returning to the status quo ante.

With respect to the literature on parties and elections, perspectives on continuity versus change—or stability versus volatility, as the case may be—can be classified based on the emphases placed on longer and shorter term drivers. Early studies took a macro-sociological approach, which emphasized change-resistant social cleavages. Anchored in the structural frameworks of Max Weber and Talcott Parsons, this approach attained wide acceptance in the 1960s–1980s. A second paradigm arose in the 1980s as a means to account for waves of party system change in Western Europe. This perspective stressed the changing economic and value orientations of individual citizens and, as such, conceived of election outcomes as the result of the issue positions taken by individual voters. And a third represents a partial return to and updating of the first. This 'dynamic cleavage' perspective strikes balance between the two by reasoning that abrupt exogenous shocks are incorporated into ongoing, slower moving, party system changes. We elaborate on each of these.

1.1.1. *Social Cleavages and Transformational Change*

The first perspective can be traced back to Seymour Martin Lipset and Stein Rokkan's (1967) analyses of Western political systems of the 1960s. For Lipset and Rokkan the puzzle was not why there was so much change but why, in the face of successive tumultuous events over the centuries, had political systems seemingly achieved such stability. Their answer had to do with political parties and the social cleavages that support them. The parties garnering votes, they observed, were stable not because they faithfully reflected the 'hot-button' issues of day but because they aligned with the social divisions salient at the time of enfranchisement at the turn of century. These factors are billed as resistant to change with respect to their influence on the vote. Members of the industrial working class, for example, tended to vote for parties on the left and do so with high levels of regularity, albeit at lower levels than in the past. Likewise, religious affiliation may provide an iron-clad linkage to party choice, as has been the case between practising Catholics and right-of-centre parties in many European countries. And in linguistically divided societies, language structures communication and political affiliation in ways few other divisions can (Lijphart 1979).

Lipset and Rokkan's cleavage-based argument influenced scholarship for generations, and justifiably so (e.g. Bartolini and Mair 1990; Caramani 2004). Social cleavages of class, religion, region, and language are enduring rather than ephemeral. And stability was normatively preferable to the volatility that scuttled democratic politics in Europe during the interwar years. Electoral stability has long been held up as a bulwark against democratic backsliding (Huntington 1968). Such fears were rampant in the 1930s with the rise of fascism, in the 1950s and 1960s out of concern for communism, and now again in the current era as many fear a return to the illiberal politics of the interwar era. Economic and political challenges may arise, the argument went, but social cleavages and the political allegiances frozen in national party systems would endure.

1.1.2. *Issue Politics and Rapid Change*

The emergence of new parties in the 1970s and 1980s, however, required scholars to rethink the general tendency towards stability. To make sense of the rise of new parties and decline of others, researchers heralded short-term factors—issues and economics—now rivalling long-term social divisions in shaping voter decisions (Dalton, Beck, and Flanagan 1984; Franklin et al. 1992). With generational change and cohort replacement came a rise of so-called postmaterial postmaterialist values. Value change in tandem with an increasingly sophisticated public, the argument goes, produced more activist and less deferential electorates and rendered partisan heuristics less essential (Franklin et al. 1992; Dalton 1984). A decline in materialist values has weakened the influence of ideological divisions (Inglehart 1984; 1990). Expressed in terms of the funnel of causality (Campbell et al. 1960), these short-term factors such as the confluence of party and citizen positions on issues like health care, immigration, the environment, or European integration, along with evaluations of economy and other performance indicators, are located most proximately to the vote.

This issue-based approach, then, assigns a good deal of capacity to the individual to make informed decisions and to update beliefs in response to changing conditions. With respect to spending priorities, people can devise issue-specific preferences and can make adjustments to these priorities unanchored by long-term cleavages. A prominent example here is the thermostatic model of public preferences which maintains that changes in policy priorities adjust in response to government spending as a thermostat would to changes in temperature—that is, counter-cyclically by heating up when spending levels cool off, and vice versa (Soroka and Wlezien 2010). All told, if the voter's choice among parties and candidates is shaped by a mix of long- and short-term elements (LeDuc and Niemi 2014, 140), this *issue politics* approach places disproportionate emphasis on the latter.

1.1.3. *Dynamic Cleavages and Layered Change*

Recent years have witnessed a return to cleavage-based or sociological understandings of political behaviour. This research shares with Lipset and Rokkan the notion that disruptive processes like revolutions or exogenous shocks are reflected in party system change (Hooghe and Marks 2017). While rising education levels, changing values, and the weakening of political parties' programmatic appeals do affect political choices, the reasoning goes, cleavages still matter. Insomuch as voters today face a wider array of party options and are uncertain about what governments can deliver, social divisions lend a measure of predictability to an otherwise unpredictable landscape. Indeed, social structures may matter more now than at any time in the past thirty years.

What has changed is the relative importance—or saliency—of different social divisions. This is particularly the case when it comes to social class. As is well known, class divisions have long structured politics in industrial Western democracies, with members of the working class backing social democratic and labour parties and those of the middle and upper classes pledging support for conservative, Catholic, Christian Democratic, and other bourgeois parties. However, linkages between traditional notions of class, tied to the rise of industry, have now been in decline for decades (e.g. Nieuwbeerta and

Ultee 1999). While some take this as evidence of the decline of long-standing cleavages, others argue that cleavages have instead been recast along new divisions.[1]

In terms of the latter, Kitschelt (1994, 1995) maintains that social divisions in Western democracies have evolved such that a libertarian/authoritarian cleavage has risen to rival the importance of the industrial left/right or 'social-ist politics/capitalist politics' divide. To Kitschelt, the decline in support for left-labour parties in Europe is due not to a shift away from economic consid-erations and towards cosmopolitan ideas or post-material values but may be traced to changes in the economic structure in general and to national labour markets in particular. Shifts away from low-skilled blue-collar jobs and towards higher skill object processing and interactive occupations mean that traditional class appeals no longer guarantee a winning electoral strategy.

Kitschelt's work offers a theory of electoral change without discounting the importance of the class cleavage. Rather than waning in importance, class divisions are reconceptualized into more fine-grained divisions in the labour market. Linear conceptions of class identities based on a hierarchy of skill and/or location within systems of authority over the processes of production (Erikson, Goldthorpe, and Portocarero 1979) have been replaced with schema emphasizing occupational task structures and relative skill specificity. In the post-industrial era, more refined occupational classes and skills determine not only the income of individuals, but further determine the cost of exogenous shocks (Iversen and Soskice 2001; Kitschelt and Rehm 2014; Oesch 2006; Pardos-Prado and Xena forthcoming). In particular, employment among sociocultural professionals and managers has grown while large numbers of low and semi-skilled jobs have disappeared. This change has produced more fragmented and less mobile social structures in many post-industrial econ-omies (Oesch 2015). Labour market dualization also created an additional social cleavage based on employment security. Even among workers with similar levels of skills and occupational task, work contract types influence the vulnerability of workers to risk, resulting in conflicting policy interests between those with secure and insecure jobs (Rueda 2007; King and Rueda 2008; Chung and van Oorschot 2011; Näswall and De Witte 2003).

The renewed focus on social structures thus understands cleavages to be more complex, less linear, and closer tied to positions in the labour market, on the one hand, and identity politics, on the other. This revised, or updated, version has been referred to as a 'dynamic' concept of cleavage formation (Bornschier 2010; Kriesi et al. 2008, 2012). As with Lipset and Rokkan, new issues arise from social conflicts produced by long-term social change.

---

[1] As discussed below, others locate the decline of class-based voting not in social divisions but in the policies and rhetoric of mainstream parties (Evans and Tilley 2017).

Table 1.1. Theoretical Perspectives on Electoral Change

Theoretical Framework	Key actors	Prospects for change	Causal orientation	Nature of change
Social cleavages	Social cleavages based on socio-economic and cultural structures and political parties representing them	Low	Bottom–up	Transformational and durable: persists until next critical juncture
Issue politics	Voters, who respond rapidly to changes in policies or economic conditions	Very high	Bottom–up	Rapid and temporary, driven by issue positions and policy performance
Dynamic cleavages	Political parties, which react to emergence of new exogenously determined social divides	Somewhat high	Bottom–up	Layered and accumulative: exogenous shocks are filtered by and alter extant cleavages
Elite Cues	Political elites, who shape mass opinion and voter demands and manage public expectations	High	Top–down	Rapid and potentially durable, dependent on electoral success

With respect to changes brought on by crises, 'the potential impacts of the multiple crises on European politics were embedded in processes of change that had been going on long *before* the onset of the Great Recession' (Hutter and Kriesi 2019, 4, emphasis added).

With broad brush strokes, this section has highlighted how contributions to research on parties and elections in the established democracies vary in terms of the key actors and with respect to the prospects for electoral change. The first three rows in Table 1.1 summarize these differences and bring them into sharper relief.

1.2. Continuity, Change, and the Global Financial Crisis

Returning to the task at hand, what do we know about the scope and duration of the political consequences of the GFC? The spate of studies initially following on from the crisis characterized the events as a temporary interruption of normality (Bermeo and Bartels 2014; Bartels 2014; LeDuc and Pammett 2013; Talving 2017). For instance, in one of the first collections of empirically grounded essays to take stock of the crisis from the perspective of electoral politics, Bermeo and Bartels conclude that the immediate political reactions to the crisis were muted among the Western democracies. 'In most countries, popular reactions to the Great Recession were surprisingly muted and moderate' (Bermeo and Bartels 2014, 3). In another contribution to the volume, Bartels (2014) examines the outcomes of elections in forty-two OECD countries immediately following the recession and concludes that, by and large, these outcomes are best interpreted not as a mandate for any particular policy response but more simply as retrospective assessments of the incumbent governing parties. Examining election outcomes in twenty-four European democracies between 2008 and 2011, LeDuc and Pammett (2013) arrive at a similar conclusion. While governing parties generally saw their share of the vote decline, the authors find the effect was 'surprisingly modest' compared with previous election cycles. And despite the size of the negative economic shock, the financial crisis 'was not the central focus of the campaign discourse due to uncertainty about the recession's full impact' (LeDuc and Pammett 2013, 498). And according to Talving's (2017, 695) analysis of European Election Studies data, there was 'very little abrupt change' in the effect of the economy on the vote in economic effects over time.[2]

Other research following on the heels of the events in 2007–2009 addressed the influence of the crisis on public preferences. Analysing panel data from the United States, Margalit (2013) shows that the social policy preferences of individuals who experienced a job loss were affected, but only temporarily. Analyses of survey data from other countries report similar findings: in the face of personal hardship, policy preferences often shift leftwards, at least initially (Alesina and Giuliano 2011; Alt et al. 2017; Martén 2019; Naumann et al. 2015). This research shows that the impact of crisis experiences was such that it shifted preferences over policy solutions, a finding reinforced in Chapter 4 of this volume. The literature is less clear, however, in terms of whether and how shifts in preferences translate into the choices between programmatic-oriented party options (cf. Lindvall 2014). Most work finds policy shifts to be temporary rather than permanent. Furthermore, there is little evidence that crisis-induced policy change produces changes in the voter's decision, a point we explore in Chapter 7 (see the review in Margalit 2019).

In short, the first wave of research on balance characterizes the years spanning the crisis period in a way consistent with normal politics. Continuity trumped change; voters responded as they usually do, by punishing sitting governments for the economic fallout and by updating their preferences in response to changes in their life situation. Any changes can be considered short-term in nature. In terms of models of change, this accords most strongly with the 'issue politics' perspective.

This initial take on the crisis, however, underestimates its full effects on government policies. After a brief period of fiscal stimulus, austerity ruled the

---

[2] Interestingly, early studies on the mass political effects of the crisis in Russia, an authoritarian regime, similarly conclude that it did little to change the public's views of regime leaders (McAllister and White 2011; Rose and Mishler 2010).

day as policymakers privileged financial stability over short-term growth, over redistributive policies to stave rising inequality, and over demand-side relief. Indeed, as the financial crisis evolved into a sovereign debt crisis, it became clear that the most fundamental political consequence of economic malaise had to do with the fragility of the postwar social contract. This social contract held that, in exchange for allowing a free market to largely shape consumer behaviour and labour markets, citizens had a right to certain protections from their government including the provision of state-funded public services, safety nets to catch the unlucky, and redistribution of incomes through taxation and benefit systems. While this bargain has been challenged since the 1980s, the shift to austerity after 2009 potentially signalled the beginning of its end in many Western democracies (Streeck 2014).

In Greece, evidence in support of fundamental change was brought into sharp relief. Banks responded to the crisis and revealed structural weaknesses in the economy by hiking interest rates. The interest rates on ten-year government bonds, which had been stable for years at around 5 per cent, rose steadily from the beginning of 2010 to the end of 2012, reaching nearly 30 per cent. At the same time, Greece's membership in the common currency Eurozone took away the option of adjustment by way of currency depreciation. The end result was skyrocketing debt levels which, by 2017, had plateaued at a debt-to-GDP ratio just over 175 per cent.

The primary means of rescuing the Greek economy was through large-scale bailout programmes engineered by the European Commission, European Central Bank (ECB), and International Monetary Fund (IMF): the so-called 'Troika'. With the approval of the Eurozone members, Greece received three large-scale bailouts from 2010 to 2015, totalling over €300 billion. The price for this financial support was a steady diet of austerity. Taxes were raised, pensions cut, and public service pay slashed. Greece's public sector workforce was hit especially hard, with layoffs affecting around 25,000 civil servants.

Cuts to social programmes and public employment have challenged the very basis of representative democracy in Greece. Since the end of the dictatorship and return to democracy in 1974, the country had been led by one of two political parties, PASOK on the left and New Democracy on the right. Both parties built up loyal constituencies through the expansion of state largess, realized in the form of generous pensions and a large public sector. Troika-imposed conditionality meant that such strategies of constituency-building were no longer viable. The political effects of austerity were swiftly felt. During the six years between the end of 2011, with the ouster of Prime Minister George Papandreou's PASOK Government following the first bailout package, and the end of 2016, Greece was led by one grand-coalition, two non-partisan caretaker governments, and most recently governments led by the SYRIZA, a left-wing socialist party established little more than a decade before. While the drama of its politics exceeded that found anywhere else, the forces leading to Greece's modern tragedy were present across the OECD. Whether it is Spain or Portugal, Ireland or Italy, the economic turbulence of the years spanning 2008 and 2013 changed the bases of electoral politics.

As the calendar turned from 2016 to 2017, many election watchers braced themselves for a wave of change. The June 2016 referendum on Britain's membership in the European Union was a bombshell which invited considerable speculation about its meaning. The decision to exit the EU was not initially backed by any of the mainstream political parties. Did it amount to victory for the anti-integration, anti-foreigner politics of populist right-wing parties? Did this signal the beginning of the end of the postwar liberal order, combining open borders with social protection? Or was it an indirect rejection of years of austerity, social expenditure cuts, and declining real wages? Five months later many of these same questions were asked after the unexpected victory of Donald Trump in the United States' presidential election. These elections were watershed events which had repercussions beyond the two countries. In the wake of Brexit and Trump, many anxiously anticipated the outcomes of a slate of elections in 2017. The Dutch election in April, followed by the French and German elections in May and September, served as key touchstones in a narrative in which a 'populist wave' was sweeping across the liberal democracies. The snap British election in June 2017, called just two months earlier, was a belated entry to this story, and its unexpected result again suggested that previous assumptions needed to be reconsidered.

Of course, reality was more complex than this simple narrative implied. In the Netherlands, the Liberal Party of sitting Prime Minister Mark Rutte fended off the challenge of Geert Wilders's upstart anti-Muslim, anti-integration Party for Freedom. In France, Emmanuel Macron, a centrist liberal, prevailed over Marine Le Pen and the anti-immigrant, anti-globalization Front National Party. In Germany the centre-right Christian Democrats remained the largest party and could form a governing coalition, returning Angela Merkel for a fourth term as Chancellor. But the radical right, Alternative for Germany, became the third largest party, entering the Bundestag for the first time. Later in 2017, conservative populist parties scored significant gains in Austria and the Czech Republic. And in Britain the outcome of the June 2017 vote, in which the governing Conservative Party lost its outright parliamentary majority, was viewed both as an indictment of the country's decision to part ways with Europe and as a sign that disillusion with austerity politics was generating a revival of the left. Derided by commentators and political scientists alike as a hopeless left-wing extremist, Labour leader Jeremy Corbyn's campaign had unexpectedly lifted the party back into contention as an alternative government. Meanwhile centre-left governments took office in Sweden

(2014) and Portugal (2015), although only in the latter case as a result of a vote shift to parties of the left.

But while outcomes of recent elections resist summary by a single narrative, we would also be mistaken to sum them up as politics as usual. While the Dutch Liberal Party received more votes than any other, fragmentation ruled the day as no fewer than thirteen parties earned representation in the 150-seat lower house. This degree of party system fragmentation has also affected the once-stable party systems in Greece and Spain, where systems which had been dominated by two party blocs have splintered, making the task of forming governments in these parliamentary systems all but impossible. The French election was historic, marking the first time in the history of the Fifth Republic that the centre-right and centre-left standard bearers were shut out of the second round of the presidential election. Angela Merkel's ability to form a new government in Germany had nothing to do with her party's ability to engage voters. Rather, it owed far more to the weakness of the opposition forces. Merkel's Christian Democrats lost one in five of its voters compared to the previous election in 2013. In short, these elections demonstrate a deep sense of dissatisfaction with politics as usual.

The challenge for the social scientist is to make sense of these changes. At minimum, the 'modest effects' story offered from the initial assessments of the crisis's consequences must be revised upwards. And as more recent work has argued, the crisis came on top of—and arguably exacerbated—ongoing social and economic changes already making inroads into 'normal' politics. These include, for instance, the rise of the service sector, the growth of part-time and temporary work, globalization and outsourcing, and demographic developments brought on by immigration flows and the ageing of the population. In this way, the crisis events that began in late 2007 and persisted through 2010 were layered on top of these forces and, with a lag, pushed them over the edge in the voters' minds. This narrative is consistent with a dynamic cleavage formation account of party system change (Bornschier 2010; Kriesi et al. 2008, 2012; Hutter and Kriesi 2019).

1.3. A Supply-Side Framework for Making Sense of Mass Political Reponses

Our account of the mass political consequences of the global financial crisis and Great Recession is informed by these accounts of continuity and change. In particular, we share with the 'dynamic cleavages' approach an emphasis of how parties, subject to structural constraints, respond to shifts in the structural divisions of advanced capitalism. However, we part ways with the macro-sociological approach's conception of political parties. While acknowledging that parties' room to manoeuvre is constrained by the interests of their partisan supporters and their internal political dynamics (Meyer 2013), we conceive of parties and their leaders as strategic actors capable of adjusting policies and positions for electoral gain over both the long and short term. Along with a distinct theoretical focus, our study of the mass political response ranges beyond current treatments by examining information about voters and parties before, during, and after the crisis. We expand on these theoretical and empirical innovations below.

National differences in government responses were apparent in the immediate aftermath of the financial crisis. Following the collapse of Bear Stearns and Lehman Brothers, US President Barack Obama argued for a coordinated Keynesian response to inject funds into cratering economies and to stave off further bank failures. While some of its partners, notably Britain, supported the US-led effort, in the end the $787 billion economic stimulus package approved by Congress in early 2009 was done without international coordination. Germany, France, and other continental economies opted for more incremental responses. The lack of urgency in Northern Europe was justified by these countries' reliance on the 'automatic stabilizers': the redistributive mechanisms of tax and welfare systems already in place in these developed welfare states.

These varying policy responses should matter for public opinion, perceptions, and behaviour. A venerable tradition in political economy traces differences in responses to exogenous shocks to some mix of political institutions, policy legacies, and government partisanship. For instance, compared to liberal market economies, nations with universal social protections and/or high levels of income redistribution through tax and benefit systems are better able to buffer citizens against the downturn's most deleterious effects, thereby reducing the need to undertake sweeping reforms, bailout industries, or engage in deficit spending. Likewise, left of centre governments are more likely to respond to downturns with increases in public spending and more redistributive and risk-pooling policies. In contrast, right of centre governments take strides to pursue more supply-side strategies and/or go along with extra-national pressures to cut back on social services, pensions, unemployment insurance, and the like in a general diet of austerity (Huber and Stephens 2001, 2015).

Yet while institutions and government partisanship are emphasized in studies of public policy and political economy, their impact is less clear when it comes to mass politics. The expansion of cross-national election studies has made it possible for researchers to examine the impact of institutional arrangements—including electoral rules, government concentration of power, and even regime type—on how voters choose. Results of this research raise questions about how political-economic institutions determine individual attitudes and behaviour. For example, a recent collection of empirical papers explores whether institutions affect how elections work as instruments of representation and accountability. Collectively, the studies' major finding is that formal political institutions 'are far less relevant for people's political behaviour and their perceptions and evaluations of the process of democracy than often presumed' (Thomassen 2014, p. viii). Dalton and Anderson (2011, 250) summarize findings from a collection of analyses of electoral choice across three dozen democracies, noting that one of the 'most striking empirical findings is the importance of the clarity of choice', which they capture in terms of party polarization. Similar findings based on cross-national analyses of survey data, often collected as part of the Comparative Study of Electoral Systems, the main source for this book, are reported by Dalton, Farrell, and McAllister (2011), Vowles and Xezonakis (2016), and Hobolt, Tilley, and Banducci (2013). Rather than formal political institutions, a common thread running through these analyses is the importance of characteristics of the party system in structuring the choices voters make. So while institutions and partisanship may be important determinants of *policy* response, these factors do not have the same purchase for understanding the *voters'* response.

We reason that the source of this divergence can be traced to party politics. Research on the comparative political economy of the welfare state considers elections mainly in terms of the left-wing and right-wing partisan make-up of governments they produce. The traditional approach states that left- and right-leaning parties hold contrasting positions on welfare issues, depending on the interests of their respective electorates. Until recently, however, studies of social policy have ignored changes in party strategies and party constituencies over time. As Häusermann, Picot, and Geering (2013, 227) conclude from a review of the welfare state literature, insights from research on electoral change have been almost completely ignored by welfare state scholars. Fortunately, a research agenda has emerged in response to this oversight. Championed by welfare state scholars, this 'politics of advanced capitalism' approach considers how party agency and fluid electoral constituencies help explain labour market developments, the evolution of and changes in government spending levels, and policy reforms in the twenty-first century (Beramendi et al. 2015). Canonical frameworks for the political economy of advanced capitalism, such as Varieties of Capitalism (VoC) (Hall and Soskice 2001; Iversen 2005; Iversen and Soskice 2015) and their intellectual forbearers (Cameron 1978; Katzenstein 1985), emphasize the effects of formal institutions and firm-level interactions on outcomes. In this VoC approach, political parties are important insomuch as they represent and advance policies in accord with specific, definable constituencies stemming from a unidimensional, occupational-based social structure.

In contrast, a 'politics of advanced capitalism' approach to understanding policy outcomes calls for the primacy of *electoral* partisan politics wherein vote-seeking parties compete for office in times when the workings of capitalism are uncertain. In this approach, the electoral arena receives focus as 'the locus where institutional and structural constraints meet public demands' (Beramendi et al. 2015, 12). This literature shares elements in common with the dynamic cleavage approach in that the social structure remains tied to economic production and exchange. However, since political competition is not unidimensional, occupational groups can, with the assistance of opportunistic political elites, craft distinct electoral coalitions. For instance, low-skilled wage earners may form alliance with highly educated sociocultural professionals in support of state intervention in the market, as has been the case in Germany. Or business may leverage its relationships with petit-bourgeois shop owners, on the one hand, and sociocultural professionals, on the other, to crowd labour out of the axis of political competition, as has been the case in the United States. But the shaping of these alternative coalitions is not preordained; rather, they are an outcome of existing state capacities and party alignments. Shifting social divisions, in turn, mean that today's party systems are not simple reflections of dominant social cleavages but instead must realign to accommodate issues that were initially not centrally related to social and economic policymaking. 'As a result, governments are now confronted with a deeply transformed configuration of preferences and power relations, which constrains the set of feasible policy options' (Beramendi et al. 2015, 388; also Gingrich and Häusermann 2015).

Differing from both neo-Marxist and VoC frameworks, this emerging research agenda accords special attention to the interaction of the supply and demand sides of democratic politics; that is, to politicians' policy proposals on the one hand and citizens' preferences on the other. For present purposes, this recognition of the 'supremacy of electoral partisan politics' (Beramendi et al. 2015, 62) provides an opening for a framework for understanding *mass* political responses to abrupt economic change.

1.4. Shaping Mass Political Responses: Party Cues and Policy Behaviour

Our theoretical approach builds on this theory of constrained partisanship in its emphasis on party politics—a factor often ignored in previous political economy literature in favour of the effects of domestic institutions and the organization of interest groups. Thus, our examination of electoral outcomes supplements a 'politics of advanced capitalism' emphasis on electoral politics with an understanding of voter choice founded on the idea of strategic parties.

However, our theory parts from the 'politics of advanced capitalism' framework in some important ways. First, the 'politics of advanced capitalism' approach views political preferences as exogenous to party behaviour. Preferences are instead considered to be rooted in individuals' socio-economic and occupational experience. Parties in electoral competition then identify voters' preferences and position themselves accordingly (Beramendi et al. 2015). By contrast, we argue that parties can *shape* individuals' preferences as well as their political behaviour through policy and rhetoric. In other words, individuals' preferences and vote choices are affected not only by their own socio-economic experience, but also by elite cues. In line with spatial models of party competition, we argue that party actions constrain or redirect voter decisions. Party scholars have long recognized that parties do not occupy fixed places in policy space but move strategically to attract votes and respond to other parties (Downs 1957; Adams and Somer-Topcu 2009). And voters do respond. Party position shifts can alter the relationship between social divisions and party choice (Elff 2009; Evans and Tilley 2017; Jansen, Evans, and de Graaf 2013). As a gauge of electoral success, pragmatism often prevails over principle and parties can champion different policies over time (Green and Jennings 2017), and this should be especially true during crises.

We also extend the focus of political economic research from the impact of institutions and party actors on policy outcomes (e.g. Bermeo and Pontusson 2014) to examine how political elites' response shape mass political behaviour. As students of public opinion have argued, on many if not most issues the public is only tangentially informed. Further, opinions on many issues lack internal coherency, or ideological constraint (Converse 1964). This opens up a space for influence—or manipulation—by political elites. Public opinion research emphasizes the importance of cues from opinion leaders. Zaller's (1992) reception-acceptance-sampling model posits that a person's expressed opinions about a topic are a sample of the messages about that topic that the person has recently received and accepted. The probability of receiving a specific message on a topic is a function of the frequency with which the message is voiced and the individual's level of sophistication or awareness.

The influence of elite cues on attitude formation is related to the nature of information processing. Systematic information processing requires considerable effort to search for details and facts about an issue. In comparison, heuristic information processing of the sort received from trusted elites is more passive (Kam 2005). Individuals rely on salient cues or information shortcuts that are given externally. Not surprisingly, researchers maintain that individuals are more likely to rely on heuristic information processing when developing opinions (Chaiken and Ledgerwood 2012). Complex issues provide openings for opinion formation from elite cues. On multifaceted issues like foreign policy (Zaller 1992) or immigration (Hellwig and Kweon

2016), public attitudes are likely to be more influenced by how elites frame or prime the issue than by objective policy information. Their capacity to selectively report and strategically manipulate information about the causes and consequences of certain issues provide elites a degree of latitude to shape mass opinion.

Building on these insights, we argue that political parties have the potential to shape the extent that economic shocks reflected in voter attitudes and behaviour. Parties stake out positions on the issues. Parties assert the need for more or less spending and in which policy areas: more or less redistribution of wealth, more or less accommodating positions with respect to foreign influences, and so on. Party words and actions no doubt derive from the interests of their constituencies. However, links between interests and opinions become more tenuous during times of heightened uncertainty, that is, when the established rules of the political-economic game are called into question. Such is the case of the era in advanced capitalism which began in the fall of 2007 with the GFC wherein assigning credit or blame for economic outcomes is difficult and, thus, subject to elite manipulation (Hellwig and Coffey 2011). During such times, we argue, the benefits of the status quo decline and the potential gains from strategic action increase. Indeed, the bond between the positions of parties and their supporters in the electorate should weaken during periods of economic uncertainty. Rather, parties are strategic. Vote-seeking parties trade off, or leverage as the case may be, the value of their reputation for electoral gain.

The bottom row of Table 1.1 summarizes our 'strategic parties' lens and places it in comparison with the other perspectives. By imparting agency on individual parties, this orientation leads to a consideration of the set of tools at their disposal for shaping the mass political response. First and foremost, through the formation of governments, parties make policy. In what follows, we focus on parties' choices in response to the crisis. As the recounting of American and Franco-German responses to the financial crisis indicates, governments wishing to respond to the downturn have, broadly speaking, two options: (i) they could retain or otherwise prop up existing systems of social protection to compensate those most adversely affected, or (ii) they can engage in deficit spending in an attempt for fiscal stimulus. With respect to policymaker response, the first is less active yet arguably no less effective than the second.

In Figures 1.1 and 1.2 we display summary indicators of these two policy options: austerity (or stimulus) and relative redistribution by taxes and income transfers. The mix of policy efforts directed at social protection—which include pensions, unemployment and disability insurance, and other retributive schemes—are summarized by using the reduction in inequality (Gini) after taxes and transfers (Solt 2019). Higher scores indicate that

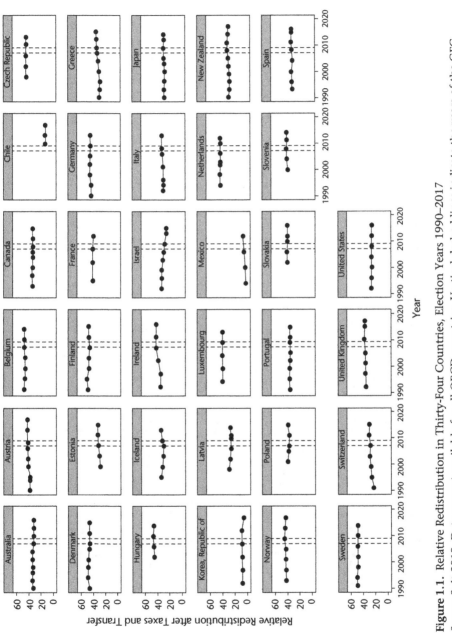

Figure 1.1. Relative Redistribution in Thirty-Four Countries, Election Years 1990–2017
Source: Solt 2019. Data are not available for all OECD countries. Vertical dashed lines indicate the years of the GFC.

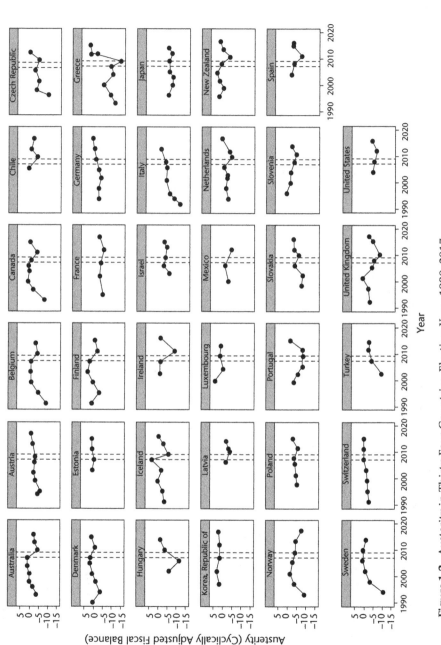

Figure 1.2. Austerity in Thirty-Four Countries, Election Years 1990–2017
Source: IMF. Data are not available for all countries. Vertical dashed lines indicate the years of the GFC.

government policies through taxes and income transfers have effectively improved income redistribution. This measure captures the degree to which incomes are equalized as a result of government welfare efforts. Unlike spending indicators, this measure is unaffected by unemployment rates and the population of pensioners that cause welfare spending to vary even if entitlement policies remain the same.

Figure 1.1 makes clear that in some countries, like those of north-western continental Europe, policy regimes serve to reduce market inequality by 50 per cent or more, as gauged by the Gini coefficient (note that y-axis scales are adjusted by country). In other countries, however, policy efforts are less effective at minimizing income differences across individuals. In Chile, Mexico, and South Korea, tax and transfer systems bear little on the distribution, with Switzerland and the United States performing only somewhat higher on this score. It is also worth noting that, though not as large as cross-country difference, we find evidence of temporal change as well.

Fiscal stimulus packages also vary over time within countries. This is evident in Figure 1.2, which tracks the expansion ('stimulus') and contraction ('austerity') of spending, measured in terms of the cyclically adjusted fiscal balance as a percentage of potential GDP. The indicator, provided by the IMF, removes the effects of 'one-off' factors such as exceptional fiscal transactions and deviations from trend in capital transfers: equivalently, an estimate of the fiscal balance that would apply under current policies if output were equal to potential (IMF 2019). The measure is coded such that higher values signal the absence of stimulus, or 'austerity': it serves as an estimate of 'fiscal consolidation'. We observe some general patterns: with important exceptions (e.g. Germany, Sweden) policymakers in most countries attempted to blunt the initial effects of the crisis through deficit spending. This was followed up by a quick about-face as campaigns for fiscal discipline to tamp down spending ruled the day. As the figure makes clear, the shift towards austerity was most abrupt across the European periphery: Spain, Portugal, Ireland, Iceland, and, especially, Greece.

Figure 1.3 highlights the extent of policy change from the pre-crisis period to post-crisis. This figure shows that Greece had the most abrupt change before and after the crisis. The country had a significant stimulus during the pre-crisis period, but after the crisis it became the country with the strictest austerity measures. A similar pattern, though to a lesser extent, is found for Italy, Hungary, and Turkey.

Party elites can also shape mass responses through their rhetoric. On this point, parties condition mass opinion through their choice of issue emphasis. Parties vying for office compete on not one but multiple dimensions. They make choices between competing on the same issues as their competitors—say, on social policy responses to the crisis—or, alternatively, to campaign on

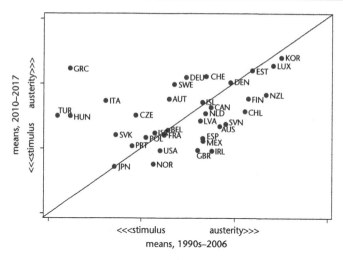

Figure 1.3. Fiscal Responses Before and After the Crisis
Source: IMF.

a different set of issues—say, the environment or immigration. Figure 1.4 provides an illustration of this point, as well as offering a snapshot of our empirical approach. The graphs report party positions on social welfare communicated in election campaigns during 2011–2016, in the crisis's aftermath. Parties that score higher on welfare positions are those which emphasize welfare state expansion over limitation, deficit spending (demand management) over orthodoxy, and growth over equality.[3] In each graph, parties with left-leaning ideologies are at the top and those right of centre are at the bottom.[4] If parties merely aligned with long-standing cleavages, then we would expect a positive association between ideology and welfare positions. However, the graphs show this not to be the case. For only a handful of countries do we find perfect alignment of parties' welfare positions and their ideological stance (e.g. Australia, Turkey, and the United States). For the other cases, we find that parties' ideological positions correspond loosely at best to their welfare positions. For instance, parties in Austria, both left- and right-wing parties, all have relatively pro-welfare positions. This reflects the nature

---

[3] To be specific, *Welfare position* is measured by subtracting the party's share of (quasi)sentences in their programme allocated to 'welfare state limitation', 'economic orthodoxy', and 'economic growth: positive' from their emphases on 'welfare state expansion', 'Keynesian demand management', and 'equality: positive'. The source is the Comparative Manifesto Project (Volkens et al. 2019).

[4] We rely on party family designations from the Comparative Manifesto Project (Volkens et al. 2019). Parties belonging to left, green, and social democratic party families in grey and parties belonging to liberal, Christian democratic, conservative, agrarian, and nationalist party families in black.

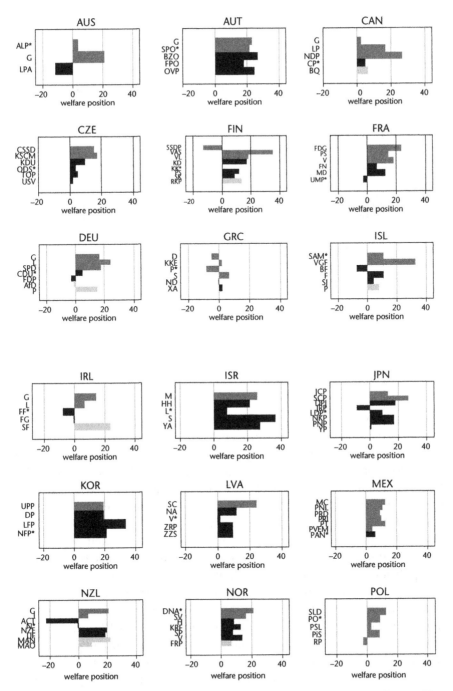

Figure 1.4. Parties, Party Ideology, and Party Welfare Positions in Twenty-Five Countries, 2011–2016

Note: Graphs display party positions produced by party statements included in their manifestos. Welfare position measured by subtracting party's score on 'welfare state limitation', 'economic orthodoxy', and 'economic growth: positive' from their emphases on 'welfare state expansion', 'Keynesian demand management', and 'equality: positive'. Parties arrayed on y-axis from left to right, with parties belonging to left, green, and social democratic party families in grey and parties belonging to liberal, Christian democratic, conservative, agrarian, and nationalist party families in black. Incumbents are marked with an asterisk. Party names are provided in Appendix 1.1.

Source: Volkens et al. 2019.

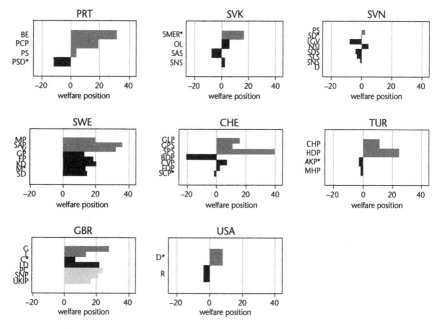

Figure 1.4. Continued

of conservative politics in Austria where the party of the right is Christian Democratic, and therefore more open to government provision for social security. In fact, some right-wing parties advocate more expansionary social protection than left-wing parties, although these tend to be smaller rather than the major mainstream players. A similar pattern is found for Israel. By contrast, in Greece, under pressure of events, the traditional party of the left that took office before the crisis had curtailed spending.

We also find over-time variation of party messaging on welfare solutions. Given the uncertainty in how to respond to the crisis, the capacity of tried and true policies—e.g, fiscal tightening from the right, spending from the left— may well have been shunned in favour of experimenting with different policies. In the aggregate, the result should be an increase in the diversity, or *range*, of policy proposals put forward by party competitors. We can get a sense of these by again considering the manifestos-based *Welfare position* measure. But rather than charting different parties over time, we assess the polarization of views within party systems.[5] The top half of Figure 1.5 reports means over four sets of elections across the OECD: those occurring in the 1990s,

[5] Following Dalton (2008), polarization is defined as the square-root of the summed squared differences of each party's *Welfare position* from the party system mean Welfare position, weighted by vote share.

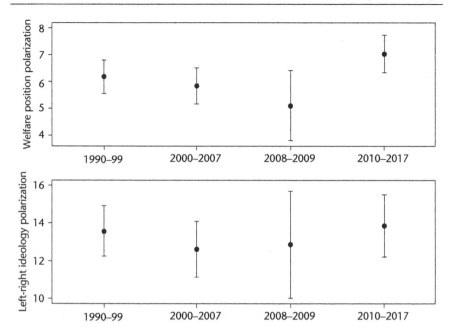

Figure 1.5. Party Polarization, Welfare Positions, and Right–Left Positions

Note: Graphs report polarization (mean deviation) of party system welfare position (top graph) and left–right ideology (bottom graph) across thirty-three OECD countries.

Source: Volkens et al. 2019.

the 2000s pre-crisis, the years of the GFC shock (2008–9), and post-2009. We see that, indeed, polarization of social policy responses increased during the recovery years—a strong indication of its growing contestation. In contrast, we observe no change in the diversity of party position-taking on the general left–right dimension (bottom half of Figure 1.5). As we discuss in greater detail in later chapters, these displays indicate that ideology cannot alone predict the welfare positions of parties, particularly under pressure of an economic crisis.

1.5. Parties and Voters: Before, During and After the Crisis

As noted, the Great Recession served as a common shock external to the back-and-forth of electoral politics. Yet lest we thought otherwise, the summary data presented so far show that parties and the governments they formed did not react similarly to this common shock. Nor did they maintain a constant response over time as the crisis progressed (see Figure 1.2). We suspect that, both in terms of policy initiatives and rhetoric, party actions should have an disproportionately large effect on mass politics during times of uncertainty, such as during and after the tumultuous years of 2008–10 across most Western democracies. Elite actions need not be static but may adjust over time, and to a degree greater than anticipated by Rokkanean cleavage-based perspectives. Governments may initially adopt a position of austerity, regardless of whether it aligns with the preferences of their electoral constituency or, for that matter, regardless of it being externally imposed. And they may later abandon such a course in favour of delivering short-term relief through deficit spending. Or parties may experiment with different issue emphases during election campaigns to stay atop of fast-moving realities. In short, as Tooze notes, parties matter. In this section, we reconnect with the voters and propose a model of voter choice in post-crisis political economies informed by our supply-side approach.

Our prime mover, economic change, approximates a common exogenous shock to all political-economic systems participating in the global capitalist economy. The impact of the shock on domestic politics, however, is filtered through distinct national contexts (Bermeo and Pontusson 2010). Post-crisis politics looked very different in the United States compared to Germany, compared to Spain, and so on, and in ways not simply reducible to the depth of the crisis, the organization of national economies, or, for that matter, social divisions in the electorate. Thus, we focus on how party actions through their policies and through their position-taking strategies structure the mass political response.

Further, we take seriously the crisis response not only in the crisis's immediate wake but during the recovery as well. In order to assess the full effects of the GFC and Great Recession on mass politics, it is necessary to consider both policy response and policy rhetoric, and to do so with respect to the initial shock and the follow-on recovery. We discuss this point both theoretically and empirically in latter chapters. Nevertheless, to briefly explain it, during the shock period, there is a 'clarity of responsibility' problem. Since many countries are simultaneously affected, voters are likely to perceive that the crisis, at its onset, is largely caused by exogenous factors, and so voters' blame of incumbent parties may not be too strong. As a result, the political impact of crisis might be smaller and incumbent parties' policy response may not be evaluated by voters with a great weight. However, as the crisis develops in long term, there is more room for politics. Especially during the recovery stage, as the variation in recovery rates across countries increases, voters are likely to blame political elites for poor economic recovery. The search for alternative political choices accordingly may increase and parties' policy responses and messages take on greater importance.

Figure 1.6 illustrates this scope of inquiry; solid black lines represent paths examined in this book; dashed grey lines are other connections which lay outside our scope. With respect to the mass political consequences, the lion's share of current scholarship remains focused on the impact of the shock itself.

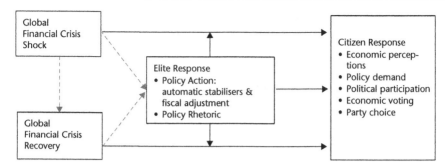

Figure 1.6. Scope of Inquiry

Note: Solid black lines represent paths examined in this book; dashed grey lines are other connections which lay outside our scope.

The role of the path to recovery has received far less attention. A consideration of the recovery—or lack thereof—opens up space for a sustained role for political elites. On this score, scholars have examined how policymakers in different countries succeeded or failed in placing national economies on firmer standing. Few studies, however, have probed the influence of elite position-taking (rhetoric) in directing the voter response. The aim of this book is to consider both of these time periods, and to give equal consideration to policy reality *and* policy rhetoric in shaping the mass political response.

1.6. Organization of the Book

The chapters that follow are organized in three parts. Part I, which includes this chapter and the next, provides the essential background on the economic crises of the young twenty-first century and revisits these events through the lens of electoral politics. The present chapter has reviewed the arc of scholarship on electoral change and continuity and laid out our general approach to the study of public opinion and voter choice post-industrial democracies of the early twenty-first century during and, especially, *after* the crisis. Chapter 2 offers a selective overview of the crisis, directed at its consequences for political competition. We examine the origins and immediate effects of the global financial crisis and the 'Great Recession' that it spawned. We document variations in its impact across the OECD, both in and outside of Europe, and the responses of governments, particularly in relation to income redistribution. We show that over the period 2007–17, in general party systems became larger, electoral volatility rose, and support for incumbent governments declined. With broad brush strokes, this overview sets up the individual-level analyses. Chapter 2 concludes by introducing the data from post-election surveys compiled as part of the Comparative Study of

Electoral Systems (CSES) data on which most of the analyses in Chapters 3–8 are based.

Part II examines the mass political consequences of the Great Recession with a focus on its influence on public perceptions and preferences. For both outcomes, we deploy the scope of inquiry sketched above. Chapter 3 is devoted to objective and subjective feelings of insecurity. The capitalist system of production and exchange requires a set of market actors willing to take on risk. Just as risk can be understood as part and parcel of capitalism, so too does it play an important role in the logic of the modern welfare state. Brought to the fore by the financial crisis, insecurity figures more prominently in electoral choice today than in any time in recent memory. But what affects feelings of insecurity? Perhaps not surprisingly, research shows that occupational-based insecurity shapes subjective perception (Rehm 2016). Yet cross-individual and cross-national variation remains in how the former is directly translated into the latter. Crisis depth and the success or otherwise of recovery have country-level effects, but we also show that individuals' sense of economic precariousness is shaped in large part by party elites. Parties can increase or weaken the impact of the crisis on subjective insecurity through use of social policy and elite cues. Though the impact varies by the stage of the crisis development and types of policy efforts, more spending on welfare mitigates the impact of adverse economic conditions on perceived insecurity. Along with concrete policy efforts, parties can also signal cues to help calm voters in times of uncertainty. By emphasizing concerns for social protection relative to other matters, through their campaign discourse and actions when in government, parties quell fears of future economic loss (e.g. Johns and Kölln forthcoming).

Chapter 4 takes up the question of policy preferences. In representative democracies, citizens select representatives according to the promises of the policies they will deliver. The structuring of preferences by parties should be especially apparent during election campaigns. Crisis depth and recovery explain a good deal of the cross-country differences, but we extend the politics of advanced capitalism's model of constrained partisanship to argue that preferences are shaped both by the individuals' positions in the social structure but also by the set of feasible options from the menu provided by competing political elites. Party cues matter little for the crisis, but significantly shape policy preferences under conditions of recovery. Leveraging a rich battery of survey items across multiple issue areas, we show that party cues operate in different ways to structure public preferences towards public health expenditure and support for the unemployed.

In Part III we turn from examining voter insecurities and preferences to investigate how they matter for political behaviour. As in previous sections, our scope of inquiry is broad but accords specific attention to the role of parties' strategies. In Chapter 5 we take up the matter of electoral participation. Part II probed the retrospective and prospective bases of voter choices at the polls. It is also necessary, however, to examine the decision to participate in elections in the first place. The post-election nature of the CSES data enable us to do that, and at the individual level. For this analysis, after macro-level analysis drawing on all our OECD cases, we turn to the integrated modules of the CSES, taking our analysis back to the early 1990s. After a brief review of the usual suspects driving voter participation, we develop a model of turnout in post-crisis elections. Supplementing standard arguments on individual resources and electoral competitiveness, we bring in the effects of party appeals, subjective insecurity, and popular demands, relative redistribution, austerity versus stimulus, and the accumulation of government debt.

Chapter 6 considers how competence appeals matter for voter choice in post-crisis elections. In an era when the feasible range of policy options has shrunk, many students of electoral choice claim that 'performance politics' reigns supreme. That is, it is not the positions that parties stake out on the issues that matters, but how competent they are as policy managers, particularly managers of the economy. Here, competence is measured by macro-level economic performance (Clarke et al. 2009; Green and Jennings 2017). And this argument finds confirmation in the first-wave research examining election data before and after the economic crisis (Bartels 2014; Hernández and Kriesi 2016; LeDuc and Pammett 2013). We re-examine the influence of competence appeals for post-crisis elections using a more detailed individual-level dataset than afforded by previous studies. Our investigation shows that, while economic conditions matter especially in their long-term impact, their effect on the vote is highly conscribed and contingent on the strategies of party elites on the supply side. However, the degree to which government policy and rhetoric condition the adverse effect of the crisis depends on types of policy efforts as well as the stage of the crisis development. Overall, we find that discretionary spending can effectively mitigate the impact of the crisis in stagnating economies, particularly during the crisis.

After identifying the limits of pure performance-based models of voting in Chapter 6, Chapter 7 examines how the policy demands translate into voter support. Where previous studies have examined how economic perceptions and occupational divisions matter for policy preferences (e.g. Rehm et al. 2012; Rehm 2016), we show that the range of party offerings limits the extent to which these individual-level factors predict voter choice. Instead, we show how the positions parties take and the issue dimensions they emphasize impact the voter's calculus.

The concluding chapter discusses the lessons from the crisis for democracy and comments on whether the elections under analysis represent a 'new equilibrium' in electoral politics or whether we should expect a reversion to pre-crisis politics. Throughout, emphasis will be placed on how variations in national responses and variations in party systems conditioned the influence of the crisis on voter choices and election outcomes.

Appendix

Table 1.A1. Names of Parties from Figure 1.4

Australia	ALP: Australian Labour Party; G: Greens; LPA: Liberal Party of Australia
Austria	G: Greens; SPO: Social Democrats; BZÖ: Alliance Future Austria; FPÖ: Freedom Party of Austria; ÖVP: Austrian People's Party
Canada	G: Greens; NDP: New Democratic Party; CP: Conservative Party; LP: Liberal Party; BQ: Bloc Québécois
Czech Republic	ČSSD: Czech Social Democratic Party; KSČM: Communist Party of Bohemia and Moravia; KDU: Christian and Democratic Union; ODS: Civic Democratic Party; TOP: TOP 09; USV: Dawn—National Coalition
Finland	SSDP: Social Democratic Party of Finland; VAS: Left Alliance; VL: Green Alliance; KD: Christian Democrats of Finland; KK: National Coalition Party; PS: True Finns; SK: Swedish People's Party in Finland; RKP: Centre of Finland
France	FDG: Left Front; PS: Socialist Party; V: Greens; FN: National Front; MD: Democratic Movement; UMP: Union for a Popular Movement
Germany	G: Green Party; L: Left Party; SPD: Social Democratic Party; CDU: Christian Democratic Union/Christian Social Union; FDP: Free Democratic Party; AfD: Alternative for Germany; P: Pirate Party
Greece	D: Democratic Left; KKE: Communist Party; P: PASOK; S: SYRIZA; ND: New Democracy; XA: Golden Dawn
Iceland	SAM: Alliance—Social Democratic Party of Iceland; VGF: Left-Green Movement; BF: Bright Future; F: People's Party; SJ: Independence Party; P: Pirate Party
Ireland	G: Green Party; L: Labour Party; FF: Fianna Fáil; FG: Fine Gael; SF: Sinn Féin
Israel	M: Meretz; HH: Jewish Home; L: Likud; S: Shas; YA: There Is a Future
Japan	JCP: Japanese Communist Party; SDP: Social Democratic Party; DPJ: Democratic Party of Japan; JRP: Japan Restoration Party; LDP: Liberal Democratic Party; NKP: New Komeito; PNP: People's New Party; YP: Your Party
Latvia	SC: Harmony Centre; NA: National Alliance; V: Unity; ZRP: Zatlers' Reform Party; ZZS: Union of Greens and Peasants
Mexico	MC: Citizens' Movement; PNL: New Alliance Party; PRD: Democratic Revolutionary Party; PRI: Institutional Revolutionary Party; PT: Workers' Party; PVEM: Green Part of Mexico; PAN: National Action Party
New Zealand	G: Green Party; L: Labour Party; ACT: ACT New Zealand; N: National Party; NZF: New Zealand First; UF: United Future; MAN: Mana; MAO: Maori Party
Norway	DNA: Labour Party; SV: Socialist Left Party; H: Right Party; KRF: Christian People's Party; SP: Centre Party; V: Left Party; FRP: Progress Party
Poland	SLD: Democratic Left Alliance; PO: Civic Platform; PSL: Polish People's Party; PiS: Law and Justice; RP: Patriotic Movement
Portugal	BE: Left Bloc; PCP: Portuguese Communist Party; PS: Socialist Party; PSD: Social Democratic Party

Slovakia	SMER: Direction—Social Democracy; OL: Ordinary People and Independent Personalities; SAS: Freedom and Solidarity; SNS: Slovak National Party
Slovenia	PS: Positive Slovenia; SD: Social Democrats; LGV: Gregor Virant's Civic List; NSI: New Slovenia-Christian People's Party; SDS: Slovenian Democratic Party; SLS: Slovenian People's Party; SNS: Slovenian National Party; D: Democratic Pensioners' Party of Slovenia
South Korea	UPP: United Progressive Party; DP: Democratic United Party; LFP: Liberty Forward Party; NFP: New Frontier Party
Sweden	MP: Green Party; SAP: Social Democratic Party; V: Left Party; CP: Centre Party; FP: Liberal Party; KD: Christian Democratic Party; M: Moderates; SD: Sweden Democrats
Switzerland	GLP: Green Liberal Party Switzerland; GPS: Green Party of Switzerland; SPS: Social Democratic Party of Switzerland; BDP: Conservative Democratic Party of Switzerland; CVP: Christian Democratic People's Party; FDP: Liberal Party; SVP: Swiss People's Party
Turkey	CHP: Republican People's Party; HDP: Peoples' Democratic Party; AKP: Justice and Development Party; MHP: Nationalist Movement Party
United Kingdom	G: Green Party; L: Labour Party; C: Conservative Party: LD: Liberal Democratic Party; PC: Plaid Cymru; SNP: Scottish Nationalist Party; UKIP: United Kingdom Independence Party
United States	D: Democratic Party; R: Republican Party

2

The Great Recession and Electoral Politics, 2007–2016

At its heart, capitalism cannot survive without change. The pace of change, however, ebbs and flows. Economic change accelerated throughout the latter part of the twentieth and into the twenty-first century (Rudel and Hooper 2005, 275–6). Beginning in the middle of the twentieth century and facilitated by advances in technology, the countries most advanced in economic and social development have experienced sweeping deindustrialization, have absorbed shifts in their economies away from agriculture and manufacturing toward the service sector, and have seen salaried work decline and part-time and temporary work rise. Globalization and the outsourcing of jobs have redistributed production supply chains around the world. Economic change has proceeded apace with demographic change: declining fertility rates, ageing populations, and rising immigration flows.

These economic and social shifts have generated political changes. Following a period of stability after the Second World War, by the turn of the twenty-first century, electoral politics in many advanced representative democracies had become increasingly unpredictable. Some party systems had begun to fragment, in some cases dealign, and in others realign. In Western Europe, electoral volatility has increased, particularly since the beginning of the century (Dassonneville 2015), leading to increased electoral instability and significant party system change (Chiaramonte and Emanuele 2015). Newcomers to the party scene, often occupying the extremes of the ideological spectrum, have attracted increasing support. The success of these challenger, or 'niche', parties has often been at the expense of centre-left Social Democratic parties but has not excluded a similarly declining vote share for those of the centre-right.

The global financial crisis that began in late 2007 and stretched through 2009 developed on top of these evolving social and economic changes and amounted to an additional external shock. By interacting with underlying trends already disrupting the conduct of electoral politics, the GFC intensified

Democracy Under Siege? Parties, Voters, and Elections After the Great Recession. Timothy Hellwig, Yesola Kweon, and Jack Vowles, Oxford University Press (2020). © Timothy Hellwig, Yesola Kweon, and Jack Vowles.
DOI: 10.1093/oso/9780198846208.001.0001

instability. Some party systems changed dramatically, like Greece, Spain, and Ireland. But others, like Australia, New Zealand, or Hungary, did not. Some governments fell, while others survived. Variations in policy responses from country to country reflected, to some degree, the extent of exposure to the crisis, the responsiveness of existing institutional and policy frameworks, prior fiscal balances, the level of government debt, other choices made by public and private sector actors, and the partisan leanings of governments in office at the time (Bermeo and Pontusson 2012).

This book examines how a combination of incremental and rapid social and economic changes have reshaped electoral behaviour throughout the advanced capitalist democracies. The previous chapter advanced a theoretical framework designed to do so. Before applying our framework and assessing its utility, this chapter provides the essential political and economic context. We first examine the origins and immediate effects of the global financial crisis and the 'Great Recession' that it spawned. Moving the focus beyond the almost exclusive European focus of the research so far, we examine the impact of the crisis across the member countries of the OECD, and the ways in which that variation is shaping the contexts of individual-level behaviour.[1] We then examine patterns of electoral volatility and the changing nature of party systems before turning to consider the reasons why some governments were defeated and why others survived. We conclude by introducing our main sources of data: cross-sectional individual-level survey data from twenty-five national elections in OECD democracies from 2011 to 2016 sourced from the Comparative Study of Electoral Systems (CSES), Module 4; macro-data for thirty-five OECD democracies from 1990 to 2016; and a pooled time series of further CSES survey data Modules 1–4 from twenty-four OECD countries between the mid-1990s and 2016, augmented by additional elections from CSES Module 5 and from country national election studies.

2.1. Setting the Stage: Continuity and Change in Advanced Capitalism, 1945–2007

The global financial crisis was not only a shock to governments and the public at large: it also sent shockwaves through the economics profession (Bezemer 2010). Mainstream neo-classical economics tends to ignore the effects of finance on the real economy. Instead it relies on equilibrium models

---

[1] In terms of its implications for electoral politics, cross-national empirical scholarship on the crisis is characterized by a European and, within that, EU focus. This is due in part to the depth of the crises' impact on EU economies but also to the availability of comparable individual-level survey data (see e.g. Anderson and Hecht 2014; Hobolt and Tilley 2016; Dancygier and Donnelly 2014; Talving 2017).

that assume markets will function effectively with minimal government intervention. Indeed, most neo-classical economists blame market failures on excessive government regulation, despite historical evidence that deregulation is the best predictor of financial crises (Reinhart and Rogoff 2009). The economics establishment had assumed that the free market policy framework of the early 1980s had produced steady, non-inflationary growth and had stabilized economies around the world (Williamson 1990). The key evidence for this stability, or 'great moderation', of the business cycle is lower volatility across macro-economic indicators in the largest OECD economies since the early 1980s (Stock and Watson 2003). However, the degree to which this new policy framework contributed to the lower volatility is subject to debate. Improved management of monetary policy and increases in labour market flexibility arguably played a role. Yet so too did factors outside of policy-makers' control, such as the influence of technological advances on inventory management of traded products (Summers 2005).

Meanwhile, average growth rates in the more advanced economies declined in comparison to the previous three decades. Figure 2.1 displays growth in real

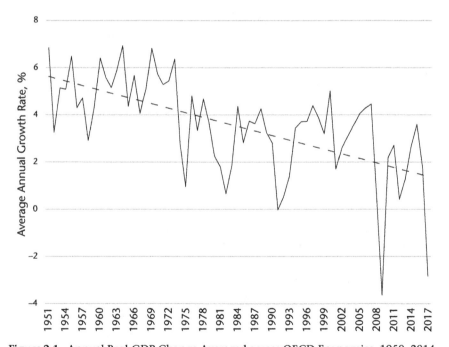

Figure 2.1. Annual Real GDP Change Averaged across OECD Economies, 1950–2014

Note: Figure reports the unweighted average across OECD member countries, as per membership in 2016. Data for Czech Republic, Estonia, Hungary, Latvia, Poland, Slovakia, and Slovenia are missing. Growth rates calculated as annual change in GDP at constant 2011 prices. Dashed line reports linear trend, Growth = 5.56–0.07* Year, $R^2 = 0.39$.

Source: Feenstra et al. 2015.

GDP from the early 1950s to 2017 averaged over the countries that were members of the OECD in 2016.[2] Despite regular ups and downs, there has been a decline in growth rates over the past sixty or more years. While much of the earlier growth can be attributed to underutilized capacity during the recovery after the Second World War, but by the 1960s and 1970s this explanation can be discounted. The shift to more market-orientated polices after the 1970s was intended to address the slowing of growth in that decade, but largely failed to do so: Figure 2.1 shows the step downward in the 1970s persisting.

Figure 2.1 does not entirely confirm a moderation in growth fluctuations post-1980, probably because it includes and weights equally the smaller OECD economies that continued to experience volatility in macro-economic indicators. Previous recessions also stand out: 1975, associated with the first oil crisis, 1982, and 1991. The precipitous drop in growth in 2009 illustrates clearly the big impact of the global financial crisis.

Forming the background to these developments, since the Second World War the rules governing the global economy have changed significantly. As devised in 1944 at Bretton Woods, the postwar economic framework contained several elements no longer in place today. Adhering to principles of a regulated market economy, it established a system of fixed currency exchange rates pegged to the price of gold and the US dollar with tight controls on capital movement. Keynesian policies of counter-cyclical demand management could be applied with low unemployment as a central policy goal. In the case of a strongly growing economy, Keynesian economists advised that governments should increase taxes, reduce expenditure, and pay down their debts. When economies faltered, governments could stimulate the economy using monetary and/or fiscal policy, the latter involving tax cuts and/or increases in government expenditure, if necessary going into deficit and borrowing to do so. Controls on capital flows limited the ability of financial markets to constrain these decisions.

From the 1970s onward, more market-orientated neo-classical economics began to prevail in business circles among academics and policymakers alike, albeit with differences in timing and intensity across countries. The ascendancy of neo-liberalism revived the ideas of the classical economic liberalism of the nineteenth century. Advanced countries deregulated their economies, reduced

---

[2] Defining the case selection as membership in 2016 includes a number of less developed and post-communist countries not part of the developed world in the earlier period and having grown more strongly post-1980. We would expect this to reduce the variance 'explained' and the slope of the time trend and indeed it does: an alternative plot confined to OECD members in 1980 accentuates the differences in average growth between the pre- and post-1980 periods. In the period after the global financial crisis, developed country growth has dropped even further (Hannon 2016).

international trade barriers, privatized state assets, discouraged trade union membership, and removed restrictions on capital flows. Economists advised governments to keep inflation under control and pay less attention to unemployment, thus minimizing counter-cyclical economic stimuli, while showing little concern about recurring asset bubbles that run the risk of triggering financial crises when perceptions of inflated asset values turn downward.

The global financial crisis therefore had deep foundations in the structure of the global economy. As a currency that can be held by governments and other institutions as foreign reserves, the US dollar was fixed against the price of gold until 1964, artificially boosting its value, allowing the US to operate a loose monetary policy underpinning increases in government expenditure to fund social programmes and the Vietnam War. This proved unsustainable, and in 1971 the US unilaterally abandoned the fixed exchange rate system. Not long after, the price of oil rose significantly, reducing growth in oil-dependent developed economies, a challenge that stimulus policies failed to counter. Restrictions on international capital flows began to be removed and those flows increased, further spurred by the higher price of oil. By the 1990s most capital controls had been eliminated. Advances in communications technology further facilitated the management and manipulation of monetary flows by international banks and financial institutions.

In 1999 the United States Congress repealed the Glass-Stegall Act. Enacted in 1933, Glass-Stegall prohibited commercial banks from engaging in wider investment activities. While its provisions had been progressively weakened, its repeal meant that boundaries between banks providing services to depositors and business and those involved in speculative investment were greatly weakened, if not extinguished. In Britain, earlier changes in the regulation of banking and finance in 1986 also encouraged the merging of commercial and investment banks, and led to the increased importance of the City of London in international finance. In 1997 an incoming Labour Government established the Financial Services Authority to provide broad oversight. Flaws in its design meant it focused on traditional banks and failed to monitor their interactions with the investment banks and hedge funds involved in 'shadow banking': institutions operating outside traditional regulatory boundaries (Pozsar et al. 2013).

Abandonment of the Bretton Woods model of fixed exchange rates and capital controls failed to counter lower growth in developed economies, and encouraged global trade imbalances, the inflation of asset values, and an increase in high-risk lending activities. Capital flowed from countries with trade surpluses to countries with large capital markets generating high returns (Iversen and Soskice 2012). Lower volatility in macro-economic data applauded by neo-liberal economists took attention away from increased volatility in current account balances and capital flows.

2.2. The Global Financial Crisis, 2007–2009

The scene was set for the crisis of 2007. As the new century began, structural problems in the world's largest economy, the United States, again became a matter of concern. A trade deficit had emerged, funded by cheap loans from capital-rich countries. Levels of private debt rose. An investment bubble in the technology sector burst in 2000 and 2001, after which interest rates were kept low to stimulate the economy. While the federal-sponsored mortgage banks charged with facilitating home ownership, Fannie Mae and Freddie Mac, operated as private providers with an implicit government guarantee, competition from other banks led to lower standards for loan approvals across the mortgage market. The use of financial instruments known as 'derivatives' increased, with the intent of spreading risk over multiple assets. Their effect was to conceal the risk as much as to spread it. With household incomes stagnant, many Americans continued to borrow and spend on the strength of what appeared to be ever-increasing house values. The infection spread to other countries, with unprecedented levels of household debt developing in Denmark, Iceland, Ireland, the Netherlands, Norway, Estonia, Hungary, and Latvia (OECD 2013).

The 'subprime' mortgage market began to collapse in 2006, and in early in 2007 several large US mortgage companies filed for bankruptcy. By late 2007 banks were becoming reluctant to loan to each other to cover short-term imbalances between deposits and loans. In September of that year, Britain's Northern Rock became the first bank to be unable to cover its commitments, precipitating the country's first bank run in over a century. Northern Rock was nationalized a few months later. In the United States, concerns that investment bank Bear Stearns would collapse led to its fire sale to another bank, J. P. Morgan Chase, a move encouraged by the US Federal Reserve.

The crisis came to a head in the United States in September 2008. The US Government bailed out Fannie Mae and Freddie Mac, and the Bank of America saved investment firm Merrill Lynch by means of a takeover. Another big investment bank, Lehman Brothers, filed for bankruptcy. On 15 September Washington refused to act, leading to a large drop of confidence in financial markets and a domino effect throughout the banking system. Consequently, the US Government reversed course and bailed out banks to prevent a collapse of the financial system. The British Government also began bailing out banks, taking several into public ownership. Revealing the extent to which financial institutions and money markets had become globalized, stock markets fell, international trade shrank, and international capital flows diminished. By the end of the year the crisis had spread throughout Europe, and the global economy was in recession. As Figure 2.1 shows, in 2009 the global economic contraction was the worst for any year since the Second World War.

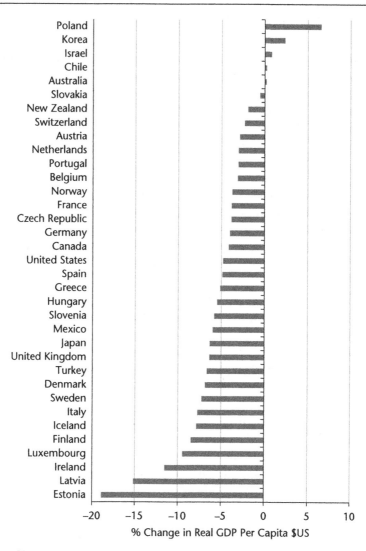

Figure 2.2. The Great Contraction: OECD Economies, 2007–2009
Source: OECD 2017.

While Figure 2.1 depicts trends in economic performance, cross-country averages mask the variation in economic performance across the OECD that forms the key context for our later analysis. Figure 2.2 illustrates the variation throughout these economies by comparing GDP per capita in purchasing power parities between 2007 and 2009. As much of the crisis can be attributed to an exogenous shock in international housing and then broader financial markets, the variation across countries is striking.

A handful of economies escaped unscathed: Poland, South Korea, and Australia, all of which are represented in the data to be analysed later in this book. As the country's prime minister at the time, Donald Tusk, was quick to point out, Poland was an island of stability in an otherwise volatile European economy. Poland's resilience may be traced to several factors, including monetary policy autonomy thanks to being outside the European common currency Eurozone, high levels of EU-funded infrastructure expenditure, low labour costs, and low public debt levels. In South Korea, an initially strong economic contraction and a fall in the value of its currency were countered by central bank efforts to stimulate the economy by lowering interest rates (Cho 2012). In combination with low debt and a healthy long-term structural balance, this was sufficient to stave off the crisis. The banking industry had learned from the 1997 Asian crisis and was not greatly exposed. Korea also benefited from the counter-cyclical policy of its largest trading partner, China. Australia's robust economic performance can be explained by its well-regulated banking system and its high exposure to the Chinese markets demanding products from an extractive resource boom. Israel benefited from a combination of prior responsibility in government fiscal policy, low public and private debt, strong baseline growth, low interest rates, high foreign exchange reserves, and a strong banking system not exposed to high-risk investments (Fischer 2008). Chile also benefited from high commodity prices, a strong fiscal position, and a well-regulated banking system.

Among the initially worst affected cases, Ireland, Iceland, Finland, and Latvia are also represented by CSES survey data to be analysed in later chapters. Ireland and Iceland were dramatically affected by banking crises and collapses in their housing markets, while Finland suffered a dramatic collapse in manufacturing on which its economy was heavily dependent. In the case of Finland, the crisis appears to have acted as a trigger that exposed the vulnerability of its forestry, metals and electronics industries to international competition (OECD 2014).

These country cases occupying the extremes are consistent with the comparative evidence. Countries with high levels of public and private debt, easy credit, and more dependent on manufacturing exports seem to have suffered the most in the initial phase. Commodity exporters, countries with flexible exchange rates, and those which had responsible fiscal policies prior to the crisis seem to have suffered less (Berkmen et al. 2012).

2.3. Governments React: Policy Responses to the Global Financial Crisis

How did policymakers respond? The first response to the crisis was coordinated by G20 summits in November 2008 and April 2009, with most participating governments agreeing to implement a stimulus package. Tax cuts were a stronger element of stimulus, often associated with cuts in expenditure. Government support for the financial sector also played a larger role than in previous recessions. Recapitalization and guarantees amounted to the equivalent of nearly 60 per cent of GDP in the UK, 50 per cent in Sweden, 20 per cent in Germany, 18 per cent in France, and 16 per cent in the United States (Pontusson and Raess 2012, 27).[3] Elsewhere the depth of the crisis was much more extreme. The cost of bank guarantees and recapitalization in Ireland peaked at 229 per cent of GDP (Barnes and Wren 2012, 292). Iceland's banking crisis was the most serious. The government could only afford to bail out the three major banks' domestic activities and imposed strict controls on the movement of capital.

Welfare systems constitute the most significant automatic stabilizers that cover unemployment and loss of income, on which a heavier load automatically develops in a recession. As indicated in Figure 1.1, states with more fully developed welfare states, like those in Nordic Europe, therefore have more inbuilt policy instruments that can contribute to stimulus. Our analysis in later chapters will build in the extent to which tax and welfare systems redistribute income by way of automatic stabilization, and we show the extent to which redistribution shaped individual-level responses. The discretionary element of stimulus is made up of new expenditure and planned expenditure brought forward to help maintain economic activity, and represented by the long-term fiscal balance: the structural deficit or surplus estimated over the business cycle, the latter defined by the period between economic expansions and contractions. Countries with less generous welfare systems, such as the United States, necessarily relied more heavily on a discretionary stimulus (see Figure 1.2). Similarly we expect stimulus by this means to have both individual-level and consequent political effects.

European Union (EU) membership levies an additional constraint on the policy response: penalties may be triggered by budget deficits over 3 per cent of GDP and debt above 60 per cent.[4] Adding to injury, the European Commission underestimated the scope of the crisis, rejecting calls early in 2009 from the US and the OECD to increase its stimulus package. Individual countries were therefore left to bear the burden. Some were more able to do so than others. Those with high levels of automatic stabilization and recent records of responsible fiscal policy were unable to cut taxes or increase expenditure, the former being the most effective strategy. For instance, the most exposed Scandinavian countries such as Norway and Finland had sufficient capacity

---

[3] Comparing country responses to the GFC to those of earlier recessions prior to the early 1980s, Pontusson and Raess (2012) interpret the responses as 'liberal' Keynesianism as compared to the 'social' Keynesianism prevalent in the 1960s and 1970s.

[4] In practice, penalties were often not enforced and noncompliance tolerated, but in September 2011 there was further agreement more effectively to apply these provisions.

for an effective stimulus beyond the immediate crisis, while countries in southern Europe with less effective tax systems and with a tendency to record regular budget deficits did not: for example, Italy and Portugal (Cameron 2012).

2.4. The Evolution of Tough Times: From Financial Crisis to Sovereign Debt Crisis

The shock of the global financial crisis was first felt by banks and investment firms, followed by stock markets. This in turn affected international trade, capital flows, and economic growth. What followed next was a crisis of government or 'sovereign' debt as governments took steps to stave off chaos by rescuing their banks: by spring of 2010, the crisis had migrated from the private to the public sector. Fears about the consequences of high levels of government debt raised interest rates for governments needing loans. The crisis spread as countries not hitherto affected now saw interest rates rise in accordance with previously acquired public debt up to 2007.

Figure 2.3 displays how sovereign debt increased within countries since the 1990s, as indicated from gross general government debt as a percentage of GDP (IMF 2019). Across the whole OECD, government debt averaged close to 50 per cent of GDP in 2006, rising to nearly 64 per cent by 2010, and nearly 71 per cent in 2016. The figure highlights considerable variation across countries, both in terms of levels, and changes. Debt levels increased substantially in two out of three OECD countries, and continued or took a decisive downward track in only three (Israel, Switzerland, and Turkey).[5] In another six countries debt had been declining from high levels in the 1990s, and picked up again modestly when the crisis hit (Sweden, Denmark, Norway, Belgium, Chile, and New Zealand). With respect to all other countries, debt had been rising even before the GFC (for example, Germany, Austria, and the UK) or, where falling before, rose significantly when the crisis hit. In some cases, the change was dramatic. From 2007 to 2016, US gross sovereign debt rose from 65 to 106 per cent of GDP. UK debt was 41 per cent in 2007, 107 per cent by 2016. Irish debt was 23 per cent in 2007, 104 per cent in 2014, although had dropped to 73 per cent by 2016. Greek debt was 103 per cent of GDP in 2007, and 181 per cent in 2016.

The sovereign debt crisis was most evident in Greece. Banks responded to the crisis and revealed structural weaknesses in the economy by hiking interest rates. The interest rates on ten-year government bonds, which had been stable for years at around 5 per cent, rose steadily from the beginning of 2010

---

[5] All three of these countries had debt at 70 per cent of GDP or more in the late 1990s that had fallen to moderate levels of about 40 per cent of GDP by 2016.

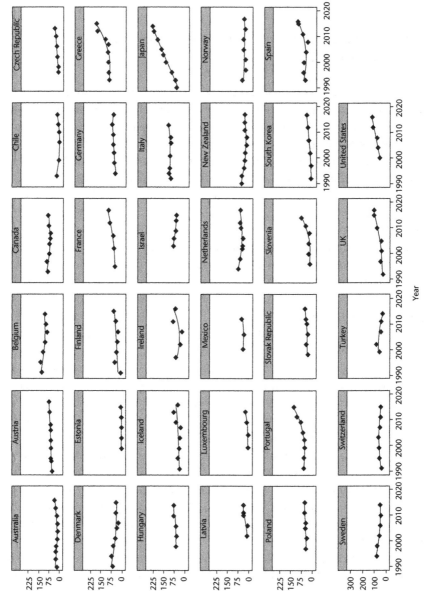

Figure 2.3. Sovereign Debt in the OECD, 1990–2016 (Gross Government Debt as % of GDP)
Source: IMF 2019.

to the end of 2012, reaching nearly 30 per cent. At the same time, Greece's membership in the Eurozone took away the option of adjustment by way of currency depreciation. The end result was skyrocketing debt levels. The primary means of rescuing the Greek economy was through large-scale bailout programmes engineered by the European Commission, European Central Bank (ECB), and International Monetary Fund (IMF), the so-called 'Troika'. With the approval of the Eurozone member states, Greece received three large-scale bailouts from 2010 to 2015, totalling over €300 billion. The price for this financial support was a steady diet of austerity. Taxes were raised, pensions cut, and public service pay slashed. Greece's public sector workforce was hit especially hard, with layoffs affecting around 25,000 civil servants.

Cuts to social programmes and public employment have challenged the very basis of representative democracy in Greece. Since the end of the dictatorship and return to democracy in 1974, the country had been led by one of two political parties: PASOK on the left and New Democracy on the right. Both parties built up loyal constituencies through the expansion of state largess, realized in the form of generous pensions and a large public sector. Troika-imposed conditionality meant that such strategies of constituency-building were no longer viable. The political effects of austerity were swiftly felt. In the six years between the end of 2011, and the ousting of Prime Minister George Papandreou's PASOK Government following the first bailout package, and the end of 2016, Greece has been led by one grand-coalition, two nonpartisan caretaker governments, and until its defeat in 2019, governments led by the SYRIZA, a left-wing socialist party established only in 2004.

While the drama of its politics before, during, and after the crisis exceeded that found anywhere else, the forces leading to Greece's modern tragedy were present across the OECD. There was also concern that countries like Italy, Spain, and Portugal might be unable to service their debts. This led to further interest rate increases for those countries and raised perceptions of a risk of default. In an effort to put a lid on debt levels, many governments by 2010 pared back their stimulus packages, cut expenditures, and embraced austerity (see Figures 1.2 and 1.3).

Expansion of the monetary supply through central bank purchase of bonds or assets continued to provide stimulus in the UK, the US, Japan, Sweden, and Switzerland, but after an initial bond purchase in 2009 the European Central Bank (ECB) refused at first to mount an expansionary strategy in the Eurozone. In 2011 the ECB instead raised interest rates, an act which only inhibited recovery. It was not until the first quarter of 2015 that the ECB used its asset purchase programme, or quantitative easing, to inject a modicum of stimulus into the nineteen-member bloc. As a policy tool, monetary expansion had the effect of reducing interest rates, thus stimulating business investment and housing markets. But expansionary policies did not benefit governments

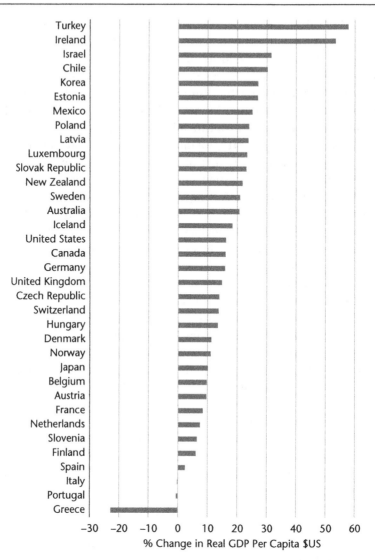

Figure 2.4. The Uneven Recovery: OECD Economies 2009–2016
Source: OECD 2017.

with debts perceived to be unsustainable, for which interest rates remained high. European governments could seek bailouts from organizations such as the European Commission, the European Central Bank, or, internationally, the International Monetary Fund.

As a gauge of economic recovery, Figure 2.4 displays the change in real GDP per capita at purchasing power parities between 2009 and 2016. Those countries least affected during the first two years of the crisis remained relatively prosperous (recall Figure 2.2). Over the longer seven-year period, more than half the OECD countries rebounded and surpassed their 2007–9 average income levels, although in some cases the recovery was very modest. Two of the worst-affected countries in 2009, Finland and Italy, remained so, with the latter a victim to the sovereign debt crisis. The Portuguese, Spanish, and especially Greek economies cratered as well. The recovery in the Nordic countries was also sluggish. Iceland, as one of the countries hardest hit in 2009, was no longer in the worst affected category, although still lacked a full recovery. Low growth in Denmark is partly accounted for by its fixed exchange rate with the euro: despite maintaining its own currency, Denmark is effectively part of the Eurozone. As a result it was not able to use monetary policy as a stimulus. Norway's situation in 2015 reflects the decline in international oil prices in 2014, on which its economy had become highly dependent: up to 2012, its recovery had been more in accord with that of its neighbour, Sweden.

For Ireland, Figure 2.4 shows an apparent increase in average real GDP per head of 50 per cent compared to 2009. Given the seriousness of the Irish crisis, Ireland's membership of the Eurozone, and the austerity that followed the crisis and bank buyout, this performance is remarkable. The Irish case has several unique features. First, while part of the Eurozone, Ireland has been able to maintain an extremely low corporate tax rate by international standards, at 12.5 per cent. This makes it highly attractive for investment, particularly compared to the rest of Europe. Second, the apparent recovery is the result of a very strong surge between 2014 and 2015—so strong that it has provoked considerable scepticism (Halpin 2016). Because of the significance of large-scale corporate investment in the relatively small Irish economy, GDP per head is not necessarily the best estimate of average incomes at the household level in that country: gross national income (GNI) is often recommended as a better alternative (OECD 2005).

2.5. Beyond the Economic Aggregates: The Effect of the Crisis on the Distribution of Wealth

Understanding the range of country experiences following the GFC is essential for comparing political consequences and policy responses. But it stops short of revealing variation in the impact on individual citizens. The effect of the crisis on the objective and subjective well-being of individuals has economic and political consequences. Subsequent chapters estimate these effects directly by use of individual-level survey data, but here we provide the broader context. The onset of the Great Recession reignited debates about social and economic inequality, particularly within the advanced post-industrial democracies. Where inequality has been associated with declining or stagnant living standards among those on low incomes, and the declining adequacy of social safety nets, insecurity and risk has intensified. As depicted in our theoretical framework from Chapter 1, we take these economic changes as key drivers of potential political change.

One diagnosis of the root cause of the global financial crisis lies in increasing inequality in the developed democracies. Since the 1980s, because of neo-liberal reforms in labour markets, tax, and benefit systems, the gains from growth have accrued disproportionately to those on higher incomes. This reduces consumer demand from those on lower and middle incomes, and may further depress growth rates. Policy reforms have also served to widen the gap between those whose income derives from investment and those who rely on their labour. Regarding the former, asset prices have inflated, and as a result those seeking to own their homes take on more debt relative to their incomes. Generous loan conditions have encouraged taking on debt. This partly accounts for the slow recovery following the GFC. Much of the renewed growth shows many of the same signs that led to the crisis: housing price bubbles and high levels of household debt.

Meanwhile economic inequality has risen in most, though not all, OECD countries (OECD 2016). Figure 2.5 displays country changes, with those becoming more unequal at the top and those achieving greater equality, through one means or the other, at the bottom. Increasing inequality can be produced by the poor doing worse or standing still, with the rich doing better. A reduction in inequality might simply be the result of the rich losing ground, as appears to have been the case in several countries worst affected in the immediate aftermath of the GFC. For example, against the trend toward greater inequality, Iceland's remarkable shift towards more equality since the GFC appears to reflect both the destruction of wealth and the persistence of a robust tax and welfare system.

This can be confirmed by closer inspection of OECD data: between 2007 and 2014 in Iceland the household disposable income of the bottom 10 per cent dropped by 5 per cent, and by almost 18 per cent among the top 10 per cent. Meanwhile in the United Kingdom the extent of austerity delivered by the Conservative Government did not prevent a small increase in tax and transfer redistribution, nor a small decrease in inequality. But lower inequality in the UK was as likely to be attributable to declining incomes among the top 10 per cent, whose incomes declined somewhat more than the bottom decile (by 3.8 per cent compared to 2.4 per cent), as it was to government taxes and transfers (OECD 2016, figure 2). By contrast, many societies emerged from the crisis years with higher levels of inequality. For instance, despite increased taxation and welfare expenditure, Greece shifted towards a significantly higher level of inequality with the bottom 10 per cent worse off than the top decile (28 per cent worse off compared to 21.6 per cent). And while annual growth rates in Spain returned to pre-2007 levels, gains were

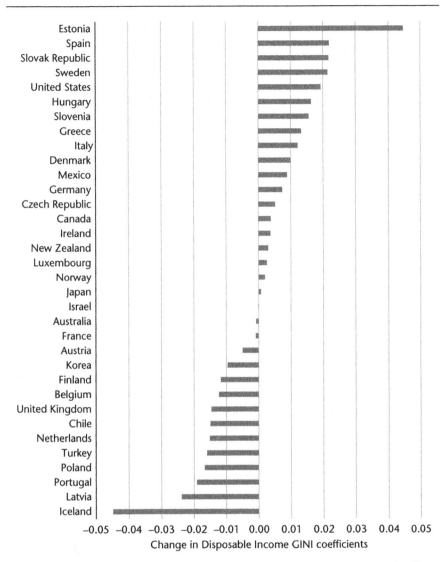

Figure 2.5. The Distribution of Wealth: Change in Disposable Income Gini Coefficients, 2007–2014
Source: OECD 2016.

concentrated at the top: incomes increased by 21 per cent for the top 1 per cent while the bottom two-thirds of income earners lost in real terms (OECD, LIS).

The range of distributive outcomes shown in Figure 2.5, with nearly as many OECD countries becoming more equal as those becoming less over these seven years, is consistent with the range of government policy responses discussed above and in Chapter 1. We expect these policy responses, as well as the language parties use to counter the crisis effects, to also condition individual perceptions, attitudes, and behaviours.

2.6. The Political Fallout: Party Systems, Electoral Volatility, and Incumbent Survival

As the preceding discussion highlights, the economic and social fallout from the GFC has been both substantial and diverse. To what extent are differences in these economies' capacities to rebound from the external shocks reflected in political attitudes and electoral behaviour? To address this question, macro-economic conditions, levels of and changes in economic inequality, and the capacity of tax and transfer systems (automatic stabilizers) to mitigate the impact of the GFC inform our key country-level parameters in our analyses in the chapters to follow. But first, to contextualize the analysis of individual reactions later in this book, the remainder of this chapter provides an over-view of the *political* consequences of the crisis, summarized by three key indicators: party systems, electoral volatility, and government support in elections.

We first consider changes in the party system as conveyed by the number of parties. Inasmuch as the crisis was met with political uncertainty, we might expect the outfall of the economic crisis to increase the number of parties as voters shop around for the best solution to what appeared to be a new problem. This would increase opportunities for new parties to pitch their wares. Or, alternatively, the crisis events may well have led to a reduction in the number of parties as voters weigh the predictability of the familiar over taking a chance on a new option. The picture, it turns out, is mixed. Figure 2.6 plots the average effective number of parties in the OECD democracies across two periods: the years before the crisis, from 1991 to 2007, and those follow-ing the crisis's onset, between 2008 and 2016.[6] In fourteen countries the party system moved toward greater fragmentation, as indicated by those located above and to the left of the diagonal. Yet in eleven countries the number of electoral competitors declined and in six there was little or no difference.

The mixed picture revealed in the figure suggests the transmission between economic shocks and political party systems is more complex. In order to take account of other factors we model the effective number of parties as a function of a set of economic and political factors. Starting from 1990, the first year elections took place in the formerly communist democracies in Central and Eastern Europe, we construct a dataset of all general elections in thirty-three

---

[6] The measure is Laakso and Taagepera's (1979) effective number of electoral parties, which weights parties by their vote shares.

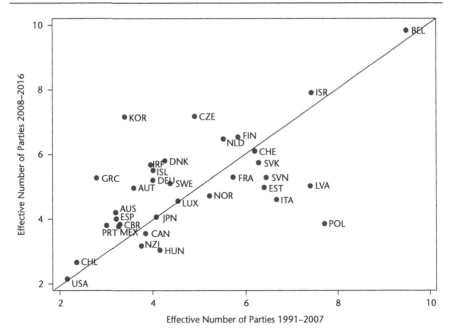

Figure 2.6. The Effective Number of Parties in OECD Countries Before and After the GFC
Source: Gallagher 2017.

OECD countries through 2016.[7] Per our conjecture advanced in Chapter 1, that crisis politics is as much about recovering from a downfall as it is absorbing the initial shock, we include indicators for the shock (elections in 2008–9) and the recovery (2010 and later) periods. To assess economic decline, we include a pair of variables. *GDP per capita change* is measured as the country's real change in GDP per capita between elections. *Government debt* is gross public debt as a percentage of GDP, which we include in the model in its natural log given the skewed nature of the variable. Finally, we control for the electoral system, measured as proportional representation systems scoring 1 and others 0 (with PR systems expected to yield more parties), regime type (presidential system), and the age of democracy, with countries with first elections in 1990s scored 1 and all others 0. To account for omitted variables and potential sources of heteroscedasticity owing to the structure of the data, all models are estimated with country fixed effects.

---

[7] Specifically, our sample are the OECD member countries as of 2015. This includes Australia, Austria, Belgium, Canada, Chile, Czech Republic, Denmark, Estonia, Finland, France, Germany, Greece, Hungary, Iceland, Ireland, Israel, Italy, Japan, South Korea, Latvia, Luxembourg, Mexico, the Netherlands, New Zealand, Norway, Poland, Portugal, Slovakia, Slovenia, Spain, Sweden, Turkey, the United Kingdom, and the United States. We exclude Switzerland owing to the power-sharing nature of the parties at the federal level.

Table 2.1. The Impact of the GFC on the Effective Number of Parties, OECD Countries, 1990–2016

	(1)	(2)	(3)	(4)
Shock period	0.020	0.074	0.111	−1.216*
	(0.185)	(0.189)	(0.192)	(0.705)
Recovery period	0.409***	0.593***	0.454***	−1.813***
	(0.135)	(0.126)	(0.130)	(0.671)
ΔGDP per capita	0.012	0.007	0.016*	0.009
	(0.009)	(0.008)	(0.009)	(0.009)
(Ln)Government debt	0.135	0.236	0.133	0.077
	(0.164)	(0.163)	(0.174)	(0.161)
PR system	1.163***	1.250***	1.178***	1.342***
	(0.411)	(0.420)	(0.423)	(0.424)
Presidential system	−1.530***	−1.650***	−1.529***	−1.673***
	(0.244)	(0.240)	(0.253)	(0.274)
New democracy	0.631	1.009**	0.663	0.391
	(0.492)	(0.495)	(0.530)	(0.519)
GFC Shock × New dem		−0.848***		
		(0.321)		
Recovery × New dem		−0.980***		
		(0.301)		
GFC Shock × ΔGDP/capita			−0.032*	
			(0.017)	
Recovery × ΔGDP/capita			−0.008	
			(0.022)	
GFC Shock × Debt				0.315
				(0.195)
Recovery × Debt				0.540***
				(0.155)
Constant	2.926***	2.584***	2.906***	3.237***
	(0.495)	(0.491)	(0.526)	(0.506)
R^2	0.852	0.864	0.853	0.860
N	263	263	263	263

Note: Cells report parameter estimates from OLS regression models with country fixed effects. ***$p<0.01$, **$p<0.05$, *$p<0.10$, two-tailed test.

OLS regression estimates appear in the first column of Table 2.1. As expected, the number of parties is shaped in part by institutional factors: compared to majoritarian systems, PR electoral rules mean an additional party in the system. Presidential systems also have a reductive effect on the number of parties at the national level. Our interest, however, is with the impact of the crisis variables. While the number of parties during the shock years did not differ from the pre-crisis era, we find that the recovery period, ceteris paribus, was associated with an increase in the number of parties. This post-crisis increase in the size of party systems is robust to a range of model specifications and, as Model 2 indicates, strongest in the established democracies.

The last pair of models adds a layer of complexity and examines the joint impact of time period and the economic performance indicators, *Change GDP/ capita* and *Government debt*. Given the interactive nature of the models, we

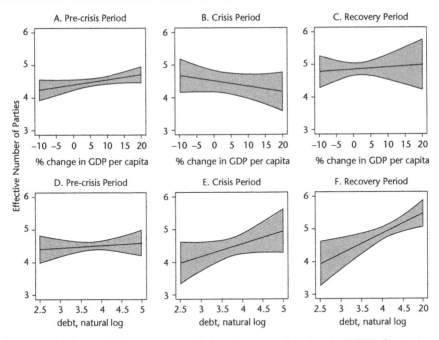

Figure 2.7. Marginal Effects on the Effective Number of Parties in OECD Countries Before, During, and After the GFC

Note: Graphs produced using estimates from Table 2.1 Models 3 (top row graphs) and 4 (bottom row). Shaded areas report 95% confidence intervals.

report results via marginal effects in Figure 2.7. The top row uses estimates from Model 3 to plot the expected number of number of parties as change in per capita growth varies produced by the regression models—separately for time periods before, during, and after the GFC. The bottom row displays the same but for *Government debt*, produced from Model 4. The change in per capita income since the last election has little influence on volatility, regardless of period. Public debt, however, contributes to party system fragmentation. As shown by the upward sloping line in Figure 2.7F, this effect is sharpest during the recovery period. This finding lends support to claims that the crisis's influence on party politics increased with time, arguably due to a shift from preferring competent management in the immediate wake of the shock to being disillusioned with established party politics (see also Chapter 7).

A more revealing way to discern the effect of the crisis on political systems may be in terms of electoral volatility. Figure 2.8 displays the change in net vote volatility, as measured by the Pedersen index.[8] As with the number of

---

[8] The measure is calculated as $\frac{\sum_{k=1}^{n}|p_{k,t-1}-p_{kt}|}{2}$ where n is the number of parties and p_k represents the percentage of votes received by party k in time periods $t-1$ and t. Our thanks to Scott Mainwaring for sharing his unpublished data with us.

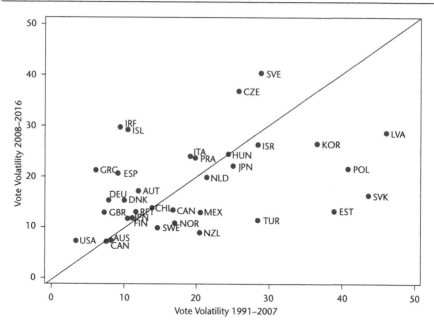

Figure 2.8. Vote Volatility in OECD Countries Before and After the GFC
Source: Emanuele (2015), Mainwaring et al. (2017), and updated by the authors.

parties, we separate the data into two, averaging across elections between 1990 and 2007, on the one hand, and 2008 and 2016 on the other. Inasmuch as elections post-crisis were marked by greater degrees of vote volatility, we would expect all countries to lie above and to the left of the diagonal. And indeed, that is where we find many political economies heaviest hit by the crisis, including the 'PIIGS' of Portugal, Ireland, Italy, Greece, and Spain. Volatility also increased, albeit slightly, in elections in many countries at the centre of the global and regional economies (e.g. France, Germany, Britain, and the United States). Of those political systems where volatility declined after the crisis, most were newer, less established democracies with higher-than-average volatility before as well as after 2007 (e.g. Estonia, South Korea, Latvia, Poland, Slovakia, Turkey).

Globally, however the main message from the two-period comparison is one of no comparison. The scatterplot resists a simple message. Was it the more severely hurt economies that experienced more volatility? To help address this question, we again conduct a multivariate analysis. We specify a model identical to that for the number of parties, regressing net volatility on its lagged values, the crisis factors, and contextual controls. Table 2.2 reports the regression estimates. Model 1 shows, not surprisingly, that young democracies experience higher levels of volatility relative to established party systems. In these countries, however, party system change is less attributable to the crisis than to

Table 2.2. The Impact of the GFC on Vote Volatility, OECD Countries 1990–2016

	(1)	(2)	(3)	(4)
Shock period	−4.473***	−4.399***	−2.732	−11.766
	(1.591)	(1.595)	(1.757)	(6.571)
Recovery period	−0.566	1.682	1.540	−42.738***
	(1.477)	(1.359)	(1.457)	(8.837)
ΔGDP per capita	−0.100	−0.157	0.116	−0.150*
	(0.103)	(0.098)	(0.116)	(0.090)
(Ln)Government debt	2.422	4.106**	3.890*	1.558
	(2.152)	(2.037)	(2.063)	(1.927)
PR system	−0.741	0.458	0.900	2.026
	(4.873)	(4.727)	(4.389)	(4.736)
Presidential system	−7.327**	−9.210***	−9.652***	−9.291***
	(2.867)	(2.754)	(2.799)	(2.777)
New democracy	27.091***	29.786***	22.646***	22.825***
	(6.566)	(7.918)	(6.310)	(6.347)
GFC Shock × New dem		−0.817		
		(6.389)		
Recovery × New dem		−12.134***		
		(3.728)		
GFC Shock × ΔGDP/capita			−0.331	
			(0.325)	
Recovery × ΔGDP/capita			−0.807***	
			(0.223)	
GFC Shock × Debt				1.964
				(1.738)
Recovery × Debt				10.213***
				(2.093)
Constant	1.596	−3.658	−3.895	6.545
	(6.548)	(6.178)	(6.249)	(5.967)
R^2	0.571	0.607	0.605	0.625
N	251	251	251	251

Note: Cells report parameter estimates from OLS regression models with country fixed effects. ***$p < 0.01$, **$p < 0.05$, *$p < 0.10$, two-tailed test.

historical factors. With respect to the impact of the GFC, the older democracies of Western Europe and North America bore the greatest effects. Model 2 estimates indicate that the Pedersen volatility index was more than four points lower during the shock compared to times previous ($\beta_{\text{old democracies}} = -4.4$, $p < 0.01$).

With respect to economic conditions—growth and debt—the baseline (naïve) model in column 1 indicates no effects on party system volatility. However, Figure 2.9, which uses estimates from the last two columns of Table 2.2 to display effects conditioned on period, uncovers notable impacts. The top row shows that prior to 2008 there is no connection between per capita growth and vote volatility. With time, however, the crisis–volatility connection strengthens such that worse conditions contribute to higher volatility. For economies that rebounded after the shock, like Ireland or Poland, our model predicts that post-crisis electoral volatility was no greater than before. The bottom row shows that government debt was also an important factor driving

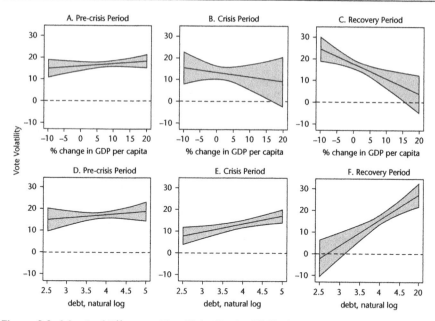

Figure 2.9. Marginal Effects on Vote Volatility in OECD Countries Before, During, and After the GFC

Note: Graphs produced using estimates from Table 2.2 Models 3 and 4. Shaded areas report 95% confidence intervals.

electoral uncertainty: the higher the debt level, the greater the vote volatility. Again, this influence is sharpest in the recovery period. At debt levels of 12 per cent of GDP (2.5 natural log), or approximately that of Estonia post-2010, the model predicts electoral volatility of nearly zero on the Pedersen index. For countries with excessive debt, such as Spain's post-crisis levels of 115 per cent of GDP (4.75 natural log), the model predicts a score of 25.

Multivariate analyses help unpack the effects of the crisis on party systems and electoral volatility to reveal notable crisis-related influences. In line with our scope of inquiry advanced in Chapter 1, the destabilizing effects of GFC evolved such that it exerted a greater impact on party systems, ceteris paribus, during the *recovery* than in the initial wake of the shock. Party systems have fragmented further, and voting choices have become less predictable.

These systemic changes likely carry implications for the survival of governments and, in turn, the kinds of policies enacted in response. A good deal of research has been devoted to understanding government turnover following the GFC, both by way of case and comparative studies (e.g. Bartels 2014; LeDuc and Pammett 2013; Magalhães 2014). Examining pre- and post-GFC elections in a set of twenty-eight OECD countries, Bartels (2014) finds that voters generally held sitting governments accountable for economic collapse:

incumbent governments in countries where the crisis was most strongly felt tended to lose votes and lose office. Timing was also important: elections closest to the deepest point of the crisis were even worse for incumbents. And though centre-left governments might have been punished more, Bartels takes this to mainly be a matter of luck rather than systematic rightward shift in public ideology. In contrast, Lindvall (2014; also Lindvall 2017) argues that voters shifted to the right in the first three years after the crisis and then began to move back to the left, analogous to experience in the Depression of the 1930s. With respect to policy responses, post-crisis fiscal stimulus did benefit incumbents, austerity having the opposite effects, although these findings are more tentative (Bartels 2014). Budget deficits were also related to punishment of incumbents in post-crisis elections (Kriesi 2014, 312).

Chapter 6 revisits debates about the crisis and electoral accountability in detail with benefit of individual-level data from the CSES. Here, we re-examine the effect of the crisis on vote shares for government parties. We extend the elections under consideration both backward to the early 1990s and forward in time to votes in 2016. In so doing, we present a more appropriate test of whether and to what extent the crisis itself influenced incumbent support. Figure 2.10 summarizes incumbent performance across thirty-two OECD countries. The vertical axis reports the share of those elections that occurred in a given year in which the incumbent government prevailed. We see that in elections post-2007, incumbent governments had a 0.5 probability or less, on average, of retaining office. The crisis, therefore, may have had an effect on election outcomes. Further, the differences in election outcomes pre- and post-elections is not clear. If a 'GFC effect' is to be revealed, we must probe more deeply.

We do so, as above, by way of pooling elections across the OECD and performing regression analysis. The dependent variable is incumbent vote share, where incumbency is defined in most cases as the largest party in government. In cases where governing coalitions included two parties with roughly similar representation, we combine their vote shares (Bartels 2014). In those systems with strong presidents (Chile, France, South Korea, Mexico, and United States), we treat the incumbent government as the party of the president. Along with the same set of covariates as above, models include government right–left ideology. Our ideology measure is produced using data from the Comparative Manifesto Project and based on the 'rile' score developed by Laver and Budge (1992). The measure, which is weighted according the party's contribution to government portfolios, is taken and updated from Seki and Williams (2014) and rescaled on a 0 (left) to 10 (right) continuum. Lastly, to account for past electoral success, models include parties' vote shares in the previous election.

Table 2.3 reports results. The first model presents a baseline specification. The period dummies fail to uncover differences across pre- and post-crisis

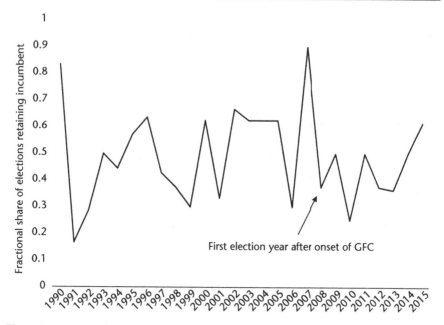

Figure 2.10. Incumbent Government Survival in the OECD, 1990–2015

Note: Graph reports share of elections in a given year in which the incumbent head of government party retained its position in office.

Source: Calculated by authors.

periods. Debt incurrence, however, exerts a strong and expected negative influence on incumbent support. Model 2 follows as previously specified but, again, there is scant evidence of different impacts across periods for new and old democracies. Models 3 and 4 report findings for the interactive specifications, marginal effects from which are displayed in Figure 2.11. Echoing previous work, we find that governments were more sensitive to economic conditions—captured here by change in per capita GDP and by debt—during the crisis periods relative to times previous. Our analysis reveals that this sensitivity continued into the recovery period. Economic voting, and the economy as a mechanism of electoral accountability, appeared to re-emerge in the aftermath of the crisis (see also Chapter 6).

With respect to debates about whether voters during the crisis years favoured governments of different ideologies, we find little evidence. The coefficient on *Government ideology* is no different from zero, regardless of time period (see Model 5). Government partisanship, however, does condition the influence of the economy. For left-leaning governments, the economic downturn had an adverse effect. However, for governments on the right, their ideology may have served to counter the adverse impact of occupying office during the crisis. Producing the marginal effects from Model 6, Figure 2.12 shows that

Table 2.3. The Impact of the GFC on Incumbent Vote, OECD Countries 1990–2016

	(1)	(2)	(3)	(4)	(5)	(6)
Shock period	0.586	0.313	−0.828	11.661*	−3.581	1.073
	(1.014)	(1.076)	(1.129)	(5.107)	(6.421)	(1.002)
Recovery period	−1.326	−2.455	−2.972*	17.211*	−13.464	−1.130
	(1.299)	(1.478)	(1.351)	(6.918)	(9.498)	(1.345)
Change GDP/capita	0.123	0.143*	−0.005	0.146*	0.120	1.917***
	(0.071)	(0.068)	(0.070)	(0.067)	(0.067)	(0.514)
(Ln)Government debt	−2.668***	−2.713***	−2.849***	−1.666**	−2.617***	−2.904***
	(0.584)	(0.590)	(0.618)	(0.599)	(0.575)	(0.575)
PR system	−0.461	−0.614	−0.823	−1.011	−0.624	−0.316
	(1.207)	(1.219)	(1.192)	(1.197)	(1.179)	(1.182)
Presidential system	4.850**	5.115**	4.515**	4.738**	4.869**	4.656**
	(1.648)	(1.701)	(1.602)	(1.632)	(1.658)	(1.617)
New democracy	−4.269**	−6.314**	−4.007*	−4.806**	−4.117*	−4.104*
	(1.607)	(2.018)	(1.589)	(1.598)	(1.600)	(1.607)
Gov't ideology	0.174	0.160	0.078	0.083	−0.771	2.227**
	(0.726)	(0.723)	(0.755)	(0.717)	(0.717)	(0.724)
GFC Shock × New dem		3.134				
		(2.169)				
Recovery × New dem		4.710				
		(2.805)				
GFC Shock × ΔGDP/capita			0.320*			
			(0.152)			
Recovery × ΔGDP/capita			0.410*			
			(0.203)			
GFC Shock × Debt				−2.781*		
				(1.240)		
Recovery × Debt				−4.536*		
				(1.758)		
Shock × Gov't ideology					0.811	
					(1.308)	
Recovery × Gov't ideology					2.400	
					(1.957)	
ΔGDP/capita × Gov't ideology						−0.362***
						(0.096)
Lagged vote share	0.721***	0.707***	0.706***	0.720***	0.738***	0.716***
	(0.048)	(0.049)	(0.049)	(0.048)	(0.048)	(0.045)
Constant	15.764**	16.808***	18.780***	12.745*	19.855***	6.715
	(4.835)	(4.880)	(4.933)	(4.994)	(5.112)	(4.997)
R^2	0.578	0.585	0.597	0.594	0.587	0.614
N	239	239	239	239	239	239

Note: Cells report parameter estimates from OLS regression models with standard errors clustered by country in parentheses. ***$p < 0.01$, **$p < 0.05$, *$p < 0.1$, two-tailed test.

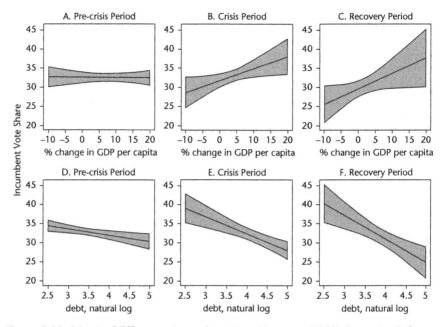

Figure 2.11. Marginal Effects on Incumbent Vote Shares in OECD Countries Before, During, and After the GFC

Note: Graphs produced using estimates from Table 2.3 Models 3 and 4. The vertical axis reports expected values of *Incumbent vote*. Shaded areas report 95% confidence intervals.

for left-of-centre governments (ideology scores < 5), a strong economy helps their fortunes but a weak one—as was the case during the crisis—has a negative effect. Right-leaning governments, in contrast, gained from the downturn but not from the recovery. If voters were 'blindly retrospective' (Achen and Bartels 2016; Bartels 2014), we would therefore expect left and centre-left governments to be punished more simply because they tended to be more in office than those to the right. Nonetheless, the figure suggests governments to the right did manage better. In Chapter 6 we go beyond this account explore additional factors governing how the crisis mattered for government survival at the level of individual voters.

2.7. A Look Ahead

The overview presented in this chapter highlights the breadth and depth of the GFC and Great Recession on national political economies among the advanced capitalist democracies. Growth rates remain more tepid than during the pre-crisis period, the recovery has been uneven, and in many places levels

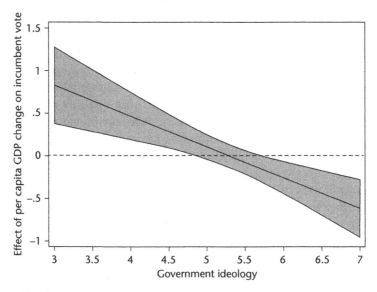

Figure 2.12. The Marginal Effect of Per Capita Change in GDP on Incumbent Vote Share Conditioned on Government Ideology

Note: Graph produced using estimates from Table 2.3 Models 6. Shaded areas report 95% confidence intervals.

of inequality have been exacerbated. Yet while the consequences for domestic economic conditions are apparent and, with time, have proven quite durable, the influence of the impact of the crisis of 2007–9 on electoral politics is a different question altogether. Did the GFC matter? At first glance, the evidence of a 'GFC effect' on electoral politics is muted. Comparisons of party systems before and after the crisis years reveal few systematic differences. We find, though, the impact of the GFC on party systems, electoral volatility, and government success in elections to be conditional on extenuating factors such as government partisanship and the age of the democratic regime. We find, for instance, that the GFC had the systematic effect of increasing the number of parties, although this relationship was strongest not during the crisis years but following them during the recovery (see Figure 2.7). We also find a longer term effect of the crisis on electoral volatility, conditioned by the severity of the shock as captured by the incurrence of public debt (see Table 2.2 and Figure 2.9). The old democracies with more established party systems have been hit particularly hard.

Both macro- and micro-level data used in this book improve on earlier research on the GFC's political effects by broadening the set of cases examined beyond Europe and by extending the time frame to capture more recent electoral contests. This chapter has used aggregate data to map general trends. In order to further examine the attitudes and behaviour of citizens, we rely on post-election survey data of the approximately 140,000 individuals from twenty-four OECD democracies from 1990 to 2017 in Chapter 5, 6, and 7. Most data were made possible by the Comparative Study of Electoral Systems (CSES) Module 1 to 5. We included six additional election studies that were missing in the original modules to make a dataset of 118 country-surveys in all (see Appendix, Table A2.3). Whereas previous work on the consequences of the Great Recession has focused on the short-term effects by limiting cases to the first elections held after the 2007 crisis, the range of time periods covered by our data allows us to examine the long-term after-math effect of the crisis, and compare it to economic voting in normal times, that is during the pre-crisis period. In addition, the broad regional scope of this book that goes beyond Europe enables us to examine a wide range of contextual factors that interact with individual characteristics to condition the GFC effect.

In Chapter 3 and 4, which examine individual policy preferences and per-ceived economic insecurity, we use post-crisis election surveys from Module 4 of CSES (see Appendix Table A2.2). The fourth module of the CSES series was designed specifically to investigate the effects of the GFC on mass political behaviour. It allows the estimation of individuals' levels of security and inse-curity, by way of job characteristics such as skill specificity and exposure to outsourcing, as well as through people's associated perceptions of the likeli-hood of income loss. We can also estimate the role of variations in household incomes and asset ownership. The module also includes a unique battery of social policy and distributional preferences. Hence, while Chapter 5, 6, and 7 leverage the CSES's breadth of coverage to examine salient factors like eco-nomic insecurity on voter choice, the analyses in Chapter 3 and 4 uniquely draw on the tailored items in the fourth module to test the full range of implications of the theoretical framework outlined in Chapter 1.

The diverse set of macro- and micro-level data used in this book allows us to model both institutional and contextual effects on individual-level political behaviour into the analysis, particularly by way of interactions. This enables us to account for the country-level effects of the automatic stabilizers such as tax and welfare systems, and the extent of discretionary stimulus. All country elections used in analyses for each dataset are listed in in the appendix to this chapter. Due to data availability, each data sample has omitted country elec-tions as noted in the appendix. These missing cases notwithstanding, OECD countries outside of Europe are fully represented, providing a useful corrective to earlier research on the consequences of the GFC that has often had an exclusive continental focus. The cases include some of those countries worst hit by the GFC—Iceland, Ireland, and Greece—as well as countries, like Pol-and, that escaped almost untouched.

Appendix

Table 2.A1. Country and Years Included in Macro-Level Analysis

Country										
AUSTRALIA	1990	1993	1996	1998	2001	2004	2007	2010	2013	2016
AUSTRIA	1990	1994	1995	1999	2002	2006	2008	2013	2017	
BELGIUM	1991	1995	1999	2003	2007	2010	2014			
CANADA	1993	1997	2000	2004	2006	2008	2011	2015		
CHILE	1993	1999	2006	2010	2013	2017				
CZECH REP.	1990	1992	1996	1998	2002	2006	2010	2013	2017	
DENMARK	1990	1994	1998	2001	2005	2007	2011	2015		
ESTONIA	1990	1992	1995	1999	2003	2007	2011	2015		
FINLAND	1991	1995	1999	2003	2007	2011	2015			
FRANCE	1995	2002	2007	2012	2017					
GERMANY	1990	1994	1998	2002	2005	2009	2013	2017		
GREECE	1990	1993	1996	2000	2004	2007	2009	2012	2015	
HUNGARY	1990	1994	1998	2002	2006	2010	2014			
ICELAND	1991	1995	1999	2003	2007	2009	2013	2016		
IRELAND	1992	1997	2002	2007	2011	2016				
ISRAEL	1992	1996	1999	2003	2006	2009	2013	2015		
ITALY	1992	1994	1996	2001	2006	2008	2013			
JAPAN	1990	1993	1996	2000	2003	2005	2009	2012	2014	2017
LATVIA	1998	2002	2006	2010	2011	2014				
LUXEMBOURG	1994	1999	2004	2009	2013					
MEXICO	1994	2000	2006	2012						
NETHERLANDS	1994	1998	2002	2003	2006	2010	2012	2017		
NEW ZEALAND	1990	1993	1996	1999	2002	2005	2008	2011	2014	2017
NORWAY	1993	1997	2001	2005	2009	2013	2017			
POLAND	1991	1993	1997	2001	2005	2007	2011	2015		
PORTUGAL	1991	1995	1999	2002	2005	2009	2011	2015		
SLOVAKIA	1990	1992	1994	1998	2002	2006	2010	2012	2016	
SLOVENIA	1992	1996	2000	2004	2008	2011	2014			
SOUTH KOREA	1992	1997	2002	2007	2012	2017				
SPAIN	1993	1996	2000	2004	2008	2011	2015	2016		
SWEDEN	1991	1994	1998	2002	2006	2010	2014			
SWITZERLAND	1991	1995	1999	2003	2007	2011	2015			
TURKEY	1991	1999	2002	2007	2011	2015				
UK	1992	1997	2001	2005	2010	2015	2017			
USA	1992	1996	2000	2004	2008	2012	2016			

Note: Greece had two elections in 2012 and 2015.

Table 2.A2. Elections Included in CSES Module 4

AUSTRALIA	2013
AUSTRIA	2013
CANADA	2011
CZECH REPUBLIC	2013
FINLAND	2015
FRANCE	2012
GERMANY	2013
GREAT BRITAIN	2015
GREECE	2012
ICELAND	2013
IRELAND	2011
ISRAEL	2013
JAPAN	2013
LATVIA	2011
MEXICO	2012
NEW ZEALAND	2011
NORWAY	2013
POLAND	2011
PORTUGAL	2015
SLOVAKIA	2016
SLOVENIA	2011
SOUTH KOREA	2012
SWEDEN	2014
SWITZERLAND	2011
TURKEY	2015
USA	2012

Table 2.A3. Elections Included in Pre- and Post-Crisis Individual-Level Analyses

	Pre-Crisis				Crisis	Post-Crisis	
AUSTRALIA	1996	2004	2007			2010	2013
CANADA	1997	2004			2008	2011	2015
CHILE	1999	2005			2009	2017	
CZECH REPUBLIC	1996	2002	2006			2010	2013
DENMARK	1998	2001	2007			2011	
FINLAND	2003	2007				2011	2015
FRANCE	2002	2007				2012	2017
GERMANY	1998	2002	2005		2009	2013	
GREAT BRITAIN	1997	2005				2010	2015
ICELAND	1999	2003	2007		2009	2013	
IRELAND	2002	2007				2011	2016
ISRAEL	1996	2003	2006			2013	
MEXICO	1997	2000	2003	2006	2009	2012	2015
NETHERLANDS	1998	2002	2006			2010	
NEW ZEALAND	1996	2002	2005		2008	2011	2014
NORWAY	1997	2001	2005		2009	2013	
POLAND	1997	2001	2005	2007		2011	
PORTUGAL	2002	2005			2009	2011	2015
SLOVENIA	1996	2004			2008	2011	
SOUTH KOREA	2000	2004			2008	2012	2016
SPAIN	1996	2000	2004		2008	2011	
SWEDEN	1998	2002	2006			2010	2014
SWITZERLAND	1999	2003	2007			2010	2011
USA	1996	2004			2008	2012	

Note: Most of elections are obtained from CSES modules (module 1 to 5). Six elections are additionally included: Australia 2010, Denmark 2011, Portugal 2011, Spain 2011, Sweden 2010, and UK 2010. All these cases are the first elections held after the 2007-financial crisis that were missing in the original dataset. Austria, Japan, Greece, Latvia, Turkey, and Italy are excluded because data were not available for either pre- or post-crisis periods. Non-OECD countries are excluded.

Part II
Public Perceptions and Policy Demands

3

Breaking the Bargain?

Economic Decline, Party Cues, and the Politics of Insecurity

Insecurity is a defining feature of post-crisis politics. In the wake of the global financial crisis (GFC) and the Great Recession that followed, insecurity emerged as a central theme in elections across the developed democracies. Pre-crisis socio-economic environments strained class bargains of postwar politics; in post-crisis environments these bargains were often broken. With the breakdown of these class bargains, insecurity supplanted security. Uncertainty about one's day-to-day well-being adversely affects individuals in a range of ways, from personal relations to making plans for the future. Perceptions of an insecure future, however, also strongly structure mass politics. Insecurity influences policy preferences, electoral participation, and voter decisions.

But what drives feelings of insecurity? There is a good deal of evidence that sustained economic downturns contribute to social malaise. According to one study, the share of Americans who lost at least one quarter of their income increased steadily from the mid-1980s through the height of the Great Recession in 2009 (Hacker et al. 2011). In many countries on the EU periphery, unemployment rates spiked, particularly among the young. Yet less is known about how adverse macro shocks combine with national contexts translate into feelings of economic uncertainty. Does macro-economic volatility necessarily beget a loss of security, thereby leading voters to a set of activities—including protests, boycotts, or voting for extreme parties and candidates—not previously considered? Or, with the 'right' mixture of policy and political response, can insecurity be allayed? Can governments increase or, alternatively, weaken the relationship between objective and subjective insecurity through use of social policy and elite cues? Does more spending on welfare or an economic stimulus mitigate the impact of objective insecurity on the public's perceptions?

Democracy Under Siege? Parties, Voters, and Elections After the Great Recession. Timothy Hellwig, Yesola Kweon, and Jack Vowles, Oxford University Press (2020). © Timothy Hellwig, Yesola Kweon, and Jack Vowles.
DOI: 10.1093/oso/9780198846208.001.0001

In this chapter we show that mass perceptions of economic precariousness are shaped not only by individual- and macro-level economic conditions but by political elites as well. Political elites take action to buffer the effects of economic downturn through concrete policy efforts. Politicians and party leaders can also help calm insecure voters through their messages, speeches, and rhetoric. By emphasizing concerns for social protection relative to other matters, parties through their campaign discourse can quell fears of future economic loss and thus weaken the impact of objective insecurity on perceived insecurity. As we examine in subsequent chapters, this has the potential to shape electoral behaviour and the make-up of governments.

We begin with a consideration of current research on economic insecurity. We then build on the theoretical framework presented in Chapter 1 to highlight how economic and political contexts interact to shape levels of subjective risk. This produces a set of expectations which we then assess using the CSES data. Statistical analyses show that the financial crisis has both short-term and long-term effects on individuals' economic perceptions. A complete understanding of crisis' political effects thus must take into account the effect of the crisis at both stages of development and recovery. Furthermore, feelings of insecurity are shaped by elite cues. Party emphases on welfare concerns serve to moderate the impact of individual risk exposure on perceived insecurity. The implication is that what matters is not so much the magnitude of the crisis, but political elites' ability to demonstrate an effective response to the crisis, manifested in the recovery rate, policy effort, and elite messages.

3.1. Understanding Subjective Insecurity

Research on economic insecurity often points to individual exposure to risk. As Hacker (2006, 20) puts it, 'insecurity requires real risk that threatens real hardship'. Experiences with adverse market conditions in the past and present times make individuals have a more sceptical view of their future economic chances (Burgoon and Dekker 2010; Helgason and Mérola 2017; Rehm 2016). The conventional wisdom, then, is that individuals' exposure to objective risk—whether through precarious employment, industry-specific skills, or lack of assets—are the main causes of subjective insecurity (Cusack et al. 2006; Fraile and Pardos-Prado 2014; Helgason and Mérola 2017; Mau et al. 2012). But the objective precarity of an individual's market status aside, favourable economic conditions can improve a person's assessment of the future economy. Conversely, prolonged economic downturn and inauspicious market circumstances like those brought by the GFC and the Great Recession can worsen feelings of insecurity (Mau et al. 2012; Scheve and Slaughter 2004). Thus the economic sources of subjective insecurity are both micro and macro.

Politics also matters. Most research on the political bases of economic perceptions focuses on individuals' partisan loyalties and political dispositions (Evans and Andersen 2006; Gerber and Huber 2010; Ladner and Wlezien 2007; Tilley and Hobolt 2011; Wlezien et al. 1997). We focus instead on the supply-side of the formation of economic perceptions. As a subjective feeling, insecurity is susceptible to being managed by political elites. Elite influence bears on citizen perceptions of insecurity through two possible paths. The first is policy implementation. Through policies that spread risk over income groups and generations, spending on welfare mitigates the impact of objective forms of economic insecurity on individual perceptions (Blomberg et al. 2012; Mau et al. 2012). While these policies are effective, political barriers mean windows for substantive reform in response to changing circumstances are rare. Short of outright reforms, political elites may also signal a concern for voter insecurity through their rhetoric by emphasizing social protection relative to other matters. As laid out in the first chapter, our general expectation is that political elites were not passive by-standers during the crisis years but, through their actions, they could shape public perceptions. Parties' commitment to their economic concerns expressed in electoral competition signals that people's economic fates will be improved despite their current precarious reality (see Bartels 2002; Carsey and Layman 2006; Margalit 2013; see also Zaller 1992). We draw on these findings from public opinion scholarship to develop expectations about the drivers of subjective insecurity.

3.1.1. *Perceived Insecurity and Individual-Level Insurance Against Risk*

Scholarship to date has identified a range of sources of adverse market experience. Among many is employment-related risk. Some argue that individuals' labour market experience varies widely depending on their employment status. Regular workers with permanent contracts and full-time employment enjoy considerable employment protection. These individuals are insulated from employment risks. By contrast, workers with temporary employment and part-time jobs, and those with longer lasting unemployment, absorb much of the employment risk resulting from deepening labour market deregulation which has increasingly been prevalent in many advanced economies. Therefore, these market 'outsiders' tend to be less secure than the 'insiders' (King and Rueda 2008; Rueda 2007; Chung and van Oorschot 2011; Näswall and De Witte 2003).[1] Occupational unemployment rates provide a related

---

[1] Indeed, the security and stability enjoyed by insiders may be due in part to the presence of a large pool of outsiders who absorb the impact of business cycle volatility on national labour markets (King and Rueda 2008; Rueda 2007).

source of insecurity. Given that individuals with the same occupation tend to have a shared risk profile, even though a person is not currently unemployed, a higher occupational unemployment rate could mean that person has a greater chance to be laid off in the near future (Rehm 2016; Helgason and Mérola 2017). As a result, feelings of insecurity are likely to be more acute among those with occupations with high unemployment rates.

Another factor is human capital. Human capital may be even more critical than employment as a safeguard during economic hard times. If one's skill set is of limited applicability beyond a particular firm or industrial sector, then the individual is more at risk of losing income from technology shocks like automation or outsourcing. These skills exacerbate perceived economic insecurity. Individuals with specific skills have lower occupational and sectoral mobility than owners of general skills. The former group faces a longer duration of unemployment or a significant decline in income in the event of job loss. The underlying implication is that workers with specific skills have a higher level of economic insecurity than those with general skills (Iversen and Soskice 2001; Cusack et al. 2006). In contrast, others maintain that specific skills empower the worker since they raise replacement costs for the employer. More replaceable workers are those who do tasks that do not require specific knowledge and that are easy to monitor. According to this view, workers with relatively specific skills are less concerned about their job security (Goldthorpe 2000; Emmenegger 2009).

Apart from labour market factors, wealth also provides protection against economic precarity. Asset ownership, particularly home ownership, has become an important part of individual welfare since the global financial crisis in 2008 (Ronald et al. 2017). As a means of self-insurance, assets provide a stock of wealth independent from the dynamics of the labour market. They act not only as a store of permanent income, but also as a hedge against labour market risk in hard times. Asset ownership enhances purchasing power that replaces incomes from labour. Whether converted into income through sale or by borrowing against them as collateral, assets serve to smooth consumption during periods of transitory income loss due to changes in labour market status (Ansell 2014; Ronald et al. 2017; Johnson and Sherraden 1992). Therefore, asset ownership likely mitigates the feelings of insecurity.

3.1.2. *Perceived Insecurity in Hard Times*

People's judgements are not only influenced by micro-level economic conditions but also by macro-level economic performance (Mau et al. 2012). Negative economic growth and high market volatility of the sort experienced during the economic crisis heighten perceived economic insecurity of not only market outsiders, but also insiders. Prolonged downturns in general and recessions in particular cause even the most robust firms to become more risk averse and delay hiring decisions. It is not surprising, therefore, that individuals in countries facing an economic crisis have a higher level of economic insecurity (Lübke and Erlinghagen 2014).

However, the extent to which the macro economic environment affects economic perceptions is mediated by political elites. Elites affect feelings of subjective insecurity in two important ways: through the policies they oversee and via their communications with the electorate. The first of these is more credible but rare; the second more common but less credible.

Redistributive policies offer a means for governments to use levers at their disposal to tend to the economic concerns of publics. The extent to which economic volatility translates into perceptions of individual risk depends in part on whether institutional mechanisms are in place to safeguard against risk. In this way, the government welfare effort affects not only people's living conditions, but also their feeling of insecurity (Mau et al. 2012; Blomberg et al. 2012). Along with serving a redistributive function, social policy insures against risks (Iversen and Cusack 2000; Moene and Wallerstein 2001). Welfare protections act as a shield against market uncertainty. Generous welfare support protects citizens in hard times through income subsidies and social benefits (Esping-Andersen 1990). Buffered by government support, therefore, the real impact of adverse labour market experience is likely to be reduced.

However, in the years leading up to and continuing through the crisis, rising economic volatility and a spate of liberalizing reforms to state social protections have weakened, rather than bolstered, the capacity of safety nets to shelter citizens from risk. Faced with higher barriers to social policy expansion, politicians can nonetheless signal to the public their concerns about the plight of the insecure. Through their discourse, cues from political elites can help calm insecure voters. Studies find that elite message and party priming matters for how citizens comprehend surrounding economic circumstances (Bartels 2002; Carsey and Layman 2006; Margalit 2013). Political elites alter and manipulate issue salience by emphasizing or de-emphasizing certain issues (Tavits and Potter 2015). During election campaigns parties publicize their issue positions in an attempt to attract voters. Signalling a willingness to address citizens' economic concerns reassures the public that elected officials are attentive to their concerns.

Elite messages also provide a source of information for individuals to assess their future economic fate. Statements made during electoral campaigns tend to be prospective-oriented, referencing issue positions the party pursues and the policies they would enact if put in a position of power. This feature of campaign messages should inform citizens' projection of potential risks. Even if the economy is performing poorly and an individual finds themself in a precarious situation, promises to expand social welfare could instil a sense of optimism for the future.

To summarize, objective economic insecurity—produced by poor economic conditions—increases perceptions of insecurity among mass publics. This claim is consistent with prevailing scholarship. It also is consistent with this book's focus on the influence of economic change on mass politics. However, heightened uncertainty accompanying the crisis offers a window for political influence—above and beyond what might exist otherwise. Members of the political establishment can take actions to suppress public perceptions of insecurity, via either policy or elite discourse. With respect to policy, spending on social welfare should mediate the extent that market uncertainty results in individual insecurity, and an economic stimulus in the face of recession should have a similar effect. With respect to discourse, messages from party elites may alleviate perceptions of insecurity through their choice of policy emphasis. The degree to which political elites' policy and rhetorical efforts mitigate perceived economic insecurity can vary depending on the depth of economic downturn. Parties' efforts to improve social protections by policy and rhetorical messages should have a considerable impact when a country is heavily affected by the crisis. By contrast, when a country is only slightly by the crisis, demonstrated in stable economic growth, emphasis on social protections likely to have little resonance with the public.

3.2. Subjective Insecurity across the OECD after the Global Financial Crisis

We test our theoretical expectations using the set of twenty-five OECD democracies included in Module 4 of the Comparative Study of Electoral Systems (CSES 2017) described in Chapter 2.[2] To measure our concept of interest, subjective insecurity, we rely on a survey item which asks: 'How likely or unlikely do you think it is that your household's income could be severely reduced in the next twelve months?' This item has the benefit of being broadly comparable across the diverse set of labour markets and political systems that characterize our set of OECD democracies. Further, as a more general item, it eschews the problems confronted by alternative measures that

---

[2] The elections in the analysis are Australia 2013, Austria 2013, Canada 2011, the Czech Republic 2013, Finland 2015, France 2012, Germany 2013, Greece 2012, Iceland 2013, Ireland 2011, Israel 2013, Japan 2013, South Korea 2012, Latvia 2011, Mexico 2012, New Zealand 2011, Norway 2013, Poland 2011, Portugal 2015, Slovakia 2016, Slovenia 2011, Switzerland 2011, Turkey 2015, the United Kingdom 2015, and the United States 2012. The module also contains the 2014 Swedish Election Study but it is not included because it does not contain the economic insecurity items.

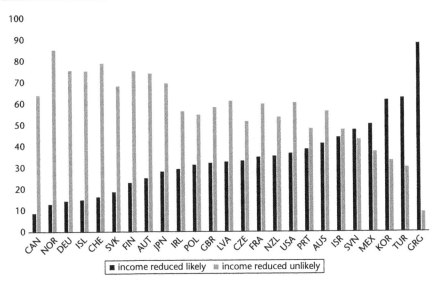

Figure 3.1. Subjective Insecurity in Twenty-Five Countries, 2011–2016

Notes: Black bars displays % of respondents who say it is (very/somewhat) likely that their household's income could be severely reduced in the next twelve months. Grey bars report % who say income loss is (very/somewhat) unlikely.

Source: CSES 2017.

operationalize risk perceptions in terms of the probability of job loss (see Walter 2017; Anderson and Pontusson 2007).[3] With the broad focus, this item also allows us to examine effects of other non-labour-market- related factors such as assets on feelings of insecurity.

Figure 3.1 displays country-level differences across the twenty-five surveys. Black bars report the percentage saying it is likely that their household income will be severely reduced in the next twelve months; grey bars do the same for those believing income loss to be unlikely. On average, about one-third of the respondents in each election study hold the pessimistic view.[4] Perceptions of insecurity vary a great deal across countries, however. At the low end, only about one in ten in Canada, Norway, and Germany feared significant income loss in the coming year. In contrast, in South Korea, Mexico, Turkey, and Greece majorities anticipated a loss of income in the next year. In Greece the share of respondents who feared a sizeable income loss was nine out of ten. Given that these surveys were fielded in elections just after a recession felt across the globe,

---

[3] CSES Module 4 also includes a version of the job loss item that asks employed respondents to reflect on their capacity to find work in the event that they were unemployed: 'If you lost your job, how easy or difficult would it be to find another job in the next twelve months?' However, respondents who are unemployed or otherwise outside the labour market do not receive this survey item.

[4] About 5 per cent of respondents answered 'don't know' or refused to answer.

the range of opinions is striking. Are factors related to the crisis—its depth and persistence—to blame? On the one hand, high levels of insecurity among the public are found in many of those countries worse hit by the GFC; these include Greece, of course, but Mexico and Slovenia also experienced economic contractions (see Figure 2.2). And on the other hand, public opinion was optimistic in some of the economies that emerged from the crisis years of 2008–9 unscathed, like Israel or Switzerland. But inferring subjective insecurity from objective economic conditions takes us only so far. For instance, there are countries, like Latvia and Poland, where perceptions of income loss were nearly identical despite large differences in terms of macro-economic performance since the GFC: a 14 per cent contraction for Latvia compared to an 11 per cent increase for Poland. And while the depth of economic pessimism among Greeks would appear to be justified, given the poor state of affairs, the Turkish economy performed much better yet its public rate among the most insecure in our sample. Indeed bivariate correlations between aggregate opinion and macro-economic change—measured, as displayed in Chapter 2, as the percentage change in GDP per capita—do not differ statistically from zero.

So while the state of the economy doubtless conditions feelings of material insecurity among the public, it does not tell the whole story. Consistent with our theoretical argument, the story becomes clearer once we add political factors. Figure 3.2 displays the aggregate opinion measures plotted against indicators of political supply introduced in Chapter 1. Graph A in Figure 3.2 considers *Austerity*, measured as cyclically adjusted fiscal balance. A positive and higher value indicates stricter austerity, while a negative value indicates discretionary spending. Figure 3.2.B considers *Relative redistribution*. As described in the introductory chapter, it represents the difference (percentage reduction) between pre-tax/transfers income inequality (Gini coefficient) and post-tax/transfers income inequality, all divided by pre-tax/transfers inequality. Data for changes in economic growth are from OECD Stats, and data for policy efforts are from the Standardized World Income Inequality Database (Solt 2019).

Figure 3.2.C aggregates subjective insecurity against a measure of elite cues. The latter is measured here using the statements from political parties delivered in the context of the election campaign. We use data from the Comparative Manifestos Project (CMP, Volkens et al. 2019) to measure the extent to which incumbent parties competing in the election emphasize social welfare concerns in their campaign discourse. Our measure combines party statements for 'Keynesian demand management', 'equality: positive', 'welfare state expansion', 'economic growth: positive', 'economic orthodoxy', and 'welfare state limitation'.[5] The sum is expressed as a share of total

---

[5] These statements are the (quasi)sentences identified by CMP coders and correspond to variable codes per409, per503, per504, per410, per414, and per505.

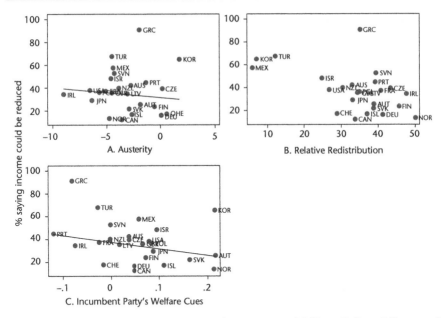

Figure 3.2. Country-Level Perceptions of Insecurity, Welfare Policy Effort, and Government Messages

Note: The vertical axis reports % of respondents who say it is (very/somewhat) likely that their household's income could be severely reduced in the next twelve months. The horizontal axes report cyclically adjusted fiscal balance (austerity) (top-left side), the tax- and transfer-induced reduction in the Gini coefficent such that higher values indate improved relative redistribution (top-right side), and governing parties' pro-welfare messages (bottom-left side). Solid lines are fitted regression lines for all cases. Austerity graph: slope = 0.08, p = 0.96; Relative redistribution graph: slope = −0.89, p = 0.01; Government messages graph: slope = −74.81, p = 0.085.

Sources: CSES 2017, IMF 2019; Solt 2019; Volkens et al. 2019.

manifesto sentences, thus providing a measure of a party's relative concern about social welfare vis-à-vis other issue concerns on the agenda (crime, terrorism, security, the environment, health care, and so on). The graph on the right-hand side displays these messages for governing parties in each country.

The bivariate relationships are informative. First, short-term stimulus or contractions (*Austerity*) appears to have little effect on subjective insecurity—*at the country level.*[6] However, the second graph indicates a negative relationship between automatic stabilizers and insecurity. The more policy effort or government attention devoted to welfare issues, the lower the levels of

---

[6] It is worth noting that not many countries apart from South Korea adopted strict austerity measures during the GFC period. Nevertheless, greater discretionary spending did not necessarily lead to lower insecurity. Countries like Ireland and the United States had more expansionary fiscal policy during the crisis period, as shown in their negative fiscal balance, than Norway or Canada, but levels of perceived insecurity are higher.

insecurity. For *Relative redistribution*, those countries where the post-tax reduction in inequality is lowest—Mexico, South Korea, and Turkey—are also three countries where citizens are most likely to anticipate a reduction in income. In contrast, in the generous welfare states of north-west Europe such as Norway, Finland, and Germany, only around one in five people report that income reduction is likely in the coming year. Greece again appears as an outlier with very pessimistic views for the future despite a reasonably effective effort on the part of policymakers.[7] In the case of government messages, we also observe a negative relationship: the more governments voice support for greater welfare efforts during their campaigns, the lower the sense of feelings of insecurity among the public at large ($r = -0.35$, $p = 0.09$, with South Korea removed, $r = -0.53$, $p < 0.01$).[8]

In sum, then, the bivariate relationships shown in Figure 3.2 are consistent with the general argument of this book in showing that public reactions to the economic crises of the early twenty-first century were not based only—or perhaps chiefly—on national economic conditions. Rather government policies and party discourse mattered.

3.3. Multivariate Analysis

3.3.1. *Data and Measures*

A full test of our arguments requires us to move beyond bivariate plots in three ways. First, since the markers of objective insecurity—unemployment, skills, wealth, and so on—are realized at the individual level, we must model subjective insecurity across individuals as well. Second, testing our argument in general in particular requires we perform a series of interactive analyses, conditioning economics on politics. And third, the argument we advanced in Chapter 1 emphasizes a need to unpack the crisis into its initial 'shock' in 2008 and 2009 and the recovery that followed thereafter.

The dependent variable is again *Subjective insecurity*, coded dichotomously where 1 indicates respondents who think that it is likely or very likely that their income will be reduced in twelve months (*high insecurity*), while 0 indicates

---

[7] Note that the negative association between insecurity and the strength of the welfare state is unaffected whether Greece is included in the comparison or not.

[8] At the time of the 2012 election, the sense of economic insecurity in South Korea was widespread, with over half of the survey respondents reporting it was likely that the next year would see their income decline. This was the case despite assurances by the governing Saenuri Party that it would address growing inequality in society. However, coming from a conservative party, these messages perhaps were not deemed credible. Consistent with this perspective, the government agenda emphasized childcare subsidies and education subsidies, and support for the elderly, rather than labour market reforms or poverty eradication. Indeed, in no country in our sample is the gulf wider between governing party statements and actual policy effort.

those who think that it is unlikely or very unlikely (*low insecurity*).[9] Countries were in various shapes throughout the different stages of the crisis. Some countries experienced a deep shock but quickly, while others suffered a long-term economic downturn. Therefore, it is important to differentiate the shock and recovery effects. Accordingly, we use two variables to assess the impact of macro-level economic conditions. The first, *GFC shock*, measures the immediate impact of the crisis on the economy by using the percentage *reduction* in GDP per capita from 2007 to 2009. Higher values indicate larger economic shocks, with respect to average income levels.[10] The second, which we label *Recovery*, captures the persistence of the crisis in terms of the percentage *growth* in GDP per capita from 2009 to the election year included in our sample. The greater value of this measure indicates the greater recovery rate from the crisis. For political contexts, we include *Austerity, Relative redistribution*, and *Incumbent party welfare cues*, all as previously described. We also tested the effect of trusted party messages by pairing the party welfare emphasis scores with survey respondents based on which party the respondent 'feels closes to'. The results are presented in the Appendix.

Models also include a set of variables to assess the impact of individual exposure to risk. *Market outsiders* refer to individuals without secure employment. Unemployed and part-time workers are coded as 1, and otherwise 0 (Rueda 2007). With respect to work hours, we recognize that voluntary part-time workers should not be considered as market outsiders, as they may not be under as much financial pressure as those forced into part-time or short-term work. To take account of different levels of economic pressures one might face, we only code an individual with a part-time job as a market outsider if her/his spouse also has precarious economic status (e.g. are unemployed or a part-time worker). We consider these individuals to be in part-time work involuntarily.[11] While market outsiders measure employment-related risk, a second measure, *Relative skill specificity*, measures portability and replaceability of skills. This variable is based on Iversen and Soskice (2001, also see Iversen 2006) which uses information contained in the occupation classifications from the International Labour Organization (ILO), ISCO-88. We measure relative skill specificity by drawing on one-digit ISCO-08 occupational codes.[12] For the purpose

---

[9] We examined alternative codings of the dependent variable, one with 'don't know' responses or refusals coded as a third unordered category and another with an ordered scale such that 1 = very unlikely (that income will be severely reduced in next twelve months), 2 = somewhat unlikely, 3 = somewhat likely, 4 = very likely. In both cases results are qualitatively identical to those we will report.

[10] We weigh the GFC shock variable by time since the crisis in order to account for memory effects.

[11] This is an alternative way to account for 'involuntary' part-time workers as our data do not include information about respondent's willingness to take part-time jobs.

[12] We thank Torben Iversen and Philipp Rehm for their assistance in coding *Relative skill specificity*.

of a robustness check, we reanalyse our main models using Oesch's class classification. As presented in Table A3.1, the main results largely remain the same (Oesch 2008; 2012). More discussion of this measure is provided in Chapter 5.

Employment security (*Outsider*) and human capital (*Relative skill specificity*) constitute two ways individuals' labour market characteristics can insure them against future loss of income. But stock of wealth can also serve this purpose. As a means of self-insurance, assets provide a stock of wealth independent of the dynamics of the labour market. However, types of assets might affect individual behaviour differently (Lewis-Beck et al. 2013). Thus, for asset ownership, we make use of the CSES module's battery of items measuring home ownership, savings accounts, business ownership, and shares of stocks and bonds. We combine the first pair to create a measure of low-risk assets and the second two for high-risk assets.

Lastly, models include a set of individual-level covariates to account for other factors that may influence feelings of insecurity. We include a series of demographic attributes for household income, education,[13] gender, age, and retirement status. In addition to these individual attributes, we note that people's assessment of the state of the economy in general and of future economic security in particular may be coloured by their sentiment towards the government. If an individual supports an incumbent party, that person is more likely to give a positive evaluation of the economy. Therefore, we also include incumbent vote, which measures whether a respondent voted for an incumbent party or not, with the expectation that these electoral 'winners' may have more positive dispositions, all else equal (Anderson et al. 2007).

3.3.2. Analysis

The structure of the data is such that individuals are nested within countries.[14] To account for this, we estimate models using hierarchical logistic regression models with random intercepts. Multilevel statistical techniques allow us to jointly model individual- and macro-level determinants of subjective insecurity and to estimate separate variance structures in order to produce unbiased standard errors. Country-specific random intercepts help reduce the threat of omitted variable bias from unobserved country characteristics.

Model estimates are visually presented in Figure 3.3 in terms of odds ratios; coefficients and standard errors are reported in Table 3.1. We first start with macro-level contextual variables. Echoing findings from the bivariate plots in Figure 3.2, coefficients on *Relative redistribution* and *Welfare cues* are negatively

---

[13] Education levels are scaled from 1 to 9, a higher value indicating a higher education level.
[14] Technically, individuals are nested within a country-election year. However, all countries included in our data only have one election year.

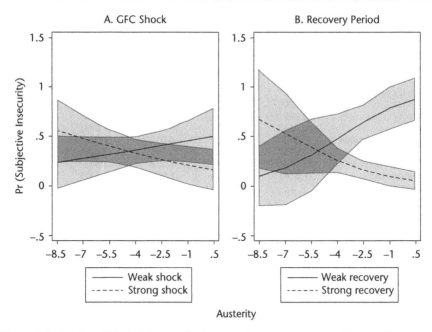

Figure 3.3. Predicted Probabilities of Subjective Insecurity across a Varying Degree of Austerity by GDP Per Capita Change Rates

Note: The figures are based on Model 3 in Table 3.1. Dashed lines display 95% confidence intervals.

signed and statistically significant, implying that redistributive policy efforts and political rhetoric help reduce individuals' perceived insecurity. By contrast, austerity (or discretionary stimuli) does not have a statistically significant impact. In terms of direct effects on perceived economic insecurity, policy outcomes (demonstrated in improved inequality) and messages are more important than spending itself. Economic conditions matter as well. Critically, however, the recovery effects are more significant and the magnitude of the impact is larger than the GFC shock effect. This finding supports our emphasis on the need to differentiate the short- and long-term effects of economic crisis.

The second column adds individual-level attributes and various sources of risk. Model results are consistent with studies that show that personal experience of risk directly shapes individual economic belief (King and Rueda 2008; Rueda 2007; Chung and van Oorschot 2011; Näswall and De Witte 2003, Iversen and Soskice 2001). All four indicators of risk exposure have statistically significant impacts, and signs of coefficients are in expected directions. Precarious employment (*Outsider*) and specific skills have a positive impact on feelings of insecurity while asset ownership, regardless of their levels of risk, tends to reduce economic insecurity. With respect to model controls, we find

Table 3.1. Modelling Subjective Insecurity

	(1)	(2)	(3)	(4)	(5)
Shock period	−0.008	−0.009	−0.053	−0.088	0.001
	(0.021)	(0.021)	(0.042)	(0.081)	(0.020)
Recovery period	−0.049**	−0.052***	−0.125***	0.042	−0.046***
	(0.020)	(0.020)	(0.046)	(0.049)	(0.018)
Austerity	−0.029	−0.033	0.149	−0.032	−0.033
	(0.054)	(0.054)	(0.118)	(0.048)	(0.051)
Relative redistribution	−0.058***	−0.057***	−0.052***	−0.037*	−0.052***
	(0.013)	(0.013)	(0.013)	(0.021)	(0.012)
Incumbent party's welfare cues	−3.386**	−3.185*	−1.578	−2.645*	−3.394
	(1.654)	(1.636)	(1.802)	(1.531)	(2.124)
Market outsider		0.247***	0.248***	0.248***	0.247***
		(0.045)	(0.045)	(0.045)	(0.045)
Relative skill specificity		0.046***	0.046***	0.046***	0.046***
		(0.010)	(0.010)	(0.010)	(0.010)
Low-risk asset (no assets)		−0.149***	−0.149***	−0.149***	−0.150***
		(0.035)	(0.035)	(0.035)	(0.035)
High-risk asset (no assets)		−0.305***	−0.305***	−0.306***	−0.305***
		(0.038)	(0.038)	(0.038)	(0.038)
Household income		−0.131***	−0.131***	−0.131***	−0.131***
		(0.010)	(0.010)	(0.010)	(0.010)
Education		−0.042***	−0.042***	−0.042***	−0.042***
		(0.007)	(0.007)	(0.007)	(0.007)
Female		0.026	0.026	0.027	0.026
		(0.023)	(0.023)	(0.023)	(0.023)
(Ln)Age		0.198***	0.198***	0.198***	0.197***
		(0.036)	(0.036)	(0.036)	(0.036)
Retired		−0.366***	−0.366***	−0.366***	−0.366***
		(0.036)	(0.036)	(0.036)	(0.036)
Lagged incumbent vote		−0.071***	−0.071***	−0.071***	−0.070***
		(0.027)	(0.027)	(0.027)	(0.027)
GFC Shock × Austerity			−0.012		
			(0.009)		
Recovery × Austerity			−0.024*		
			(0.014)		
GFC shock × Redistribution				0.002	
				(0.002)	
Recovery × Redistribution				−0.003**	
				(0.002)	
Shock × Welfare cues					−0.328
					(0.306)
Recovery × Welfare cues					0.291
					(0.198)
Constant	1.736***	1.713***	1.950***	0.963	1.352***
	(0.510)	(0.523)	(0.519)	(0.775)	(0.509)
Variance (intercept)	0.399***	0.390***	0.348***	0.317***	0.313***
	(0.114)	(0.112)	(0.100)	(0.091)	(0.090)
Chi-square	27.78***	666.19***	672.46***	677.86***	678.77***
N countries	25	25	25	25	25
N individuals	40,968	40,130	40,130	40,130	40,130

Note: Cells display estimates from multilevel logit regression with random intercepts with standard errors in parentheses.
***$p<0.01$, **$p<0.05$, *$p<0.10$

that education, retirement, and household income tend to reduce economic insecurity. Controlling for these factors, age is positively correlated with perceived insecurity: that is, older workers are likely to feel more insecure than younger ones. In addition, individuals who support incumbent parties are more likely to have positive perceptions about their future economic condition than those who do not support incumbent parties. None of the individual-level effects, however, alter the influence of the macro-economic and political variables discussed above.

Models 3, 4, and 5 of Table 3.1 assess interaction effects of macro-level contextual variables and incumbent party's policy efforts and welfare messages. Since coefficients of interactions in logistic regressions cannot be directly interpreted, we report visualized results in graphs. All graphs present predicted probabilities of expected income reduction across various conditioning variables given weak and strong economic shock and recovery rates. Here, a weak or, in this case, absent shock indicates an 8 per cent increase in GDP per capita from 2007 to 2009, as in Poland, while a strong shock indicates a 20 per cent reduction, as experienced in Estonia (see Figure 2.2). A weak recovery refers to a 15 per cent decrease in GDP per capita from 2009 to an election year, while a strong recovery refers to a 20 per cent increase.

Figure 3.3 shows predicted probabilities of expected income reduction across a varying degree of austerity. Stricter austerity increases a sense of insecurity while greater discretionary spending mitigates perceived insecurity when a country is heavily affected by an economic shock during the crisis. Though the difference is not significantly large, when a country is little affected by the crisis, we see an opposite effect of fiscal austerity. That is, stricter austerity reduces perceived insecurity. We find a similar but more pronounced pattern for recovery: government policies to tighten fiscal spending and engage in a diet of austerity reduce perceptions of material security among mass publics. Further, the impact of short-term fiscal stimulus of austerity is conditioned more by the scope of the recovery than the depth of the shock.

Figure 3.4 shows predicted probabilities of expected income reduction across a varying degree of post-tax, post-transfer changes in income inequality. Confirming the findings from Figure 3.2, higher values on *Relative redistribution* significantly reduce perceived insecurity, particularly for countries negatively affected by the crisis. What is interesting, however, is that when compared with the impact of redistribution immediately after the crisis, the negative impact of relative redistribution is moderated, if not increased, for a country with weak recovery, while its impact is heightened for a country that experienced strong recovery. The implication is that at the onset of the crisis, in-place automatic stabilizers can be an effective policy instrument to calm individuals' sense of insecurity. However, the capacity of the welfare state to

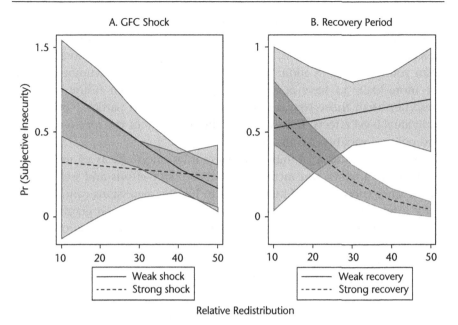

Figure 3.4. Predicted Probabilities of Subjective Insecurity across Degrees of Relative Redistribution by GDP Per Capita Change Rates

Note: The figures are based on Model 4 in Table 3.1. Dashed lines display 95% confidence intervals.

quell public anxieties is weaker when economic recovery is slow in the long term. Once again, this finding demonstrates the necessity of differentiating the development and recovery stages of economic crisis for understanding its effects on public perceptions.

Finally, we consider the impact of governing party cues. As described in the introductory chapter, political incumbents explored a range of response strategies during the post-crisis elections. For example, the governing Fianna Fáil party in Ireland went into its first post-crisis election in March 2011 and ran a campaign that defended is record by mixing blame-avoidance strategies with its efforts to enact a range of austerity policies. As a result, the party did little to signal to voters that it would improve social protections in the future. In contrast, in Austria the incumbent Social Democrats conducted a campaign in advance of the 2013 general election anchored on promises to create more jobs, adopt tax cuts for low earners, and tax increases for millionaires.

To what extent did such discourses bear on their electorates' sense of security for the future? Like policy efforts, results in the first two models in Table 3.1 show that incumbent parties' welfare cues have a negative impact on reducing perceived insecurity. However, Figure 3.5 drawn from Model 5 in Table 3.1 shows that the effect of pro-welfare messages is relatively small for a country which experienced a weak economic shock. By contrast, on welfare

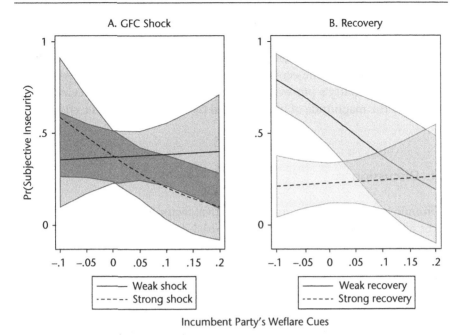

Figure 3.5. Predicted Probabilities of Subjective Insecurity across a Varying Degree of Incumbent Party's Welfare Cues by GDP Per Capita Change Rates
Note: The figures are based on Model 5 in Table 3.1. Dashed lines display 95% confidence intervals.

concerns, the government can effectively mitigate economic insecurity in a country that was hit hard by the GFC, though its impact is not significantly different from the impact on a country with a weak economic shock. However, as with *Relative redistribution*, the impact of welfare messages is weakened when a country's economic recovery is slow during the latter period. We find the strong negative impact only when a country's economy shows strong recovery.

For the purpose of comparison, we also examine the effect of trusted party's welfare messages by using a measure of trusted party messages. We pair the party welfare emphasis scores with survey respondents based on which party the respondent 'feels closes to'. The results are visualized in the graphs in Figure A3.1 in the Appendix. Unlike the impact of incumbent party messages, it appears that pro-welfare messages from trusted parties do not have a significant impact on perceived insecurity during both the shock and recovery periods. The predicted probability of expected income reduction rarely changes over the range of trusted party's welfare positions.

The findings from these multilevel analyses largely provide support for our theoretical prediction. First and foremost, context matters. Macro-level contextual variables have a significant impact in shaping individuals' feelings of insecurity. The GFC had a prolonged effect on economic perceptions for several years. More importantly, consistent with our top–down argument, the political context, as gauged by policy efforts and political rhetoric, mattered even more than the economic one. In particular, redistributive policy and incumbent party's pro-welfare messages heavily shaped perceived insecurity, but the magnitude of impact varied by stages of economic crisis.

3.4. Discussion

Economic insecurity has emerged as a critical factor in shaping policy preferences and popular support in post-industrial democracies. This importance stems from what rates as perhaps the central objective of the modern welfare state: to insure individuals, both rich and poor, against the incurrence of risk. Given shifts in national labour markets, away from manufacturing to services, and given greater constraints imposed by austerity and globalization, risk management is now more central to the workings of contemporary welfare states than is the redistribution of wealth from rich to poor.

Accordingly, this chapter has sought to examine the factors shaping public feelings of economic insecurity in times of economic crisis. Do perceptions simply follow from objective risk produced by economic crisis? And do other political, contextual factors matter as well? Our main findings are twofold. First, consistent with the conventional wisdom, we find that objective factors like employment status, relative skill specificity, and asset ownership shape perceptions of economic insecurity. Macro-economic conditions also matter as well. In particular, we find that the crisis has a long-lasting impact on economic perceptions. But the economy alone cannot account for why some individuals are less certain of their material futures than others.

Perhaps of greater importance when it comes to how democracies work, we show that, under certain conditions, political elites can mediate the effect of adverse economic conditions produced by economic crisis. In particular, we find that elite discourse and redistributive policy have a significant impact on moderating the impact of economic downturn on perceived insecurity. Greater emphasis on welfare expansion by political elites, particularly incumbent parties, and improved inequality as a result of taxes and transfers increase a sense of security. The implication is that, although risk exposure and economic impact of the crisis do affect individuals' feelings of insecurity, what matters even more is the effective response of political elites to the crisis. The next chapter builds on these findings to examine how crisis-induced perceived insecurity and political-economic contexts inform individuals' policy demands.

Appendix

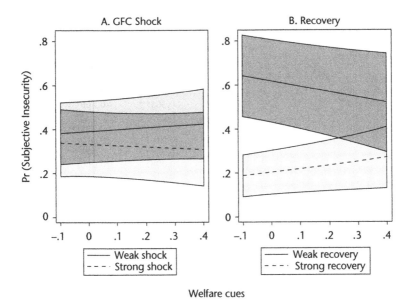

Figure 3.A1. Predicted Probabilities of Subjective Insecurity across a Varying Degrees of Trusted Party's Welfare Cues by GDP Per Capita Change Rates

Table 3.A1. Reanalysis of the Main Models Using Oesch's Class Classification Instead of Skill Specificity and Employment Status

	(1)	(3)	(5)	(7)	(9)
Shock period	−0.008	−0.010	−0.052	−0.091	0.001
	(0.021)	(0.021)	(0.042)	(0.081)	(0.020)
Recovery period	−0.049**	−0.051***	−0.122***	0.042	−0.046**
	(0.020)	(0.020)	(0.047)	(0.050)	(0.018)
Austerity	−0.029	−0.034	0.144	−0.033	−0.034
	(0.054)	(0.054)	(0.119)	(0.049)	(0.051)
Relative	−0.058***	−0.056***	−0.051***	−0.037*	−0.051***
redistribution	(0.013)	(0.013)	(0.013)	(0.021)	(0.012)
Welfare cues	−3.386**	−3.321**	−1.750	−2.787*	−3.500
	(1.654)	(1.642)	(1.814)	(1.536)	(2.128)
Social class					
High service		ref	ref	ref	ref
Lower service		0.047	0.048	0.048	0.048
		(0.046)	(0.046)	(0.046)	(0.046)
Self-employed		0.190***	0.190***	0.190***	0.191***
		(0.048)	(0.048)	(0.048)	(0.048)
Skilled worker		0.205***	0.206***	0.206***	0.205***
		(0.040)	(0.040)	(0.040)	(0.040)

(*continued*)

Table 3.A1. Continued

	(1)	(3)	(5)	(7)	(9)
Unskilled worker		0.260***	0.260***	0.260***	0.260***
		(0.051)	(0.051)	(0.051)	(0.051)
Not in labour force		0.096**	0.095**	0.096**	0.097**
		(0.043)	(0.043)	(0.043)	(0.043)
Low-risk asset (no assets)		−0.149***	−0.149***	−0.149***	−0.149***
		(0.035)	(0.035)	(0.035)	(0.035)
High-risk asset (no assets)		−0.305***	−0.305***	−0.306***	−0.305***
		(0.038)	(0.038)	(0.038)	(0.038)
Household income		−0.135***	−0.135***	−0.135***	−0.135***
		(0.010)	(0.010)	(0.010)	(0.010)
Education		−0.029***	−0.029***	−0.029***	−0.029***
		(0.008)	(0.008)	(0.008)	(0.008)
Female		0.016	0.016	0.016	0.016
		(0.023)	(0.023)	(0.023)	(0.023)
(Ln)Age		0.208***	0.208***	0.209***	0.208***
		(0.036)	(0.036)	(0.036)	(0.036)
Retired		−0.397***	−0.396***	−0.397***	−0.397***
		(0.036)	(0.036)	(0.036)	(0.036)
Lagged incumbent vote		−0.071***	−0.071***	−0.071***	−0.070***
		(0.027)	(0.027)	(0.027)	(0.027)
Shock × Austerity			−0.012		
			(0.009)		
Recovery × Austerity			−0.024*		
			(0.014)		
GFC shock × Redistribution				0.002	
				(0.002)	
Recovery × Redistribution				−0.003**	
				(0.002)	
GFC shock × Welfare cues					−0.336
					(0.307)
Recovery × Welfare cues					0.291
					(0.199)
Constant	1.736***	1.566***	1.798***	0.825	1.203**
	(0.510)	(0.528)	(0.525)	(0.780)	(0.514)
Variance(intercept)	0.399***	0.393***	0.352***	0.319***	0.314***
	(0.114)	(0.113)	(0.101)	(0.092)	(0.090)
Chi-square	27.28***	660.26***	666.13***	671.86***	672.92***
N countries	25	25	25	25	25
N individuals	40,968	40,130	40,130	40,130	40,130

Note: Cells display estimates from multilevel logit regression with random intercepts with standard errors in parentheses.
***$p < 0.01$, **$p < 0.05$, *$p < 0.10$

4

Revising the Bargain?

Policy Preferences After the Crisis

As shown in the previous chapter, the economic crisis eroded many people's sense of well-being and economic security. And, as later chapters demonstrate, the consequent political responses influenced voter decisions. However, in the advanced capitalist democracies, elections are about more than tending to the public's material needs. The direction of policy also matters. Positions over policy lie at the heart of the democratic bargain: citizens grant policymaking authority to a set of elected representatives. These representatives, in turn, are subject to removal from office for not meeting citizens' expectations. In the industrial West after the Second World War, business, organized labour, and political elites famously forged a 'class compromise' (Przeworski 1985), or what Ruggie (1982) termed a bargain of 'embedded liberalism (Hays 2009). The bargain took the form of a trade-off between global capitalism and social security, the former to encourage business and economic growth, and the latter to protect individuals against misfortune and economic change.

This bargain served the rich democracies well for decades. But governments and the citizens they represent must now navigate more challenging times. At the end of the twentieth century the ability of governments to translate citizen preferences into policy had increasingly been called into question. Globalization, deindustrialization, technological change, and other forces mean that patterns of apparent social and economic stability that have long underpinned party systems and political parties' connections to their electorates have been disrupted. In Marx and Engels's (1848) oft-cited words: 'All fixed, fast-frozen relations, with their train of ancient and venerable prejudices and opinions, are swept away, all new-formed ones become antiquated before they can ossify. All that is solid melts into air.' In such times of instability and change, many people have become more exposed to risk and insecurity than in the past, and political parties can no longer so strongly rely on the

Democracy Under Siege? Parties, Voters, and Elections After the Great Recession. Timothy Hellwig, Yesola Kweon, and Jack Vowles, Oxford University Press (2020). © Timothy Hellwig, Yesola Kweon, and Jack Vowles. DOI: 10.1093/oso/9780198846208.001.0001

consistent support of their traditional cleavage-based voters. The global financial crisis has intensified these developments. The dramatic change Marx predicted can be uncomfortable and painful. People value stability, with secure jobs, with family and friends close at hand, and with a safety net available to protect them against the consequences of bad luck or poor judgement. Disruptive change may disconnect people from established parties, a topic we explore in Chapter 7. Such change can also give people reasons to search for new political identities and cause them to lose confidence in the ability of governments to protect their interests.

Consequently, these economic and social changes were not divorced from politics. As we saw in Chapter 2, across the OECD countries voter support has become increasingly volatile as ties to established political parties weaken and new political identities emerge. And in Chapter 3 we showed that feelings of insecurity are shaped by the political context in general and elite messages and actions in particular. This chapter takes up another piece of the citizens' response: their preferences for policy. We consider how economic change interacts with party politics to inform mass preferences over key aspects of public policy. Insomuch as the economic crisis of 2007–9 contributed to feelings of insecurity, did it also raise public demands for government action? Alternatively, did citizens perceive the crisis as a signal that their government's capacities had become compromised and, accordingly, temper policy demands on efficiency grounds? Were there institutionally based variations in public opinion and policy preferences related to differences between countries in their forms of labour market regulation, and longer term histories of economic and social policy? Did the existence of automatic stabilizers cushion the impact on preferences and what difference, if anything, can be attributed to short-term fiscal stimulus? Those not immediately affected may be less likely to endorse the role of government and instead put credence in their own capacities to protect themselves from increasingly volatile markets, fostering their own self-development. But even those who suffer insecurity may come to believe they cannot depend on the state, particularly if cued in that direction by party-political elites coping with crisis conditions. Those cues could be most strongly influential on those who are most exposed to risk and insecurity. Our expectations follow from these elements of our argument.

Expectations also emerge from the logic of preference formation for social protection (Rehm 2016). We assess the impact of the crisis on mass preferences for policies in two key social policy areas: expenditure on public health services and expenditure on policies to assist the unemployed. The first of these is a prime example of universal social protection, where all are subject to the risks associated with ill-health, while the second is an example of a targeted means-tested policy protection. As indicators of social policy, health care and unemployment benefits differ in level and breadth of popular support. As government-funded health care benefits most, if not all, it tends to receive a high level of support from the public. This is not the case for unemployment. As not all are equally vulnerable to the risk of unemployment, we expect a lower level of support for spending in this policy domain. Demands for health care also remain relatively constant, whereas unemployment varies more over time, potentially making preferences more volatile. Comparing expenditure preferences for health and unemployment, we therefore expect support for health expenditure to remain high over time and be shared across segments of society, while support for programmes to assist the unemployed will be relatively low, more volatile, and more concentrated among those groups most affected by insecurity.

Our next set of expectations is shaped by the force of elite cues, the contexts of automatic stabilizers and relative distribution, and the policy choices made by governments between austerity or stimulus. Welfare policy effort in the form of relative redistribution of incomes should have a cushioning effect on the crisis, reducing the effects of risk and insecurity variables on policy preferences and underpinning higher expenditures. Conversely, low welfare policy effort should have the opposite effects. Next, government policy choices between austerity and stimulus should have (a) direct effects on policy preferences and (b) conditioning effects on the effects of the crisis, risk perceptions, and socio-economic positions on policy preferences. We also expect that elite cues will have (a) direct effects on policy preferences and (b) conditioning effects on the effects of the crisis, risk perceptions, and socio-economic positions on policy preferences.

What about the effects of crisis and recovery? It is important to note that short-term changes in health and unemployment expenditures are driven by different imperatives, and these differences must inform our analysis. In normal circumstances, we expect that the relationship between public opinion and policy change will be thermostatic (Soroka and Wlezien 2010): on balance, there will be a shift in public opinion towards more provision and expenditure when expenditure has fallen. Where expenditure and provision have increased, public opinion in the aggregate will tend to shift towards lower expenditure. In a time of crisis and recovery, politicians may consider cost-cutting to reduce expenditure on health, but the cost of health services remain high, because of the breadth and salience of demand for health services. We therefore expect that a thermostatic relationship will remain.

However, unemployment expenditure is a special case, and for this reason is not normally taken as an example of thermostatic policymaking. Unemployment expenditure is primarily driven by *demand* that greatly increased because of the economic crisis: by default, unless provision is cut, reducing policy *effort*, unemployment expenditure simply rises with the number of unemployed. The main driver of public perceptions is therefore the unemployment rate. As change in unemployment expenditure is driven by the economic conditions and rarely if at all in response to public preferences, a key element in the thermostatic relationship is missing.

With the aid of the post-election surveys collected as part of the CSES, this chapter addresses these questions in cross-national perspective. In Part III of the book, we investigate the impact of elite cues and party policies on political choice. This chapter extends the politics of advanced capitalism's model of constrained partisanship to argue that preferences are shaped by the individuals' position in the social structure but also by the set of feasible options from the menu provided by competing political elites. As with many perspectives out of the welfare state literature, constrained partisanship views public policy preferences as rooted in institutions, economic circumstances, and past policy legacies. Parting ways with this view, we argue that parties can shape citizens' preferences through policy efforts and rhetoric. Consistent with other research, we find that individual-level attributes associated with labour market positions, skills, and wealth inform policy preferences. But we also find evidence in the shape of party politics. Complemented by party cues conditioning their effects, both the depth of crisis *and* the extent of the recovery shaped some post-GFC policy demands across the OECD.

4.1. Government Responsiveness and Public Preferences

What do citizens demand from their elected officials? This question lies at the heart of representative democracy. Governments are more responsive when their actions align with the wishes of the governed and less when they do not. For much of the second half of the twentieth century there existed broad consensus in Western democracies about the role of government and its policy responsibilities. The generation that grew to maturity from the mid-twentieth century onward came of age at a time when the dynamic nature of the capitalist economy was suppressed or at least concealed. In the aftermath of the great depression of the 1930s and the Second World War, a platform for reconstruction and development was established at international conference at Bretton Woods. The Bretton Woods institutions provided a structure for what proved to be period of relative economic stability.[1] As reviewed in Chapter 2, fixed exchange rates, the encouragement of international trade within tariff barriers that might be only slowly diminished, and limits of the movement of capital across borders all provided the framework for the development of welfare states underpinned by Keynesian policies of income

---

[1] Indeed, with the benefit of hindsight, we can say that the years between 1944 (liberation of France) and 1973 (the first oil crisis) were unusually stable and prosperous.

redistribution and demand management targeted primarily on the prevention of unemployment. This emerging embedded liberal or social democratic model made possible the development of comprehensive welfare states.

The 'creative destruction' inherent in the capitalist system (Schumpeter 1942) remerged in the 1970s and 1980s, slowly at first but it soon gained speed. Trade barriers were dismantled and international capital flows deregulated, and governments began to target the prevention of inflation, not unemployment, often devolving inflation management to central banks. Tax systems became less redistributive, putting more pressure on benefit systems, increasingly integrating the two. Neo-liberal economic ideas, most strongly but not exclusively associated with the policies of Margaret Thatcher in Britain and Ronald Reagan in the United States, were used to justify efforts to roll back the welfare state, targeting those most in need and encouraging people on benefits to move back into the labour market.

More recently, the accelerating dynamism of the capitalist economy has been underpinned by technological developments that have reduced demand for unskilled labour and reduced the costs of distance, together creating the return of significant unemployment in many developed democracies. Manufacturing and primary production have shrunk, while jobs in the expanding service sector tend to be less secure and garner less compensation. Changes in the labour market and laws restricting their powers have marginalized trade unions in many countries. These long-term trends towards a reduction in citizens' economic and social security only intensified with the financial crisis of 2007–8 and its aftermath. Lack of regulation of capital flows and investment created the conditions for a financial bubble in property markets. When the bubble burst, banks and other financial institutions had insufficient reserves to maintain confidence. By various means, governments moved to cover the deficits, in several worst affected countries leading on to a further crisis of sovereign debt.

Changes in the political economy of representative democracies are linked to changes in public policy demands. The welfare state protected individuals from the vagaries of advanced capitalism. Welfare state buffers in turn implied a high level of policy responsiveness: publics demanded social protections against injury, sickness, and unemployment, and their popularly elected governments responded more or less in kind (Flora and Heidenheimer 1981). Economic decline during and after the oil-induced crises of the 1970s put pressure on governments to cut their cloth to circumstances. Publics responded to attempts to dismantle the welfare state with protest and disillusionment (Pierson 1994). This is consistent with a more general pattern uncovered in the research on government responsiveness showing that public expenditure preferences are cyclical. All else equal, reductions in expenditure are associated with shifts in public opinion, as broadly characterized the public response to 1980s fiscal retrenchment. Similarly, publics respond thermostatically to increases in expenditure by shifting towards preferences for reduction (Soroka and Wlezien 2010). We therefore investigate both thermostatic and crisis effects on mass preferences for health expenditure in the wake of the Great Recession: as noted earlier, while we may expect to see a public response to changes in the unemployment rate, this is not strictly speaking a thermostatic relationship as changes in expenditure are not driven by public preferences. With respect to crisis and recovery effects, we further examine the potential of individual and contextual protections against policy demands, as well as the extent to which supply-side factors condition the influence of the GFC on policy preferences.

4.1.1. Micro-Protections: Skills, Labour Markets, and Wealth

A wide-ranging body of research demonstrates that peoples' policy preferences are derived from their individual attributes. Regarding social protection, chief among these are one's position in national labour markets and thus occupational social class. Economic and social change of the late twentieth century have reshaped the nature of work, and traditional forms of class analysis may no longer be fit for purpose. The male workforce in manual occupations has shrunk, and women have entered the labour market in large numbers, primarily in a burgeoning service sector. The differences between lower paid manual and non-manual workers have shrunk, and the differences between owners and managerial employees have also become less socially and politically salient. To take account of these changes in this chapter we adopt a version of Daniel Oesch's five class categories (Oesch 2008, 2012). The logic behind them lies across two dimensions: an economic divide separating holders of organizational power from the working class, and a cultural divide separating high-skilled classes engaged in interpersonal work settings from low-skilled classes occupied in object-related tasks.

Iversen and Soskice (2001) also emphasize the role of human capital and the specificity of marketable skills.[2] Individuals whose marketable skill set applies to only a handful of occupations will prefer higher levels of social protection where there is strong unemployment insurance and support for retraining. Otherwise, they may be less sympathetic to high expenditure on social services. Those possessing a more general set of skills, broadly adaptable to shifting demands for labour, prefer to spend less on social protection schemes.

Occupational skills represent a specific realization of a more general phenomenon: economic risk (Rehm 2009, 2016; Hacker et al. 2013; Walter 2010).

---

[2] For Iversen and Soskice (2001), the key concept is 'relative skill specificity': how specialized an individual's skills are relative to the general skills or total skills that the same individual possesses.

Support for social protection is a function of most people's tendency to be risk averse, and the extent to which they are objectively exposed to risk. This model of social policy preferences contains a dynamic element: if risks increase as the result of events such as the great depression or the global financial crisis, so will support for social programmes intended to ameliorate those risks. However, the extent of this support is contingent on the degree of the crisis. If the crisis primarily affects the weak, without affecting the majority, support for social policy wanes and retrenchment or austerity is the most likely response. In contrast, a crisis that affects the majority where the distribution of risk is more equal should augur support for the extension of social programmes.

The social effects of a crisis are felt more widely as time elapses. The real effects of an external shock are first felt by those with low levels of material security. With time, however, the more protected—by virtue of their income levels, wealth, skills, and the like, also will observe negative effects on their lives. This means that while the initial response to a crisis may *reduce* support for social protection, preferences over time may reverse in favour of more expansive policies as the crisis deepens. The aftermath of the global financial crisis provides some support for risk-based arguments. After a brief stimulus to avert the collapse of the international financial system, the policy response in most of the affected economies was towards austerity and the right (Bartels 2014). Some recent comparative research identifies a later shift in the other direction (Lindvall 2014, 2017). Margalit's (2013) micro-level analysis of panel data from the United States, however, indicates that, while experience of risk and insecurity influenced social policy preferences, the effects were only temporary. Analyses of publics from other countries also uncover substantively meaningful, but fleeting, effects (Alt et al. 2017; Martén 2019; Naumann et al. 2015). Arguments for austerity have more public support than many might expect. It may be that, for many people, the image of the economy is finite: if there is a shortage of money, there is none to spare, particularly for the poor, who take out more than they put in. The market has a logic of its own, independent of human volition or responsibility, leading to fatalism (Framing the Economy Network and Advisory Group 2018). Presented with a crisis, this language of austerity may be briefly marginalized, but may emerge again later. At least, voters' preferences for austerity relative to deficit spending are inconsistent (Huebscher et al. 2018).

In addition to place in the labour market, accumulated wealth may also affect one's tolerance for risk and, by extension, one's preference for risk-diffusing social protections. While correlated, income and wealth are not the same, and wealth and asset levels may be a more powerful source of political preferences about social protection than income alone. This 'patrimonial' argument identifies asset ownership as an additional dimension of economic well-being (Lewis-Beck et al. 2013; Hellwig and McAllister 2019; see also Ansell 2014). Patrimonial theories provide a window into the motives of people who choose to acquire or not acquire assets. Asset acquisition has both psychological and ideological elements. The absence of any assets indicates vulnerability and a possible inability to cope, or, alternatively, a 'devil-may-care' attitude. With ownership comes a level of security and insurance against volatile market-based income. Owners of low-risk assets such as one's residence or savings insulate themselves against some risk. Ideologically, they will favour the principle of pooling risk within a society rather than establishing their own pool of assets to guard against adversity. Meanwhile those with higher risk assets may see them as a source of potential independence from any state assistance, as a 'buffer-stock' (Carroll 1997), and indeed may be ideologically opposed to collective risk-pooling.

4.1.2. Macro-Protections: Policy Preferences and the Welfare State

Along with skills, labour market security, and wealth, policy demands are shaped by the existing policy context. As Esping-Anderson's pioneering *Three Worlds of Welfare Capitalism* (1990) showed, variations in welfare state performance can be explained in part by path dependence and party politics. The varieties of capitalism framework (Hall and Soskice 2001) deepened the analysis into the structure of business but with important implications for the welfare state. Their dichotomy of liberal versus coordinated market economies was complementary to the three models of the welfare state, pushing analysis into structures of vocational training and education as well as into industrial relations.[3]

The structure of welfare state institutions within the different forms of advanced capitalism also conditions the influence of individual attributes, like skills, on policy preferences. In coordinated market economies (CMEs), people have incentives to acquire specific skills because if those skills become outdated there is government support by way of income maintenance and retraining programmes. In those economies, the relatively skilled will tend to favour the welfare state. Investing in specific skills is more risky in the more service-oriented liberal market economies (LMEs). The welfare state becomes

---

[3] Hall and Soskice (2001) defined LMEs, CMEs, and mixed countries for only a subset of the cases included here. We rely on Crowley (2006) for the addition of Slovenia as a CME, on Devore (2015) for Israel as an LME, on Schneider (2009) for Latin American countries as Hierarchical Market Economies (HME), on Drahokoupil and Myant (2010) and Bohle and Greskovits (2012) for Estonia and Latvia as LMEs, and on Kiran (2018) for the addition of Turkey as an HME, and Nölke and Vliegenhart 2009 for the classification of other Eastern European countries as Dependent Market Economies (DME). Also see Schmidt (2016) on France as a 'State-Influenced Market Economy' (SME). We collapsed all non-LME additional categories into MMEs in our exploratory analysis. This indicated that the most significant distinction was between LMEs and the rest.

increasingly confined to addressing insecurity among those on the lowest incomes, who tend to become stigmatized as undeserving. In LMEs support for these services is widespread only in cases where public services are open to all, such as for health and hospital services. This makes the difference between LMEs and other types of advanced capitalism a very relevant control variable for expenditure preferences, particularly in the case of any policy related to the labour market.

4.1.3. *The Political Supply: Elite Cues and Policy Preferences*

While important as anchors social policy preferences, micro-individual and macro-contextual accounts take us only so far. Missing is the impact of *politics*, realized here in terms of policy responses and party competition. As already stated in our first two hypotheses, this book asserts that to understand mass politics in the post-crisis era, we must consider the role of influential political elites. Political parties may either confirm or contest fatalistic assumptions that sideline human agency and the possibilities of political action. A common refrain is that the capacity of parties to inform public opinion has been stymied, be it due to cognitive mobilization (Dalton 1984), to growth in single-issue parties (Ezrow 2010), or to the sort of sweeping social and economic change analysed here. Such assertions notwithstanding, there is evidence that party systems in advanced capitalist democracies have tended to realign rather than dealign. Perhaps most prominently, researchers have posited a transformation of socio-cultural cleavages, in Western Europe especially, away from left versus right and onto what Kriesi et al. 2008 call an 'integration-demarcation' cleavage (also Kriesi et al. 2012; Kitschelt and Rehm 2015). The implication is that the cleavage structure that lies beneath party systems has changed, and become more complex, but parties themselves shape the cleavage structure by responding to and redirecting public preferences by way of cues and heuristics. Extending this logic, we maintain that the capacity of elites to shape the political debate, and the policy demands within it, should be heightened during times of crisis.

Following the theoretical framework introduced in Chapter 1, we assert that economic change—brought on by the crises in advanced capitalist nations—matters for public preferences over policy which, in part, should protect them from the aftermath of past economic shocks and the effects of those in the future. But unlike earlier work on the crisis's effects (Bartels 2014; Lindvall 2017), our argument is that the transmission between economic shocks and policy opinion is also affected by the capacity of political elites to structure the policy discourse. And as with the case of perceptions of individual insecurity examined in the last chapter, political elites can subdue or encourage policy opinions.

4.2. Data and Measures

4.2.1. *Measuring Policy Demand and Effort*

First, we provide a visual preliminary test of our expectation that support for health expenditure will remain high and less volatile, as compared to support for expenditure on the unemployed, that we expect to be lower and more volatile.

Evidence shown in Figure 4.1 supports these expectations. The graphs chart mass opinions supporting government-provided employment assistance and health care from the 1970s to 2016 in four countries for which comparable data exist. The trends indicate that opinions about the governments' role in health care has remained high and constant. In contrast, in every nation, support for government action to protect jobs and directly influence economic activity has declined over time, and with no sign of rebounding in the wake of the crisis events of the early twentieth century (also see Humpage 2015). Rather than volatility, then, we see decline.

Focusing in more closely, we next plot aggregate opinion on expenditures in these same two areas, health and unemployment, before (2006) and after

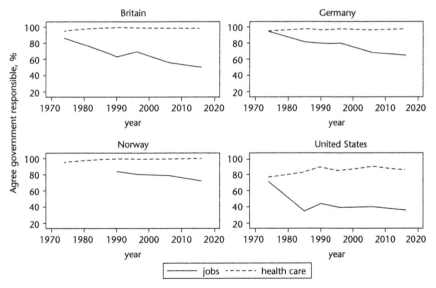

Figure 4.1. Public Preferences for Government Provision of Jobs and Health Care, % Supporting Government Responsibility

Note: Graphs display the summed % of respondents who 'strongly' and 'somewhat' agree that it is the government's responsibility to provide jobs (solid line) and to provide health care (dashed line). Figures for Germany are for Western Germany only.

Sources: Barnes et al. (1979), various ISSP surveys.

(2016) the GFC.[4] Across fifteen countries, aggregate opinion is measured as the percentage of respondents in each country who say that the government should spend (much/somewhat) more on the policy area.[5] We see, first, that as expected public support levels are generally higher for health care than for unemployment benefits. In fact, in no country do larger shares of the public prefer more spending on unemployment than on health. Second, collective preferences are relatively stable over time: publics with high (low) levels of support before the crisis are likely to have relatively high (low) support levels after the crisis. Further, attitudes on health care remain stable in most countries, and have shifted in a more conservative direction only in Japan, the United States, Norway, and Australia. Preferences for helping the unemployed are stable in about half the countries, and have otherwise shifted in a more conservative direction in the other half. No obvious explanation is apparent for these differences between countries: further analysis is required.

We now move back to data from Module 4 of the Comparative Study of Electoral Systems examined in the previous chapter. The dataset includes a battery of items on preferences for policy expenditure, from which we examine preferences for health care and unemployment similar to those examined above (Figure 4.2). The CSES survey item reads: 'Please say whether there should be more or less public expenditure in each of the following areas. Remember that if you say "more" it could require a tax increase, and if you say "less" it could require a reduction in those services.'

To get a sense of the relationship between the impact of the crisis and public sentiment, Figure 4.3 plots the size of the shock and the recovery against collective opinion scores on policy preferences. The top two graphs do so for preferences over health spending. As expected, bivariate plots reveal no discernible relationship between the size of the GFC shock—operationalized as the percentage drop in per capita growth from 2007 and 2009, weighted by the passage of time until the election in question—and preferences for spending on health (Figure 4.3A). Similarly, bivariate relationships reveal no apparent association between the recovery and health spending opinions (Figure 4.3B).

---

[4] Data are from the International Social Survey Programme (ISSP). Country cases are those for which data exist at both time periods and include Australia, the Czech Republic, France, Germany, Japan, Iceland, Latvia, New Zealand, Norway, Slovenia, Spain, Sweden, Switzerland, the UK, and the USA. We use measures from the ISSP, rather than the CSES, for purposes of over-time comparison: the English-language question wording from the 2006 ISSP survey omits the additional CSES phrase 'if you say "less" it could require a reduction in those services' (see CSES question wording below). No CSES data are available from before the GFC.
[5] This question reads: 'Listed below are various areas of government spending. Please show whether you would like to see more or less government spending in each area. Remember that if you say "much more", it might require a tax increase to pay for it.' Respondents were then asked to consider 'health' and 'unemployment benefits'. Response options are on a five-point scale ranging from 'spend much more than now' to 'spend much less than now'.

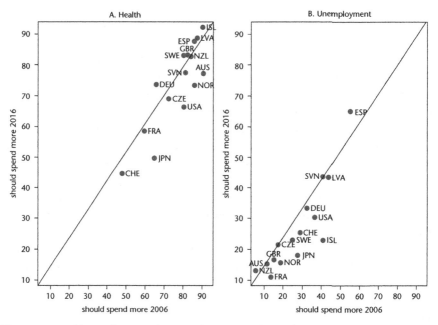

Figure 4.2. Public Preferences for Spending on Health and Unemployment, 2006 and 2011–2016

Note: Graphs report the % of respondents in the country survey saying their government should spend (much/somewhat) more on health or unemployment.

Source: ISSP 2008 and 2018.

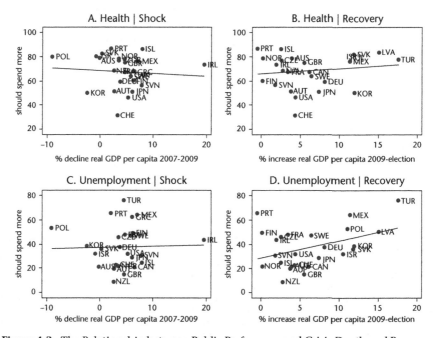

Figure 4.3. The Relationship between Public Preferences and Crisis Depth and Recovery

Notes: Vertical axes report % of respondents who say that the government should spend more on health (Graphs A and B) and unemployment (C and D). Horizontal axes report the % decline in economic growth per capita from 2007 to 2009 (A and C) and increase in economic growth per capita from 2009 to the year of the election (B and D). The latter omits the outlier case of Greece for presentation purposes.

Sources: CSES 2017 and OECD.

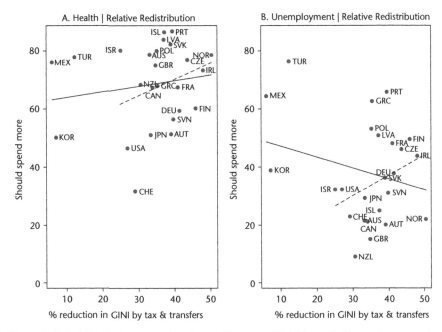

Figure 4.4. Public Preferences for Expenditure on Health and Unemployment by Relative Redistribution of Incomes

Notes: Vertical axes report % of respondents who say that the government should spend more on health (A) and (B) unemployment. The horizontal axes report the tax- and transfer-induced reduction in the Gini coefficient such that higher values indicate greater policy effort. Solid lines are fitted regression lines for all cases, dashed lines are with South Korea, Mexico, and Turkey removed.

Sources: CSES 2017, Solt 2019.

The bottom pair of graphs do the same for unemployment expenditure. Again, the shock had no apparent effect on opinions: in the aggregate, people in countries which weathered the crisis well, like Poland, had views on unemployment like those in countries that were hit hard, like Ireland. We do find, however, an apparent recovery effect: on average, publics in countries which were able to rebound from the crisis approved of spending more on unemployment policies than did those in countries with little or no improvement in per capita GDP following the shock.[6]

Before moving on to that next step, we plot preferences for health and unemployment expenditure against country welfare policy effort (Figure 4.4). We do so using the change in the Gini coefficient attributable to government tax and welfare expenditure—our estimate of the effects of 'automatic stabilizers'. The first graph implies that, while support for more spending on health care may be higher in countries with greater welfare effort, the slope is

---

[6] The fitted line displayed in Figure 4.3D is Unemployment Opinion = 28.9 + 1.4* Recovery, with both intercept and slope estimates statistically significant at $p < 0.05$, two-tailed test.

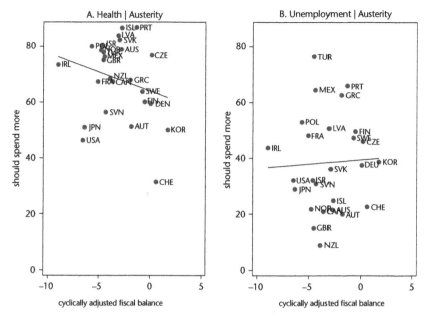

Figure 4.5. Public Preferences for Expenditure on Health and Unemployment by Degree of Austerity or Stimulus

Notes: Vertical axes report % of respondents who say that the government should spend more on health (A) and (B) unemployment. The horizontal axes report the in-sample values of austerity, defined as cyclically adjusted fiscal balance as a % of potential GDP. Higher values signal austerity, lower values signal stimulus. Solid lines are fitted regression lines for all cases.

Sources: CSES 2017, IMF 2019.

shallow and not statistically significant. On the surface, preferences for greater provision for unemployment appear lower in countries where there is greater redistributive effort, but the slope of the estimate is driven entirely by three countries with low levels of welfare effort and high preferences for more support for the unemployed: Turkey, Mexico, and South Korea. With these outliers omitted, higher levels of automatic stabilization in the form of welfare effort would be associated with somewhat higher support for spending on unemployment, as depicted by the dashed line in the figure. The slope for health remains non-significant with those deletions, and for that reason, after further exploratory multivariate modelling we drop relative redistribution from our health expenditure preference modelling.[7] Redistribution or welfare effort does not generate the cushioning effect on health expenditure

---

[7] An alternative model on health expenditure comparable to those in Table 4.2 with relative redistribution included, that excludes the three outlier countries, finds even less statistical significance than a model that includes the outliers.

preferences we expected. This may simply reflect the absence or at least the weakness of effect on health expenditure preferences for the crisis in general.

We next examine the effects of short-term fiscal policies designed to counter or adapt to economic shocks on these preferences for spending. *Austerity* is measured as described in earlier chapters, in terms of the long-term structural balance. Graphs shown in Figure 4.5 reveal an apparent relationship between this form of policy effort on health expenditure, but not on that for unemployment. Where governments are engaging in stimulus, people may feel more confident in supporting expenditure on health. In a situation of austerity, people may be taking cues that expenditure should be cut. However, since the post-election surveys constitute a series of snapshots taken at different points in the cycle of crisis and recovery, caution in interpretation is advised. Further, countries such as Chile, South Korea, and the United States have relatively weak publicly funded healthcare systems that are likely to lower expectations for higher expenditure. Again, multivariate analysis is needed to take the matter further.

4.3. Multivariate Analysis

4.3.1. *Data and Measures*

The bivariate plots of aggregated opinions set the scene. This book argues, however, that the impact of the GFC and Great Recession on mass politics is realized through elite cues and government actions, both directly and through conditioning relationships. As depicted in Figure 1.6, we expect the crisis— gauged by both its initial shock value and path of recovery—to be reflected in popular opinion conditioned by the supply-side factors of policy and rhetoric. To assess the joint influence of macro-conditions, individual-level attributes, and elite cues, we move to multivariate analysis. As described above, we measure the depth and persisting effects of the global financial crisis in two ways: *GFC shock* is the change in real GDP per capita between 2007 and the year of the election in the country in question, adjusted to take account of differences in time elapsed. *Recovery* is the extent of recovery between the election in question and 2009, again measured as the change in real GDP per capita (OECD 2017). We incorporate further policy-contextual variables that we have good reason to expect may affect preferences and expose thermostatic effects: for health, change in public health expenditure since 2007, and for unemployment, the unemployment rate over the year prior to the election, from the World Bank (2018a; 2018b).

Models contain the set of individual-level covariates introduced in the previous chapter against which we expect to find conditioning effects. These include market outsider, relative skill specificity, high- and low-risk assets,

Table 4.1. Adaptation of Oesch's Class Categories

Oesch Classifications	Module 4 CSES Codes
1. Higher Grade Service Class	Large employers, technical experts, higher grade managers and administrators, socio-cultural professionals
2. Lower Grade Service Class	Technicians, lower-grade managers, socio-cultural semi-professionals
3. Small Business Owners	Self-employed (including farmers)
4. Skilled Workers	Skilled manual, clerical, and service workers
5. Unskilled Workers	Low-skilled manual, unskilled clerks, low-skilled service

Source: Adapted from Oesch (2015).

household income, gender, and age. To test a more fine-grained class analysis with different theoretical motivations, a second model examines the impact of Oesch's five class categories in place of relative skill specificity (see Table 4.1).[8]

In the health care model, we use *Party welfare cues*, as defined previously, as our measure of elite cues. For the unemployment model the CMP codes enable us to home in on party statements about policies to address unemployment alone. To ensure that our party cue findings are not an artefact of existing ideological predispositions, models include respondents' self-identified left–right position. Lastly, perceptions of income insecurity and subjective insecurity, are measured as described in Chapter 3, as other potential candidates for conditioning.

4.3.2. Analysis

As in the previous chapter, the data structure nests individuals within country-elections. We code the dependent variable as 1 if the respondent expresses support for (somewhat/much) more public spending and 0 otherwise. Models are estimated using hierarchical logistic regression models with random intercepts. Alternative ordinal logit models on the original five-category expenditure variable produce almost identical results.

---

[8] Informed by Oesch (2015), we classify occupations into five categories according to CSES ISCO08 two-digit codes. The fit was not perfect, requiring coding of all self-employed to the small business category. While all CSES surveys we employed from Module 4 had respondent occupational codes, not all provided codes for their partners: those not providing this data were Canada, Finland, Iceland, Ireland, Sweden, and the UK. Where partner codes were available, we coded those as an estimate of household occupation where the respondent did not report an occupation. Canada, Ireland, Portugal, Slovakia, Slovenia, and the United States failed to provide data on self-employment. In those countries, only four categories could be coded, excluding (3). For the multivariate analysis below we assign no occupation and missing values to their own category to avoid case attrition.

Table 4.2 presents results for health expenditure. The first model reports results with all covariates of interest. Model 2 removes those variables not attaining statistical significance and re-estimates the model, while Model 3 substitutes in the five class categories from Oesch (2015) in place of *Relative skill specificity*. Since this inclusion does not significantly improve model fit, we reply on Model 2 estimates for interpreting our findings. Using these estimates, Figure 4.6 displays the effects of the covariates from Model 2 on the probability of survey respondents supporting higher health expenditure.

Our analyses find that austerity exerts no significant impact on preferences for health spending.[9] However, party cueing positions on welfare exerts strong effects, well outside confidence intervals. Where health expenditures have fallen since the depth of the crisis, respondents are more likely to be in favour of an increase: where expenditure has risen, the opposite is more likely. The scale runs over 2.4 points: a maximum to a minimum difference is therefore expected to have slightly less than a 2 per cent effect on expenditure support. As expected, this finding is consistent with a thermostatic model of policy response (Soroka and Wlezien 2010). Party cues and health expenditure change display the only significant country-level effects.

With respect to individual-level predictors, we find that owners of low-risk assets only are somewhat more favourable to health expenditure than those with none. Those with the highest level of relative skill specificity are more likely to support health expenditure than those with the lowest. Skilled workers are also more likely to support higher health expenditure than those in the highest service/professional/managerial category when comparing the social classes, as are those in the lowest service category. Overall, the more detailed class model adds a little more variance explained, but relative skill specificity provides the most straightforward theoretical leverage. High incomes, university degrees, and right as opposed to left ideology turn people away from support for higher expenditure, while women are more favourable than men. On the other hand, outsiders are not distinct from others, and owners of high-risk assets indistinguishable from those with no assets. Those fearing a fall in income prefer higher expenditure, as expected. However, the average marginal effects of these risk and social structure variables are relatively small, partially confirming hypothesis 4.1. Seeking to condition these risk-associated variables with party cues, we did not find the significant interactions anticipated, but still confirmed the strong direct effects for health expenditure preferences we also expected.

Table 4.3 explores preferences for more expenditure for unemployment programmes. Model 1 provides the baseline, including the shock and recovery.

---

[9] Alternative models exploring interactions with the relevant individual-level covariates fail to identify any otherwise hidden effects of these non-significant contextual variables.

Table 4.2. Preferences for Public Expenditure on Health

	(1)	(2)	(3)
Shock period	−0.009		
	(0.018)		
Recovery period	0.002		
	(0.014)		
Austerity	−0.069		
	(0.045)		
Δ Health expenditure	−0.658***	−0.647***	−0.658***
	(0.183)	(0.181)	(0.182)
Party welfare cues	0.126***	0.126***	0.126***
	(0.015)	(0.015)	(0.015)
Market outsider	−0.053	−0.053	−0.058
	(0.047)	(0.047)	(0.047)
Low risk assets (no assets)	0.125**	0.125**	0.123**
	(0.038)	(0.038)	(0.038)
High risk assets (no assets)	−0.023	−0.022	−0.010
	(0.041)	(0.041)	(0.041)
Income	−0.133***	−0.133***	−0.137***
	(0.042)	(0.042)	(0.042)
Education	−0.305***	−0.306***	−0.265***
	(0.042)	(0.058)	(0.062)
(Ln)Age	0.021	0.021	0.038
	(0.032)	(0.032)	(0.032)
Female	0.216***	0.217***	0.202***
	(0.024)	(0.024)	(0.024)
Right–left position	−0.722***	−0.722***	−0.720***
	(0.057)	(0.057)	(0.057)
Subjective insecurity	0.141***	0.141***	0.138***
	(0.039)	(0.039)	(0.039)
Relative skill specificity	0.121**	0.120**	
	(0.039)	(0.039)	
Social class			
High service			ref
Low service			0.127*
			(0.047)
Self-employed			−0.047
			(0.048)
Skilled workers			0.194***
			(0.041)
Unskilled workers			0.083
			(0.053)
Not in labour force			−0.019
			(0.043)
Constant	1.289***	1.474***	1.399***
	(0.282)	(0.211)	(0.218)
Variance(intercept)	−0.630***	−0.565***	−0.579***
	(0.143)	(0.140)	(0.143)
Chi-square	550.244	546.861	587.652
N countries	25	25	25
N individuals	38,155	38,155	38,155

Notes: Cells display estimates from multilevel logit regression with random intercepts with standard errors in parentheses.
***$p<0.01$, **$p<0.05$, *$p<0.10$

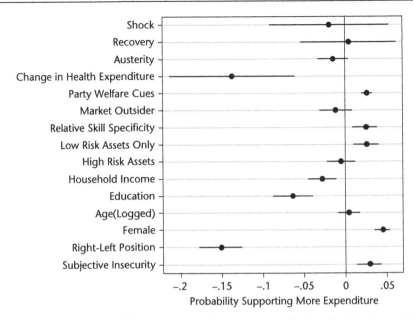

Figure 4.6. The Effect of Covariates on Preferences for Public Health Expenditure (Average Marginal Effects)

Source: Calculated from estimates reported in Table 4.1 Model 1. Dots and 95% confidence intervals represent the effect of one point across the value of the covariate in question on the probability of supporting higher expenditure. Health expenditure had a minimum decline of 0.38% in (Latvia) and a maximum increase of 2.77% (Sweden). Party cues on welfare measure maximum to minimum effects where the most right position is 0 and the most left is 1. Outsider, Low and High Risk Assets, Female are all 0 or 1. Education (an eight-point scale), Household Income (in quintiles), Relative Skill Specificity, Right–Left Scale, and Income Reduction are all also estimated from their maxima to their minima (all scaled between 0 and 1).

As a control variable, we include a dummy variable for LMEs. Given our earlier bivariate country-level findings, and confirmed by further preliminary multivariate analysis, we exclude relative redistribution and austerity-stimulus as having no significant effects. Model 2 tests an interaction indicating how shock and recovery condition the effects of party cues.

Figure 4.7 shows the marginal effects derived from Model 1. The shock variable appears to have no effects. As foreshadowed in our bivariate analysis, *recovery* has a significant effect, just inside confidence intervals. Both are plotted as interactions with party cues in Model 2 and in Figure 4.8A and B (see below). These graphs present predicted probabilities of supporting government expenditure to provide for the unemployed with weak and strong economic shock and recovery rates, as in Chapter 3. Meanwhile, the higher the unemployment rate, the more support there was for higher expenditure to address the problem. Respondents in countries with liberal market economics were less keen to see increased expenditure. In general, support for higher

Table 4.3. Preferences for Public Expenditure on Unemployment

	(1)	(2)
Shock period	0.040	0.056
	(0.162)	(0.164)
Recovery period	0.438***	0.457***
	(0.131)	(0.133)
Unemployment rate	0.121***	0.121***
	(0.024)	(0.024)
Unemployment cues	0.499***	0.697***
	(0.038)	(0.070)
LME	−0.763***	−0.766***
	(0.209)	(0.211)
Market outsider	0.457***	0.457***
	(0.045)	(0.045)
Social class		
High service	ref	ref
Low service	−0.062	−0.062
	(0.048)	(0.048)
Self-employed	−0.175***	−0.175***
	(0.051)	(0.051)
Skilled workers	0.166***	0.166***
	(0.041)	(0.041)
Unskilled workers	0.199***	0.199***
	(0.051)	(0.051)
Not in labour force	0.093**	0.093**
	(0.044)	(0.044)
Low risk assets (no assets)	−0.162***	−0.162***
	(0.036)	(0.036)
High risk assets (no assets)	−0.374***	−0.374***
	(0.039)	(0.039)
Income	−0.485***	−0.485***
	(0.042)	(0.042)
Education	−0.336***	−0.336***
	(0.062)	(0.062)
(Ln)Age	−0.098***	−0.098***
	(0.031)	(0.031)
Female	0.075***	0.075***
	(0.023)	(0.023)
Right–left position	−0.656***	−0.656***
	(0.054)	(0.054)
Subjective insecurity	0.287***	0.287***
	(0.038)	(0.038)
GFC shock × Party cues		−0.415***
		(0.127)
Recovery × Party cues		−0.109**
		(0.051)
Constant	−0.585**	−0.585**
	(0.283)	(0.283)
Variance(intercept)	−0.792***	−0.781***
	(0.145)	(0.145)
Chi-squared	1421.57	1431.59
N countries	25	25
N individuals	37,951	37,951

Note: Cells display estimates from multilevel logit regression with random intercepts with standard errors in parentheses.
***$p<0.01$, **$p<0.05$, *$p<0.10$

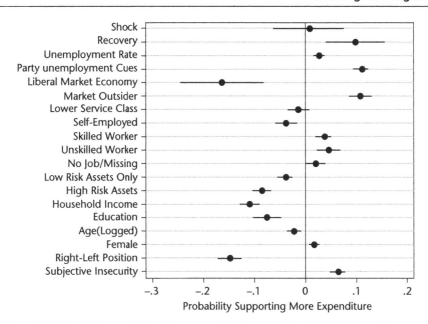

Figure 4.7. The Effect of Covariates on Preferences for Public Expenditure on Unemployment (Average Marginal Effects)

Source: Calculated from estimates reported in Model in Table 4.3. Dots and 95% confidence intervals represent the effect of one point across the value of the covariate in question on the probability of supporting higher expenditure. The weighted GFC shock variable runs between −0.91 and 2.7 with a mean of 0.45. The recovery data run between −1.99 and 2.58, with a mean of 0.48: the extent of recovery since 2009 divided by 10. The unemployment rate runs between 3.2 and 24.4%. Party cues on unemployment measure maximum to minimum effects where the position most to the right is 0 and the most left is 1. Outsider, Low and High Risk Assets, Female are all 0 or 1. Education (an 8-point scale), Household Income (in quintiles), Relative Skill Specificity, Right-Left Scale, and Income Reduction are all estimated from their maxima to their minima (all scaled between 0 and 1 and 1).

expenditure to address unemployment was low, at around 0.25 on average. Those with high-risk assets were less sympathetic to higher expenditure, as were those on higher incomes. In an unreported model, relative skill specificity had no effect. In the Oesch model, workers both skilled and unskilled were more likely to favour higher expenditure than those in the higher classes, and the self-employed less likely. Outsiders and those expecting income losses favoured high expenditure, as expected. Income, asset ownership, university education, and right–left ideology had the expected effects. The average marginal effects of these risk and social structure variables were on average about twice those observed in the health expenditure model, as anticipated.

Consistent with our top–down argument, party cues again register strong effects, both on their own, and when conditioned by crisis and recovery. But as for health expenditure, there were no conditioning effects on individual-level risk factors. While the direct and unconditioned effects of crisis appear no

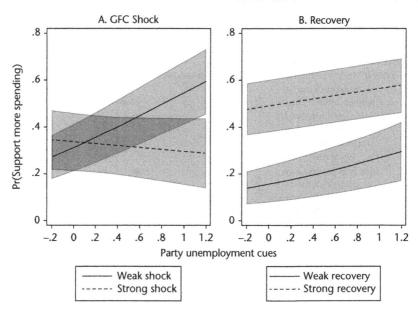

Figure 4.8. Marginal Effects of Party Unemployment Expenditure Cues on Support from Unemployment Expenditure Conditioned by Shock and Recovery
Source: Table 4.3, Model 2.

different from zero in Model 1 and Figure 4.7, as shown in Model 2 and in Figure 4.8A, there turns out to be a strong interaction between party cues on unemployment and the depth of the crisis (Figure 4.8A). Where the crisis was strong, cues for more expenditure had no significant bearing and, if anything, had the opposite effect: a strong incentive for parties otherwise friendly to provision for the unemployed to moderate their appeals. Cues were most effective where the crisis was less severe. If we were also to plot the shock level of the median country, the effects of the cues would still be both substantive and significant. In those countries still experiencing a serious and significant shock, cues from either left or right had the effect of driving preferences, as expected. Figure 4.9B shows a different effect for recovery. In this case, the strength of the recovery was the main driving force of preferences, with party cues having small effects in the expected direction but the slopes falling within confidence intervals.

4.4. How do Parties Shape Preferences?

This chapter identified two policy domains through which to test our expectations: health and employment. Everyone risks suffering from ill-health or injury, and the odds of needing health care for those purposes cannot be anticipated. As a result there is a broad consensus and much evidence, some provided here, that public support for government expenditure on health is likely to be relatively strong and not vary widely between risk groups. In contrast, people are less likely to support expenditure to provide for the unemployed, because, again, most people do not anticipate being unemployed or, if they do lose their job, will expect to find another without difficulty. Our analysis supports these claims.

Our argument is simple: to the extent that the experience of crisis and the recovery shaped preferences for health and unemployment expenditure, they did so partly but significantly through the words and actions of political party elites: through dissemination of the language of party programmes, and through the policy efforts of governments. Not all our expectations were borne out. Following the literature generated in the wake of the GFC, we anticipated that 'automatic stabilizers'—welfare effort or relative redistribution—and policy choices between austerity and stimulus could have significant effects. Relative redistribution might have been expected to provide a cushion, and a culture more prone to cue a more expansive policy response to crisis, thus generating stronger support for government expenditure. It did not. Similarly, governments' choices of austerity or stimulus had no significant effects on policy preferences: had it done so, one would have expected austerity would to have cued greater opposition to expenditure, stimulus more support.

As expected, accounting for policy preferences produced different explanations for health and unemployment. For health expenditure, the story is straightforward. Crisis and recovery experience had no effects on preferences. Policy demands were not tempered or weakened. Normal politics prevailed. Party cues did have strong effects, but there was no conditioning through the phases of the crisis. Similarly, we found a thermostatic relationship between preferences and policy, seemingly unaffected by the crisis or recovery. There were some differences in support for expenditure, those most exposed to and conscious of risk and insecurity being more prone to support higher expenditure but, again, no elite conditioning through those pathways.

We expected that expenditure on unemployment would produce more substantial findings. A shock effect for the years 2008 and 2009 appeared, but it was conditioned by the directions of party cues, and only where the shock was relatively weak. Expectations were initially tempered, but later the pattern became more complex. With a strong shock, preferences for unemployment expenditure were weak and countervailing cues had no impact. There was also a recovery effect, but in this case the direction of party cues had no significant bearing: the effect was contingent on the strength of the recovery alone, favouring higher expenditure the stronger the improvement. As with health, those more exposed to risk and insecurity were more prone to support higher expenditure and group effects were stronger, yet there was no elite conditioning through those pathways. Support for unemployment expenditure was also enhanced by the unemployment rate itself, but this was constant regardless of the depth of the crisis or the strength of the recovery. But as people saw unemployment rise, as it did in those countries most affected, they tended to agree that more should be spent.

Examination of the effects of party cues was major objective of inquiry in this chapter. We found strong effects. As far as can be gleaned from this evidence, the effects of party cues in the collection of post-crisis elections were much as might be expected, given traditional assumptions about centre-left and centre-right elite positions. But these positions could matter, encouraging people whose faith in the role of government to meet the challenge of recession would otherwise have been weakened, while, on the other side of the left–right dimension, giving support to those who saw in the crisis an opportunity to weaken the state and reassert the role of markets.

Part III
Political Choices in Uncertain Times

5

There is No Difference?

The Global Financial Crisis and Electoral Turnout

Previous chapters have emphasized how political parties have managed responses to longer term social and economic change and the experience of the Great Recession. In so doing, parties have shaped how the consequent disruption of people's lives bears on public perceptions of security and policy preferences. Some parties have signalled a capacity to defend social protection through welfare policy and thus support for the unemployed, and sought to reassure their voters that they will be sheltered from the vagaries of the market. Other parties have emphasized the need to cut expenditure, and taken the opportunity to promote their ideological agenda to reduce the size of government. Right-leaning parties consequently advocate that government actively weakens assistance for those facing the worst of the consequences, finding support among those who are sceptical of the value of government action and whose incomes, education, and jobs have largely insulated them from risk. Governments on both the centre-left—such as Labour in the UK— and centre-right—such as Ireland's Fianna Fáil—have been willing to bail out banks and other financial institutions, at the cost of increasing sovereign debt. In several countries governments adopted austerity policies justified on grounds of necessity, regardless of their ideological traditions, as the case of PASOK- and then SYRIZA-led governments in Greece illustrates.

The diversity of experiences created the potential for gaps between expectations based on past policy platforms and current crisis-driven policy responses. Governments ran the risk of failing to meet the hopes and expectations of those they claimed to represent. Policy shifts can be justified as short-term, driven by an obvious emergency, but what if the justification is poorly communicated or, worse, not believed? What if political parties, both of mainstream left or right, palpably fail to differentiate themselves in the face of crisis, following the logic of 'there is no alternative'? Are governments no

Democracy Under Siege? Parties, Voters, and Elections After the Great Recession. Timothy Hellwig, Yesola Kweon, and Jack Vowles, Oxford University Press (2020). © Timothy Hellwig, Yesola Kweon, and Jack Vowles. DOI: 10.1093/oso/9780198846208.001.0001

longer perceived as active agents, but instead the equivalent of middle managers, passing on the directives of those higher up the chain? If people see no difference between the options on offer, or worse, no apparent ability of those in office to make a difference, and where alternative challenger parties are weak or absent, why should they bother to vote? Even if challenger parties are viable, for many they may not be credible, and on the margins people may opt instead to walk away, seeing little or no hope in party politics, believing that alternative governments can no longer be told apart, lacking independent agency. Accordingly, in this chapter we examine the important question of voter participation. This chapter introduces Part III of this book, examining the impact of the crisis on various aspects of voting behaviour—turnout, incumbent support (Chapter 6), and party choices (Chapter 7).

Electoral turnout is salient for outcomes at two levels. On one level, regardless of change in overall participation, the composition of electorates could be changing because individuals in some social groups are voting less, while others could be voting more or at least holding steady. As this and other studies have shown, the consequences of the crisis and its aftermath have not been borne equally. Dislocations tend to affect the young more than the old, those on low incomes rather than the well-to-do, and the asset-poor rather than the asset-rich. And the connections between socio-economic differences and participation in elections are well-established in the political science literature (e.g. Verba et al. 1995; Leighley and Nagler 2013; Smets and Ham 2013). Indeed, a growing body of work finds that socio-economic categories like occupational class are better predictors of turnout than of choices between political parties (Dalton 2020, 163; Evans and Tilley 2017; Heath 2013, 2018). From this it follows that the experience of crisis likely hits hardest those who are already less prone to vote and, further, who may well have become less likely to participate over time. The crisis and aftermath could therefore have affected the socio-demographic composition of turnout.

As pioneers in the field of electoral research observed long ago, those who do not vote do not count: when they know what sorts of people vote or do not, politicians and political parties will pay most attention to the former (Key 1949, 527; Burnham 1987, 99). Representative democracies run the risk of failing to be inclusive of those who may require the most attention of governments to help them meet their needs, and who are likely to be the most vulnerable in the face of an economic shock. Turnout decline among the most vulnerable is often linked to concerns about rising inequality (Solt 2008). Imposition of policies to reduce government deficits and cut government expenditure affect the most vulnerable, further reducing their propensities to vote. This reduces the incentive for government to attend to the needs of the vulnerable, constructing a vicious circle that drives turnout downward, most of all among the poor.

There is good reason to believe, then, that the global financial crisis and its aftermath have exacerbated existing inequalities in the composition of turnout. But the GFC may also have affected turnout levels overall. Across countries continuously democratic since 1970, electoral turnout has been in decline (Vowles 2018). One explanation for steadily declining electoral turnout stands out from the rest and forms a backdrop to the supply-side argument of this book: a widening gap between the preferences of the mass electorate and those of political elites (Sanders and Tóka 2013; Ezrow and Hellwig 2014). The economic and social changes identified in earlier chapters have made governing more difficult in the early twenty-first than in the mid-twentieth century. Public expectations about protection and security have become more costly and difficult to meet. Even before the crisis, by failing to fully or even partially meet such expectations, many citizens have come to perceive that politicians are turning away from their voters.

The global financial crisis is frequently cited as evidence supporting a broader argument that since the late twentieth century the capitalist economy has become (even) more responsive to the interests of economic elites and less responsive to those of ordinary people (Streeck 2014). Examples abound. For instance, in Greece, a Socialist-led government in 2009 began a process of rolling back the generous welfare state protections and entitlements popular with most of the electorate. In Ireland, the implosion of an asset bubble has required politicians to become attentive to bond ratings—arguably against the wishes of the median voter. In the United States, Britain, and many other countries financiers and banks had been taking excessive risks and after the dust settled, without their consent, ordinary taxpayers were left with the bills. Critics of contemporary representative democracies argue that political parties have become increasingly remote from those that they seek to represent. This, some reason, leads to a 'hollowing' out of Western democracy (Mair 2013) or, even more strongly, to an era of 'post-democracy' (Crouch 2004).

The reasons for abandoning voting have many sources: the claim of 'no alternative' to painful economic reforms and 'no difference' in parties' policies, supporting allegations that because of globalization the range of policy options has been shrinking towards only those acceptable to financial markets. Such arguments have come from both right and left: the former in approval; the latter seeking to shift the argument into opposition to capitalism itself. The common thread is the notion of policy constraint: because of events, markets, or other external forces, governments are unable to protect the interests of all their citizens. Those in power are no longer perceived as being able to affect outcomes: their policy options have narrowed, and it matters little whether the left or right hold office.

The insight that turnout decline may be a consequence of general perceptions, and not necessarily because of social and economic inequality, informs research that links the perception of constraint to cognitive capacities and levels of political knowledge (Häusermann et al. 2017). Returning to a compositional perspective, this suggests that perceptions of constraint, and their attendant impact on participation, are realized mainly among the more educated and thus more informed members of the electorate. To the extent such people may also be sceptical about the power of government, theories of motivated reasoning also suggest they will accept such prompting. Moreover, those with higher levels of political knowledge are normally more aware of the stakes in an election and aware of differences between parties and candidates (Popkin and Dimock 1998). If events conspire to reduce the differences and lower the stakes, those with the highest levels of knowledge will be most aware of this, and most likely to respond by lower turnout.

From these lines of argument we arrive at a set of expectations. Following the assumptions above, the global financial crisis should have intensified a general decline in electoral participation. The greater the economic downturn, the greater the fall in turnout. However, this crisis–turnout association should vary within countries. The impact of the crisis on turnout should be more pronounced among those most aware of its effects. Here, we posit two possible pathways, one affecting those most harmed materially by way of direct experience, and another affecting those who, by virtue of their knowledge levels, are most aware of the gravity of the economic downturn. If both were to be present, these two pathways could offset each other or at least muffle any compositional changes.

Our inquiry is therefore twofold: first, has overall turnout declined as the result of the GFC? Second, has its composition changed? As Offe (2013) points out, it is possible to answer 'no' to the first question but 'yes' to the second. If turnout levels in national elections have indeed declined, we should expect to see a disruption and intensification of that trend during 2008 and 2009 and after. Turnout decline may characterize citizens generally or it may be concentrated within groups that perceive more strongly than others that governments have become less responsive to their electoral demands than in the past. Differences in the extent of recovery could also make it possible to leverage investigation of the longer term implications: if turnout went down in certain countries or among certain groups, did it show signs of recovery post-crisis?

We next outline in more detail the theoretical foundations that inform these conjectures, and discuss the literature that has sought to engage with it in the aftermath of the GFC. After some descriptive analysis, we apply our argument about the importance of cues and actions of political elites to understand turnout dynamics before, during, and after the GFC. Turning to our analysis, macro-data pooled over time and places establish the broad patterns. Finally, we provide an analysis of micro-level data from twenty-four countries covering 112 elections during the period 1990–2016, again collected under the auspices of the Comparative Study of Electoral Systems, and supplemented with data from national election studies of those country-elections for which data were not contributed to the CSES.

5.1. Globalization, Policy Constraint, and Electoral Participation: Insights from the Literature

Our starting point is the theory of electoral competitiveness (Franklin 2004). Assigning a central role to political parties, competitiveness here is not just defined in terms of the closeness of the race: it is also a question of how much the outcome of an election matters to those considering their vote, and how much difference they perceive between the options, a focus directly relevant to the matters under scrutiny here. Consistent with the rational choice theory of electoral turnout, the benefits that a person might expect from her preferred party's victory are offset by the costs. This calculation, weighted by the individual's perception of their vote's influence, might matter given the expected closeness among parties competing in the election. If the race is close, the result is uncertain. In this scenario, a person will be more likely to vote even if she realizes that the odds that the election outcome turns on her single vote are low. But the insight most central to our argument is that, when potential voters consider the benefits, they also weigh up the policy promises of the contending parties (see Figure 1.6). If the *range* of policy offerings is wide, and if those difference are salient to the potential voter in question, she will again be more likely to vote, believing that those in power have the opportunity to make a difference.

Critics of representative democracy make a compelling argument that over the past half-century, governments in advanced post-industrial democracies have become less responsive to their citizens than in the past. While socioeconomic changes underlie these developments, parties themselves have changed. They have become professionalized and in many countries, although not all, their memberships have shrunk. Legislators are increasingly drawn predominantly from higher status occupational groups, and are failing to represent those whose jobs and circumstances have lower status and who own fewer assets than the norm (Heath 2013).

Compounding these effects is the ideological shift to the right since the 1970s. Governments have deregulated their economies, privatized previously publicly owned assets, granted autonomy to central banks in their oversight of monetary policy, and in many cases reconstructed social policy in an effort to incentivize labour force participation and reduce the extent of long-term receipt of income maintenance for those otherwise finding it difficult to support themselves. Governments are perceived to be doing less, taking less responsibility for the well-being of their citizens, and presenting narrower policy alternatives and choices.

Globalization provides a third component to the set of structural factors contributing to government constraint. Many argue that, since the 1990s, the liberalization of trade and capital flows across borders has limited governments' abilities to represent their citizens' preferences (cf. Hellwig 2014). Following on this reasoning, a growing number of studies report a relationship between globalization and turnout. In an early contribution, Steiner (2010) examined the effects of trade dependence, measures of capital market integration, and a measure of overall integration on aggregate turnout across parliamentary elections in twenty-three OECD countries between 1965 and 2006. He finds the expected evidence of decline and a link with globalization. In a follow-up study Steiner and Martin (2012) examine turnout levels in elections between 1950 and 2005 and conclude that globalization affects turnout through the narrowing of party policy differences. However, both studies' research designs do not accommodate different country-specific turnout levels, an analytical decision which leverages variation across cross-sections—e.g. differences in turnout levels between, say, France and Germany—rather than change over time—e.g. comparing levels between the German federal elections over time.

Yet globalization is a process of change over time. Emphasizing this feature, Marshall and Fisher (2015) employ time-series techniques to examine how changing exposure to world markets affects turnout levels within countries over time. Like Steiner (2010; Steiner and Martin 2012), they examine aggregate turnout levels in a sample of industrialized democracies. But Marshall and Fisher's approach differs from previous work in their use of country fixed effects, focusing on change over time. Seeking to replicate Steiner's findings in their own model, they find no effects for international trade but do find effects for foreign direct investment (FDI) flows and portfolio equity stock.[1] By considering different components of openness, the authors conclude that the link between globalization and turnout decline is due to foreign ownership, policy narrowing around lower levels of government expenditure and constraint, rather than the alternative compensation argument.

In each of the above, turnout effects are assessed at the macro-level alone, and no micro-level linkages are uncovered. For Marshall and Fisher, the micro-expectation is one of perceived constraint, yet they provide no data to test this. An assessment of the micro-mechanism governing the decision to vote

---

[1] Marshall and Fisher's robustness checks revealed barriers to inference owing to the trending of both turnout and globalization variables, and therefore adjusted their analysis as best they could for spurious correlation.

requires an examination of individual-level data. Using the Module 3 of the CSES, Vowles (2016) investigates the effects of foreign direct investment, in the context both of globalization and the GFC, not on turnout directly but instead on mass perceptions as estimated by a survey question measuring the extent of government agency: whether or not who is in power makes a difference. Vowles finds no apparent perceptions of constraint arising from FDI but a substantive and significant relationship between government debt and perceptions of government agency.

Expanding the macro-analysis of turnout to seventy-three countries between 1970 and 2011, Karp and Milazzo (2016) identify the effects of economic openness in tandem with the effects of the financial crisis. At the macro-level they find the expected negative effects for globalization, and these are intensified when interacted with a dummy variable representing the post-GFC elections: the most globalized countries suffer the most turnout decline. They also address the compositional element of turnout change associated with the pathway of vulnerability. Drawn from the CSES, their micro-level analysis covers ten countries and twenty-six elections between 2002 and 2010. Identifying the GFC years as those from 2008 to 2011, they interact their dummy variable with individual-level variables representing vulnerability, operationalized with an index based on being single, a non-union member, and unemployed. They find negative effects.

Other empirical research does not entirely confirm this pattern of declining turnout among the poor estimated over longer periods (Stockemer and Scruggs 2012), in some cases finding that turnout decline is more concentrated among the rich (Kasara and Suryanarayan 2015). In this vein, Häusermann et al.'s (2017) study also addresses the compositional aspect, this time through the pathway of cognitive perceptions. Their findings question the vulnerability theory, confirming an apparent knowledge effect. Their analyses of European Social Survey data between 2006 and 2012 find that the GFC suppressed turnout most among the educated. More educated voters were most responsive to indicators of government constraint.[2]

5.2. The GFC and Voter Turnout: Further Expectations

Financial globalization sowed the seeds of the global financial crisis. And as described above, there is now considerable evidence that economic

---

[2] Häusermann et al. (2017) combine three macro-measures to produce a scale estimating government constraint: the general government deficit, the long-term interest rates that shape bond markets, and experiences of the imposition of conditionality agreements by international financial organizations providing shorter or longer term financial support for governments in need of bailouts.

integration—along with other trends in the structure of national economies—has depressed electoral participation in the advanced capitalist democracies. Foreign direct investment and levels of government debt have been shown to have significant effects on turnout and perceptions of government agency. For governments, however, the GFC presents something of a paradox: on the one hand, the logic of 'there is no alternative' loomed large, as without their consent taxpayers were required to foot the bill for the mistakes made by economic and political elites. If the advance of globalization has created constraint on governments, the experience of crisis should have reduced state autonomy and agency even more. According to this logic, the GFC can be expected to have generated more extreme but otherwise similar effects to that of more incremental globalization, in the form of a severe shock and its aftermath. Meanwhile, on the other hand, policy tools hitherto thought abandoned were brought out of retirement during the crisis, most notably, the bailouts and in many cases the nationalization of banks, weakening the credibility of centre-right parties that would normally oppose such actions. As we saw in our overview of crisis events and government responses in Chapter 2, the crisis in many ways served as catalyst to renewed forms of policy activism.

One of these forms of policy activism was the acceptance of rising public debt—in the cause of financial bailouts, of maintaining social programmes, and/or of funding a fiscal stimulus. Given the salience of sovereign debt in the world post-GFC, and its association with perceptions of government agency (Vowles 2016), one might expect an increase in government debt to have negative effects on turnout. Where government debt is increasing it becomes highly salient in political discourse (Clift 2015), often framed in negative terms that conceive it as an impediment to economic growth (Reinhart and Rogoff 2010) or in ways that imply it limits the ability of governments to take decisive action (Alcañiz and Hellwig 2011). Meanwhile, as noted above, previous studies have not uncovered an individual-level attitudinal or mediating factor as a link between the GFC period and the turnout behaviour identified.

Along with countervailing expectations for overall *levels* of turnout in national elections, the impact of the crisis and recovery on the *composition* of turnout remains unclear. Existing evidence at the micro-level yields two contrasting hypotheses. The first is that turnout tends to fall in those countries where the accumulation of government debt is greatest. The effects of economic change are strongest among the most vulnerable, presumably by way of direct experience that demotivates them from voting (Karp and Milazzo 2016). The second is that the impact of the shock on voter participation runs through information and perceptions and is concentrated among those with the cognitive capacities to appreciate the growth of constraint (see also Häusermann et al. 2017). Contradictory micro-level findings should not be surprising. There are differences in timing and in case selection, not to mention in data sources. And the passage of time since previous studies were conducted requires a reanalysis of data over a longer period of time.[3] While the depth of the crisis experienced in 2008 and 2009 had passed, recovery was slow in many countries. A principal assertion of this book is that the full impact of the GFC on mass politics—turnout included—must be assessed over the long term.

Accordingly, we advance a further compositional pathway that extends vulnerability theory and is likely to have long-term effects: turnout rates among less knowledgeable voters, those who are younger, those on lower incomes, and those with those lower education will be the most affected by the increase of government debt. Negative connotations of government debt are more likely to be perceived among those on lower incomes because, for those people, debt is often a burden, incurred to cover short-term needs rather than to achieve long-term goals such as asset accumulation, and often cast in negative terms of failure to manage their lives (Walker 2011; Wiggan 2012). There are strong economic arguments to allow debt to increase in the context of economic crisis and recovery, if only temporarily. But less knowledgeable voters, people who tend to be younger, on lower incomes, and with lower education, are those less likely to be exposed to the arguments that justify countercyclical macro-economic policy in times of recession.

5.3. The Broad Parameters: Aggregate Turnout over Time

As used in earlier chapters, our macro dataset encompasses thirty-five OECD countries between 1990 and 2016, encompassing almost 250 elections. We have confined our scrutiny to 'first order' elections, in which we expect the highest level of turnout. These are votes which determine what party or coalition of parties controls the executive functions of government. We therefore exclude mid-term elections in the United States or purely legislative elections in other presidential systems.[4] Turnout data are taken from International IDEA, which provides measures estimated both on registration and age-eligible bases.

Figure 5.1 plots voting age population (VAP) turnout in first order elections across our dataset. Contrary to expectations, we detect no GFC effect. Electoral turnout continues to track steadily downward but with no apparent shock

---

[3] The data examined by Karp and Milazzo (2016) end in 2010; those of Häusermann et al. (2017) end in 2012.
[4] All elections included here are therefore legislative elections except for presidential elections in Chile, France, the USA, and Turkey in 2014, after it changed to a presidential system.

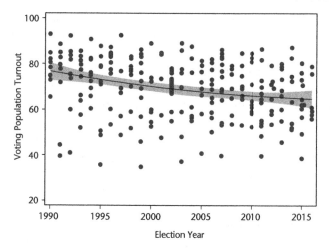

Figure 5.1. Voting Age Population Turnout in the OECD, 1990–2016, First-Order Elections
Source: International IDEA 2019.

over the period 2008 and 2009.[5] To register the experiences of individual countries, some worse affected by the crisis than others, Figure 5.2 plots these data by country. The countries are ordered from top left to bottom right by the extent of the shock, as estimated by change in real GDP per capita between 2007 and 2009. The two worst affected countries, Estonia and Latvia, experienced turnout increases. By 2015, Latvia had made a strong recovery, consistent with its turnout performance, but Estonia had experienced no significant improvement in its economy since 2009. Two other badly affected countries, Iceland and Ireland, did have turnout declines, but so did relatively unaffected countries such as Austria and Chile. Some countries experienced the worst consequences after the 2008–9 crisis—Greece, Spain, Portugal, and Italy—and in these cases turnout decline is apparent, although Spain's has been relatively minor. There is some evidence here for a GFC and turnout linkage, but there are significant outliers and exceptions.

5.4. Modelling Aggregate Turnout, 1990–2016

5.4.1. *Data and Measures*

To conduct further macro-analysis, we establish our control variables, most notably, the effects of changes in electoral competitiveness and the structure of the party system—two indicators that virtually all previous research has

---

[5] A similar unreported plot of registration-based turnout shows the same trend.

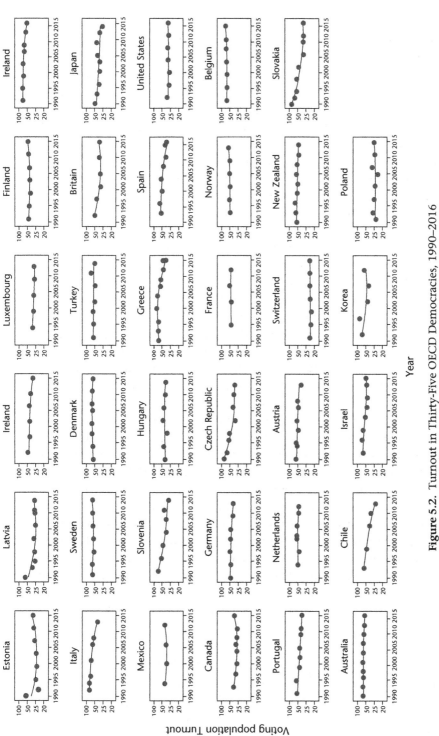

Figure 5.2. Turnout in Thirty-Five OECD Democracies, 1990–2016

Note: Country graphs are sorted by extent of exposure to the crisis.

Source: International IDEA 2019.

shown to significantly affect electoral turnout. The first of these is operationalized as the closeness in vote share between the two largest parties; the second as the effective number of elective parties (Laakso and Taagepera 1979). A close vote share should promote turnout, giving people a sense that their vote could be pivotal. Closeness or distance in vote shares may fluctuate, or it may reflect a more fundamental feature of the party system. The effective number of elective parties is a more stable factor but has two countervailing effects. On the one hand, more parties provide more choice for voters, promoting turnout. On the other hand, with more effective parties there is a weaker relationship between vote choice and the government coalition that may be formed, potentially discouraging turnout (Jackman 1987). We include the year of election to control for trending effects in turnout, which we suspect that, in most countries, is being driven downwards by generational replacement of voters we cannot otherwise estimate.[6]

Moving closer towards our main concern, we turn to the effects of the crisis and its aftermath. We measure these factors as change in real GDP per capita in purchasing power parities at 2010 constant prices since the previous election, plus a categorical variable for pre-crisis (1990–2007), the crisis (years 2008 and 2009), and the recovery (2010–16), thus establishing a period effect across the three time frames. We interact period indicators with change in GDP per capita to identify the shifts that took place in the two later periods compared to those in the reference pre-crisis period (1990 to 2007). Consistent with our emphasis on the importance of party cues (see Figure 1.6) and Franklin's (2004) point on elections' policy implications, we also include an estimate of party polarization on welfare policy, derived from CMP data, and weighted by party sizes. We also tested a similar estimate based on broader right–left differences but welfare policy polarization had the stronger effect.

The effects of the GFC on ordinary citizens were mediated by two factors: first, the so-called automatic stabilizers made up of tax and welfare systems that redistribute income and provide citizens with collective insurance for risks such as unemployment, illness, and accidents (Bermeo and Pontusson 2012). In a society with a highly effective tax, welfare, and transfer system, the effects of an event like the global financial crisis may be addressed in large part by existing programmes that protect citizens against insecurity. Following the logic of arguments about the effects of inequality and turnout, redistribution

---

[6] As a further control variable in the exploratory modelling, we initially included stocks of FDI, both inward and outward, as a percentage of GDP. As noted earlier, FDI has been identified in recent research as the most potent apparent effect of globalization on electoral turnout. The most globalized countries also tended to be more affected by the global financial crisis than those least globalized. We expected FDI to have a negative effect on turnout, as found by Marshall and Fisher (2015). It did, but well below levels of significance. It also correlated strongly with our time trend, and we excluded it from our models thereafter.

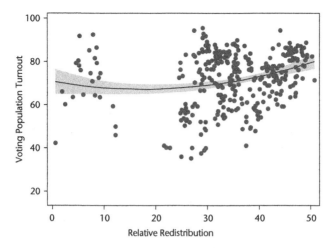

Figure 5.3. Relative Redistribution and Turnout, OECD Country-Elections 1990–2016
Source: Solt 2019, International IDEA 2019.

of income will have a positive effect on turnout. We therefore include an estimate of relative redistribution as used in earlier chapters: the percentage reduction in the Gini coefficient through taxes and transfers (Solt 2019). Figure 5.3 plots our country-election data by relative redistribution, showing a similar bifurcation between a cluster of low redistribution and higher redistribution countries as displayed in Chapter 4 (Figure 4.4), and a non-linear bi-modal relationship with turnout.

The second form of mediation between citizens and the crisis was austerity and its alternative, a fiscal stimulus: the extent to which governments were prepared to address the crisis by stimulating the economy by means of extra spending or tax cuts, usually by taking on government debt to fund the consequent deficit (Barnes and Wren 2012). The fiscal stimulus is captured by the cyclically adjusted or structural fiscal balance as a percentage of potential GDP, estimated as an austerity measure: that is, the absence of stimulus is positive, the extent of stimulus negative.

We also include gross government debt as a percentage of GDP, a factor highly salient to the second stage of the crisis (see Chapter 2, Figure 2.3), and shown to influence perceptions of governments making a difference (Vowles 2016). Averaged across the OECD, government debt rose substantially between 2006 and 2016, with considerable variation between countries. Rapid rises in government debt were common to some of the worst affected countries. We expect both austerity and government debt to negatively affect turnout, discouraging people from casting a vote because austerity tends to be justified on grounds of there being 'no alternative'. Debt has the effect of constraining governments by making them more vulnerable to fluctuations in international financial markets, and for this reason we use gross rather than net debt to represent countries' levels of exposure to those markets.[7]

5.4.2. Macro-Level Analysis

Table 5.1 reports results of modelling aggregate turnout in first order elections as a function of the afore-mentioned economic, institutional, and political factors. Our macro-level model is a pooled time series. We employ linear regression with election clusters as the panel is unbalanced, including elections separated at irregular intervals. Models report estimates with country fixed effects, so that this analysis focuses entirely on changes within countries rather than differences among them.[8] Table 5.1 reports results for voting age population (VAP)-based turnout. Models using registration-based turnout return similar results with few exceptions.

In our baseline Model 1, coefficients on the period indicators for crisis onset and recovery carry negative signs, hinting that the crisis-depressed turnout was lower during the crisis years, or at least voters did not systematically increase their participation rates after 2007. These effects, however, do not attain statistical significance in the expected direction: compared to the pre-crisis period, there is some indication turnout was lower at elections during 2008 and 2009, and from 2010 onwards. In a more restricted unreported model, however, including only the time trend and the period effect, it is the time trend that stands out, again with non-significant period effects, a picture also consistent with inspection of the scatterplot in Figure 5.1.

With respect to economic conditions, we find an apparent paradox: the higher the economic growth between elections, the lower the turnout: for each one percentage point difference in growth upward within countries, turnout is lower by 0.12 of a percentage point. This variable is estimated as change in real GDP at purchasing power parities between the election in question and the one before. There are well-known debates about the value of GDP as an estimate of economic well-being, and empirical evidence that, in the case of Ireland, the measure is flawed because of distortions associated with high levels of inward capital investment. But removing Ireland from the analysis makes no difference. Figure 5.4 is based on an interaction between the three periods and GDP growth (Model 2), and shows that the apparent negative effect of growth on turnout is confined to the pre-crisis period. Subsequently, there is no relationship over the crisis and recovery periods.

---

[7] We also examined the effects of annual general government deficit, long-term interest rates, and the unemployment rate, but detected no effects.

[8] Given the shortness of the time-series, we do not estimate models with both fixed effects and lagged dependent variables (see Nickell 1981; Plümper and Troeger 2007).

Table 5.1. Modelling Voting Age Population Turnout in the OECD, 1990–2016

	(1)	(2)	(3)	(4)	(5)
Shock period	−0.764	−1.943	−0.561	0.149	3.133
	(1.287)	(1.401)	(1.280)	(1.628)	(6.992)
Recovery period	−0.096	−1.706	0.310	1.629	13.704***
	(1.287)	(1.368)	(1.292)	(1.407)	(4.160)
ΔGDP per capita	−0.120***	−0.210***	−0.287***	−0.126***	−0.111***
	(0.039)	(0.048)	(0.092)	(0.039)	(0.038)
Relative redistribution	−0.455*	−0.460*	−0.287***	−0.504**	−0.388
	(0.248)	(0.242)	(0.092)	(0.245)	(0.242)
Austerity	−0.268**	−0.275**	−0.266**	−0.509***	−0.228*
	(0.132)	(0.129)	(0.130)	(0.151)	(0.128)
Welfare polarization	0.010	0.033	0.026	0.040	0.050
	(0.111)	(0.109)	(0.111)	(0.109)	(0.109)
(Ln) Government debt	−4.790***	−5.127***	−4.885***	−5.130***	−4.266***
	(1.144)	(1.124)	(1.135)	(1.125)	(1.130)
Two-party vote gap	−0.011	−0.008	−0.009	−0.014	−0.013
	(0.015)	(0.014)	(0.014)	(0.015)	(0.084)
Effective elective parties	−0.900**	−0.856**	−0.920**	−1.019***	−0.697*
	(0.383)	(0.376)	(0.380)	(0.377)	(0.377)
GFC shock × ΔGDP/capita		0.134			
		(0.179)			
Recovery × ΔGDP/capita		0.225***			
		(0.070)			
Redistribution × ΔGDP/capita			0.006**		
			(0.003)		
GFC Shock × Austerity				0.325	
				(0.247)	
Recovery × Austerity				0.680***	
				(0.228)	
GFC shock × Debt					−1.044
					(1.663)
Recovery × Debt					−3.469***
					(0.995)
Year	−0.177**	−0.136	−0.192**	−0.145*	−0.162*
	(0.087)	(0.087)	(0.086)	(0.086)	(0.084)
Constant	469.623***	388.428**	498.62***	408.900**	433.819**
	(172.078)	(172.032)	(171.217)	(169.980)	(167.686)
R^2	0.923	0.927	0.924	0.927	0.928
N	218	218	218	218	218

Note: Cells report coefficients from ordinary least squares regression with standard errors in parentheses. All models estimated with country fixed effects. ***p < 0.01, **p < 0.05, *p < 0.10, two-tailed test.

Figure 5.5 solves the puzzle about the effects of economic growth and relative redistribution on turnout: there is an interaction between relative redistribution and growth. Where redistribution is high, variation in growth or recession has no effect on turnout, because people are relatively insulated from economic fluctuations. Economic decline motivates turnout, however, where redistributive effects are modest or low. This confirms earlier research that identified a similar relationship between growth, social welfare expenditure, and turnout (Radcliff 1992). Consistent with the pattern in Figure 5.3,

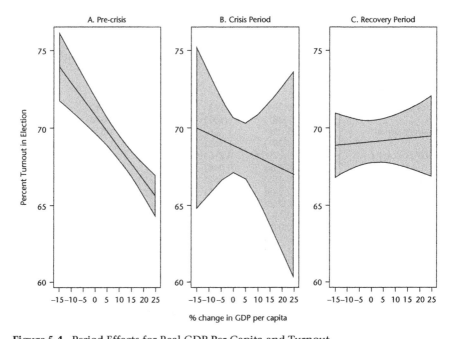

Figure 5.4. Period Effects for Real GDP Per Capita and Turnout

Note: Graphs produced with estimates from Table 5.1 Model 2. Shaded areas represent 90% confidence intervals.

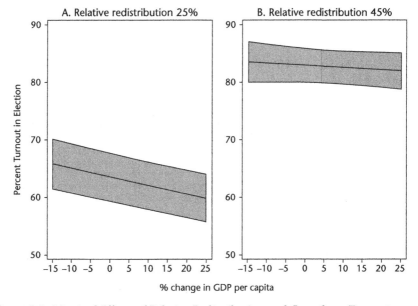

Figure 5.5. Marginal Effects of Relative Redistribution and Growth on Turnout

Note: Graphs produced using Table 5.1 Model 3 estimates. Shaded areas represent 90% confidence intervals. In order to display turnout that is on average slightly lower in countries with less relative redistribution as shown in Figure 5.3, the probability estimates have been calculated to represent Sweden (if it were at 45% redistribution) and Canada (if it were at 25%). Note that for both countries rates of redistribution are actually slightly higher.

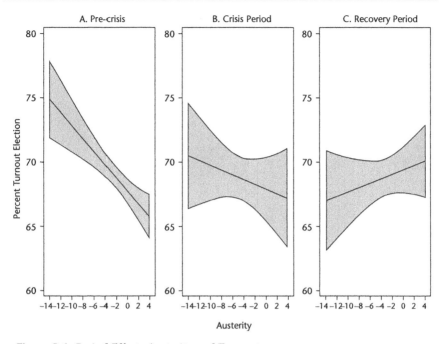

Figure 5.6. Period Effects Austerity and Turnout

Note: Graphs produced using estimates from Table 5.1, Model 4. Shaded areas represent 90% confidence intervals.

however, the turnout mobilizing effects of low growth or economic recession are confined to the pre-crisis period.[9]

Findings align more closely with expectations with respect to fiscal stimulus and debt. *Austerity* has the expected effects, stimulus being associated with higher turnout and austerity with the reverse. But as we have seen elsewhere, the impact of short-term fiscal policies on mass politics differs over time. However, interacting austerity/stimulus with the two period dummies shifts the ground somewhat. The positive effects of stimulus on turnout are confined to the pre-crisis and, less dramatically, the crisis periods, but have no appreciable effect after the crisis (see Figure 5.6). Since the stimulus was at its highest during the crisis years, this is likely to be one reason why turnout did not fall lower at the time.[10]

The effects of *Government debt* are the most dramatic (see Figure 5.7).[11] Consistent with a policy constraint argument, higher levels of debt signal a

[9] As confirmed by an unreported three-way interaction between these variables in an alternative model.
[10] We considered that the effects of austerity might be muted by correlation with the debt variable: however, excluding *Government debt* from the model reduces rather than boosts the austerity effect, indeed consigning it to non-significance.
[11] The x-axis in Figure 5.6 is logarithmic but the labels report the unlogged equivalents.

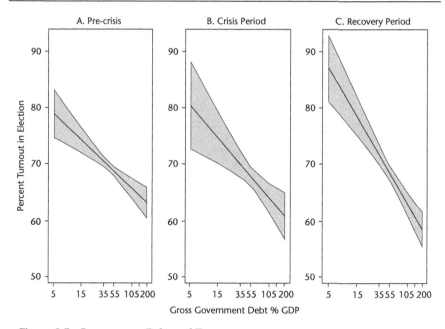

Figure 5.7. Government Debt and Turnout

Note: Graphs produced using estimates from Table 5.1, Model 5. Shaded areas represent 90% confidence intervals.

narrowing scope for policy autonomy, which in turn reduces the benefits of participation and aggregate turnout declines. This makes sense given the significant increase in government debt in most countries during the recovery period. Ancillary analyses reveal the effects of government debt remain consistent across all the time periods. However, since government debt levels have spiked in most countries since the GFC, debt has still had a more potent negative effect over the later period.

Lastly, perceptions of welfare policy difference between parties were associated with higher turnout, but the effects are again small and non-significant. In all models, the effect of the two-party vote gap is negative but not statistically significant. For party system size, we find that an increase in the number of effective parties reduces turnout.

5.5. Modelling the Decision to Vote

We now take up competing claims of the association between the GFC and voter participation that can only be tested with micro-data. This enables bringing to bear the socio-economic differences between individuals only available in these data but, perhaps even more important, the effects of mass perceptions of government agency that link experience of the GFC to behaviour. On the socio-economic front, the inequality hypothesis maintains that rapid economic downturns depress turnout among the poor and the vulnerable (Karp and Milazzo 2016). The alternative sophistication hypothesis reasons that turnout is discouraged among the more highly educated because they are most aware of the constraints imposed on governments by the crisis (Häusermann et al. 2017).

Our main source is the first release of the integrated module dataset (IMD) of Modules 1–4 of the CSES. We augment the IMD with survey items for occupation and political knowledge from the original modules. The CSES IMD provides us with data from twenty-four OECD countries and ninety-five elections, to which another seventeen elections have been added from national election studies, filling in some of the gaps.[12] Given our interest in within-country change over the period 1990–2016, we employ fixed effects at country level, using mixed effects logit with random effects for country-survey years.[13] For models with cross-level interactions, we also included random slopes. As in the macro-model, we allow for period effects with a category variable for pre-crisis, crisis, and recovery, with pre-crisis as the reference.

Regression estimates appear in Table 5.2. Models contain variables attaining statistical significance at the macro-level and add the micro-level measures described above. With respect to demographic factors, we find the relationship between age and turnout as expected given previous work: the young vote less than the old. Generalizing across countries, women are less likely to vote than men and low incomes and low education are associated with lower turnout. Human capital also matters: those whose skill set tilts towards specific rather than general skills are less likely to participate. On balance, those with high relative skill specificity tend to have lower general skills, and lower education than average, and thus relatively low occupational status: a familiar story with respect to turnout in most countries. Market outsiders, defined as the unemployed, part-time employees, and those not currently in the labour force are less likely to vote than non-outsiders. This confirms well-known findings that turnout is usually shaped by age and socio-economic position.

Turning to our factors of interest, we have seen that, compared to times previous, aggregate turnout was only marginally affected by the crisis and recovery at the elections held after 2007. As we saw in Table 5.1, the pre-crisis mobilizing effects of stimulus, and of low or negative growth, albeit only in countries with modest redistribution, disappeared after 2007. Only

---

[12] Note that missing data at both macro and micro-levels reduce the number of country/election cases listed in the table for various specifications.

[13] This is equivalent to a three-level model, albeit with country-level effects constraineed to be fixed, with random effects generating election-within-country intercepts.

government debt maintained a strong and apparently continuous contextual effect, depressing turnout in countries in which debt was increasing. Leaving growth and redistributive effort in the background, shifting to the individual level of analysis allows us to address the composition of turnout within countries, and probe more deeply into the individual-level mechanisms that link debt levels to turnout. Even if overall turnout was stable, or only in decline where debt was an increasing burden, crisis events may nonetheless have altered its composition: if so, how?

To assess, we return to the pathways that link the GFC and compositional turnout change outlined earlier: cognitive perceptions and economic vulnerability, both directly and conditioned by debt. First, it has been argued those with higher cognitive skills, as demonstrated by education, had less incentive to cast a vote due to belief that that governments had little choice in their response to the crisis. Model 2 in Table 5.2 confirms the narrowing of the effects of education on turnout at elections held in 2008 and 2009 (Häusermann et al. 2017). But the effect is small and temporary. Compared to the pre-crisis period, if anything the education gap in turnout increased in elections from 2010 onwards. Figure 5.8 shows that the slope on education for the crisis period lies within the confidence intervals for the pre-crisis and recovery periods. Further, where effects differ, the gentler slope may be the result of higher turnout among the less educated rather than lower turnout among those with university degrees.

Analyses of individual-level data revealed no interactive effects of economic vulnerability, GFC period effects, and growth. However, recalling our theoretical approach, we argue and show in previous chapters that public responses to the GFC have been fundamentally conditioned by the words and actions of political party elites and governments. Cues in the form of differences in welfare policy discourse had no effects. But in our analysis here, we have two examples of government action: austerity versus stimulus, and debt (and we have found that debt affects overall turnout).

Accordingly, the next four columns of Table 5.2 test interactions with austerity and debt across the socio-demographic variables defined as representing vulnerability. Post-estimation effects are displayed in Figure 5.9. As expected, education (Figure 5.9A), age, (Figure 5.9B), and income groups (Figure 5.9C) are all affected by the increase of government debt: the young, those with lower incomes, those with lower education became less likely to vote. Model 7 considers political knowledge (Figure 5.9D).[14] Those with low political

---

[14] Political knowledge is a four-point additive scale based on answers to three CSES questions coded 0 (wrong or don't know) or 1 (right), and standardized by country/election. For Modules 1–3, CSES political knowledge questions were selected by collaborators, one to be correct for about a third of respondents, another by about a half, and another by about 75 per cent. For Module 4, specific questions were defined by the CSES Planning Committee.

Table 5.2. Modelling the Decision to Vote, Individual-Level Data

	1	2	3	4	5	6	7
Shock period	0.341	0.430*	0.308	0.409*	0.410*	0.138	0.030
	(0.231)	(0.243)	(0.273)	(0.235)	(0.240)	(0.215)	(0.209)
Recovery period	0.081	0.081	0.471	0.212	0.105	0.014	-0.113
	(0.285)	(0.296)	(0.331)	(0.288)	(0.295)	(0.257)	(0.279)
ΔGDP per capita	-0.018**	-0.019**	-0.031***	-0.017**	-0.019**	-0.016*	-0.014*
	(0.008)	(0.009)	(0.010)	(0.008)	(0.009)	(0.008)	(0.008)
Relative redistribution	-0.099**	-0.101**	-0.072	-0.095**	-0.103**	-0.043	-0.056
	(0.048)	(0.050)	(0.056)	(0.049)	(0.050)	(0.047)	(0.049)
Austerity	-0.032	-0.031	0.008	-0.034	-0.032	-0.025	-0.034
	(0.033)	(0.034)	(0.040)	(0.034)	(0.034)	(0.030)	(0.031)
(Ln) Government debt	-0.468**	-0.431*	-0.565*	-0.635***	-0.520**	-0.210	-0.235
	(0.234)	(0.244)	(0.320)	(0.242)	(0.247)	(0.220)	(0.224)
Two-party vote gap	-0.016**	-0.014*	-0.013	-0.016**	-0.014*	-0.013*	-0.013*
	(0.008)	(0.008)	(0.009)	(0.008)	(0.008)	(0.007)	(0.007)
Effective elective parties	-0.228**	-0.207**	-0.249**	-0.236**	-0.208**	-0.228**	-0.212**
	(0.094)	(0.098)	(0.109)	(0.095)	(0.098)	(0.091)	(0.088)
(Ln) Age	1.189***	1.177***	1.415***	1.185***	1.177***	1.105***	1.202***
	(0.020)	(0.020)	(0.226)	(0.020)	(0.020)	(0.022)	(0.023)
Female	-0.069***	-0.073***	-0.067***	-0.069***	-0.073***	0.071***	-0.063***
	(0.016)	(0.016)	(0.016)	(0.016)	(0.016)	(0.018)	(0.018)
Household income	0.186***	0.187***	0.188***	-0.020	0.187***	0.152***	0.175***
	(0.006)	(0.006)	(0.006)	(0.093)	(0.006)	(0.007)	(0.007)
Education	0.261***	0.261***	0.262***	0.265***	-0.124	0.205***	0.242***
	(0.009)	(0.024)	(0.009)	(0.009)	(0.131)	(0.010)	(0.010)
Relative skill specificity	-0.030***	-0.030***	-0.030***	-0.031***	-0.030***	-0.021***	-0.026***
	(0.004)	(0.004)	(0.004)	(0.004)	(0.004)	(0.004)	(0.004)
Market outsider	-0.147***	-0.144***	-0.147***	-0.144***	-0.144***	-0.121***	-0.142***
	(0.020)	(0.020)	(0.020)	(0.020)	(0.020)	(0.022)	(0.024)
Year	-0.024	-0.034	-0.031	-0.041*	-0.032	-0.013	-0.003
	(0.021)	(0.022)	(0.025)	(0.022)	(0.022)	(0.020)	(0.026)
GFC shock × Education		-0.041					
		(0.059)					

(continued)

Table 5.2. Continued

	1	2	3	4	5	6	7
Recovery × Education		0.044 (0.039)					
Debt × Age			-0.052 (0.058)				
Debt × Income				0.056** (0.024)			
Debt × Education					0.103*** (0.034)		
Political knowledge						0.186 (0.154)	
Debt × Knowledge						0.058 (0.040)	
Who in power difference							0.295*** (0.007)
Constant	52.172 (42.399)	71.928 (43.955)	66.128 (49.202)	86.251** (42.953)	69.840 (44.039)	27.993 (39.316)	6.817 (52.354)
Variance (intercept)	0.247*** (0.037)	0.240*** (0.041)	0.094* (0.053)	0.232*** (0.039)	0.241*** (0.041)	0.184*** (0.030)	0.178*** (0.030)
Variance (slope)		0.022*** (0.004)	0.034*** (0.009)	0.009*** (0.002)	0.020*** (0.004)	0.027*** (0.005)	
Chi-square	5527.07***	4742.70***	4459.57***	4698.83***	4758.00***	4302.51***	6183.20***
N country-survey years	104	104	104	104	104	92	92
N individuals	148,541	148,541	148,541	148,541	148,541	132,205	122,897

Note: Cells report coefficients from multilevel model with individuals nested in country-years and country fixed effects. Standard errors in parentheses. ***$p<0.01$, **$p<0.05$, *$p<0.10$, two-tailed test.

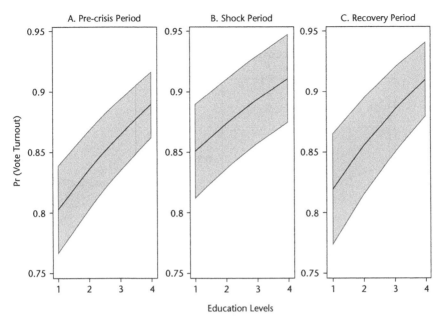

Figure 5.8. Education Period Effects

Note: Table 5.2, Model 2. Shaded areas represent 95% confidence intervals.

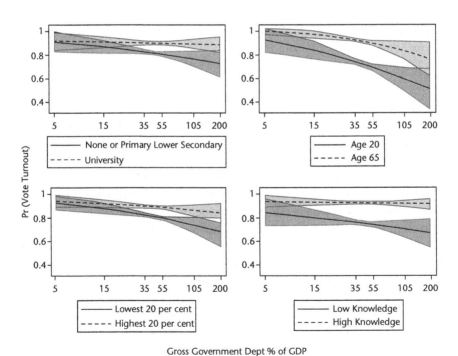

Figure 5.9. How Individual Attributes Condition the Effect of Government Debt on Turnout

Note: Table 5.2, Models 3, 4, 5, and 6. Shaded areas represent 95% confidence intervals.

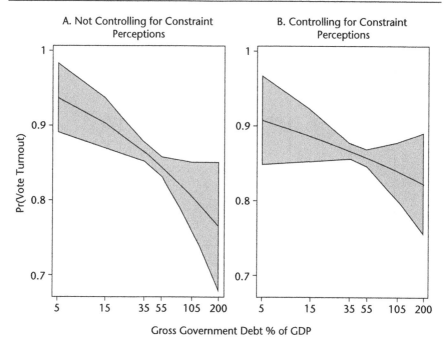

Figure 5.10. The Effects of Government Debt on Turnout, without and with Controlling for 'Who is in Power Makes a Difference'

Note: Table 5.2 Model 1 (A), Model 7 (B). Shaded areas report 90% confidence intervals.

knowledge were less likely to vote as debt levels grew. This is consistent with our expectation that negative effects of debt are more likely to be discursively constructed among this group.

Finally in Model 7 we take up the question of perceptions of government agency, using a CSES question asking whether or not who is in power makes a difference.[15] In our earlier analysis, we confirmed that, with respect to welfare policy differences between the parties, wide or narrow differences in manifesto commitments to more or less welfare had no effects on people's propensity to vote: a contrast to our earlier chapters where cueing effects were observed on vote choice between parties. In this more direct estimate of what people think and feel, perceptions of government agency and an ability to 'make a difference' come strongly to the fore. They exhibit strong effects on turnout and its addition to the model reduces the coefficient on logged debt, taking it below statistical significance. Figure 5.10 compares the effect of debt

[15] The survey item is a five-point scale, 'where ONE means that it doesn't make (a/any) difference who is in power and FIVE means that it makes a (big) difference who is in power), where would you place yourself?' Because the question was changed during Module 2, adding 'any' and 'big', Model 7 also includes a dummy variable registering this in our multivariate analysis (not shown).

on turnout from Models 1 and 7, Model 1 without the 'who is in power' variable (Figure 5.10A), and Model 7 containing it as a control (Figure 5.10B). Comparing the two slopes indicates that about half the effect of debt on turnout is channelled through perceptions of government constraint.

5.6. Implications and Conclusions

This chapter sets out to test some simple conjectures: that by intensifying the alleged gap between masses and elites, the GFC has intensified a decline in electoral participation, particularly in those countries—and those groups *within* countries—most affected. With respect to first of these, we find that despite the severity of its consequences for domestic political economies, there is scant evidence for a 'shock' turnout effect. As shown in Figure 5.2, in many places with more extreme experiences, turnout did not decline and sometimes increased either during or after the GFC. In other countries turnout did go down: no clear pattern emerged from first inspection of the data. Previous chapters have stressed the importance of elite cues in shaping opinion and, potentially, behaviour. Here we find none. By detaching themselves from the act of voting, most of those failing to vote insulate themselves from those influences. Our assumption, following Franklin (2004), was that cues might have an effect through policy differences between parties as measured by right–left and welfare polarization measures derived from the CMP.[16] However, we find that in the case of turnout, cues were not the place to search for conditioning effects: it was government action that mattered by way of the increase of sovereign debt.

The extent of the shock and the recovery had no effect on turnout by way of change in real GDP per capita. Only pre-crisis did the extent of growth or recession affect turnout, but there only in countries with low levels of relative redistribution. Similarly, austerity and its opposite, stimulus, only affected turnout pre-crisis. The experience of shock and recovery appears to have muted, not boosted, the effects one might have expected of austerity and growth on turnout behaviour. Consequently, overall turnout shows no obvious relationship with the crisis and its aftermath—with one exception, the effect of government debt: the conditioning effect that came to the fore of our analysis.

---

[16] Average levels of welfare policy polarization were moderate in the majority of countries, with a mean of 6 and a spread between 1 and 17. Overall, the crisis reduced polarization from 5.7 to 4.9, and during the recovery welfare polarization increased to 7, less than half its potential maximum. It seems likely that in most countries the extent of polarization was simply insufficient to matter for turnout.

Debt and austerity are negatively linked, of course: the role of debt during the crisis and the recovery has been to save off disaster in the case of the bank bailouts, to fund stimulus, or partly pull the punch of austerity in those countries worst affected. Government debt has increased even in countries engaged in austerity policies: Britain and the Irish Republic are good examples, although debt peaked in the latter case in 2013. Stimulus or the tempering of austerity are usually funded by increasing government debt or by tax cuts. Debt can increase without effective stimulus, however, where governments bailed out or nationalized banks and finance companies to protect them from failure. Without incurring debt, tax cuts must be matched by expenditure cuts and consequent reductions in government services. The economy in general may benefit, but the cost may be borne by those for whom the services are cut. Post-crisis, debt increased and there were expenditure cuts in many countries, and whatever evidence of stimulus that remained no longer had positive effects on turnout. But the increase of debt appears to have had quite notable negative effects.

Turning to microdata allows us to inquire why and how government debt registered such effects. But first, we tested whether the turnout effects of the GFC would be felt most strongly among those individuals suffering the most harm, and we also noted findings that apparently identified the most significant decline among the most educated. Drilling down to the individual level, we tested these two claims: one rooted in an inequality paradigm, the other focusing on the ability to cognitively process information about constraint. Despite initial indications, there were no changes in the direct effects of income or outsider status on turnout across the periods in question. With education, there was a weak association in the expected direction during the crisis, but the effect was only temporary. The power of education to predict turnout in 2008 and 2009 was slightly weaker; but, if anything, this did not support a decline in participation among the most educated.

Our analysis of how government shaped turnout produces explanations consistent with our expectations. We find that the effects of government debt on turnout depend on many components of the classic SES models of participation, including age, income, education, and political knowledge. The effects of political knowledge do not bear out expectations that constraint should be perceived most strongly among the educated or, in this case, the more informed. The less informed are more affected by debt constraint perceptions in their turnout behaviour, as are those on low incomes, lower education, and to a lesser extent, the young. Ironically, a government policy to incur debt to address the crisis and assist a recovery should be more expected to benefit people in these groups, at least on the assumption that debt enables fiscal stimulus rather than austerity, or at least reduces the burdens of austerity, and perhaps funds the continuation of redistributive social policies. There are strong economic arguments to allow debt to increase in the context of economic crisis and recovery, if only temporarily. But less knowledgeable voters, people who tend to be younger, on lower incomes, and with lower education are less likely to be exposed to those arguments.

The attitudinal variable that links government debt with turnout decline is perceptions of government agency—of governments being able to 'make a difference'. Half the effects of government debt on turnout can be accounted for by public perceptions of constraint ('who is in power makes a difference'). Our finding that young people are slightly more affected by the accumulation of government debt has further implications. If turnout is learned behaviour, and acquiring the propensity to vote or not when young has lasting effects, we may not yet be able to estimate the full consequences of the GFC for electoral turnout in the future, particularly in countries where debt continues to limit the policy options of governments.

The good news is that turnout has not responded to the exogenous shock of the global financial crisis and its aftermath by any abrupt alteration in a slow downward trend: and even this is a trend that is far from common among the OECD democracies. There is evidence of a compositional shift that does somewhat increase socio-economic bias in turnout behaviour where levels of government debt have been steeply increasing. And of course, a severe impact may not have a strong immediate effect. But with time, small consequences may accumulate into large ones.

6

The Shock, the Recovery, and Economic Voting Before and After the Crisis

The previous chapter considered the effect of the GFC on citizens' decision to participate in elections. The effect of the economic downturn on the decision to turnout was mixed. On the one hand, we find an expected adverse effect. Realized in terms of public debt, the crisis mattered much in the way a constraint argument would predict: higher debt levels depressed turnout. Policy decisions to adopt austerity also had the unintended effect of reducing electoral participation, particularly during the recovery period. On the other hand, many factors associated with the crisis—such as growth—and the policy response—such as automatic stabilizers or elite rhetoric—had little effect, positively or negatively, on the decision to turn out.

Among those who participated in politics, how did the GFC influence voter choice? Did economic crisis mean the end of the road for sitting governments? Did votes respond to economic downturns by moving to the left or right? By trusting the experience of mainstream parties or by taking a chance with upstart challengers? Were the effects stronger or weaker in short or long terms? And what, if any, role did government policies and party politics play in constraining or redirecting voter decisions? This chapter and the next address these questions. Chapter 7 investigates party choice in terms of the policy options on offer; the present chapter examines individual choices to use their vote to punish (or perhaps reward) incumbent governments.

Ten years after the fall of Lehman Brothers and Bear Stearns, a good deal of research has addressed the electoral effects of the Great Recession (e.g. Bermeo and Bartels 2014; LeDuc and Pammett 2013; Lindvall 2014; Hernández and Kriesi 2016; Dassonneville and Lewis-Beck 2014; Hutter and Kriesi 2019). Much of this work probes the influence of economy on the voters' decision, and quite appropriately so, given the enormity of the collapse. The fall in growth rates, rise in joblessness, and ballooning debt burdens meant that the

Democracy Under Siege? Parties, Voters, and Elections After the Great Recession. Timothy Hellwig, Yesola Kweon, and Jack Vowles, Oxford University Press (2020). © Timothy Hellwig, Yesola Kweon, and Jack Vowles.
DOI: 10.1093/oso/9780198846208.001.0001

survival of political incumbents was far from secure. Indeed, the conventional wisdom of how voters reacted to the crisis aligns closely with the conventional reward–punishment theory of retrospective voting: voters observed an economy in decline and voted against the incumbent. For better or worse, the Great Recession revalidated long-held but recently challenged theories of economic voting (Lewis-Beck and Lobo 2017).[1]

This chapter revisits the role of the economy and government support in light of what was the greatest period of economic volatility in the Western world since the 1930s. As a central valence indicator, the economy has received much attention in models of the vote. Indeed, a large share of extant research on mass responses to the crisis has examined the link between economic conditions and (anti)incumbent voting. We advance this research agenda both theoretically and empirically. Theoretically, we adopt the scope of inquiry as described in the introductory chapter to this volume. The immediate aftermath of the 2008–9 downturn produced a groundswell of research on the economy and voter support. While some studies find connections between the national economy and voter support to be weaker than anticipated (Anderson and Hecht 2012; LeDuc and Pammett 2013; Talving 2017), the balance of scholarship confirmed the conventional wisdom: economic crisis 'intensifies economic voting at the micro-level of the individual voter and, ultimately, at the macro-level of the national election outcome' (Lewis-Beck and Lobo 2017, 607). Economic voting, proceeded as expected. Indeed, by heightening the salience of economic conditions and linking them to national governments, elections during the crisis arguably functioned as a return to an earlier time in which the economics–elections connection was taken as a central avenue through which elections serve as mechanisms of accountability.[2]

Yet did the link between the economy and voter support persist, even as the initial shock receded into the past? Or did the economy's structuring influence on election outcomes weaken with time? Most assessments of whether and how the economy mattered following the GFC do so with reference to elections following right on the heels of the shock. This first wave of studies was not suited to assessing the long-term influences of crisis and the extent to which these economic and social forces act as a brief interruption to normal politics or instead mark a new trajectory. As we do elsewhere in this volume, we argue that it is essential to consider how popular responses evolve over time.

---

[1] For challenges to reward–punishment theories of economic voting, see Anderson 2007; Kayser 2014.

[2] In the context of the economic voting scholarship, the apparent persistence of a robust 'economic vote' during the Great Recession arguably serves to counter researchers who are sceptical of the economics–election connection due to excessive structural contingencies (e.g. Anderson 2007; Kayser 2014), political rationalizations (Evans and Andersen 2006), or both.

Most analyses of the economy and elections assume the voter to be myopic, comparing current outcomes with those in the recent past (for a review, see Hellwig and Marinova 2015). However, to understand voter response to adverse shocks requires an examination of both the depth of the shock and the competence of the policymakers' response over the course of the recovery (e.g. Bechtel and Hainmueller 2011).

Along with assessing the crisis effects over time, we emphasize the supply side of the vote and consider the role of strategic political elites. Many comment that, in a democracy, retrospective voting grants citizens the capacity to exercise control over their elected leaders and, in so doing, encourages the selection of good types of leaders (Fearon 1999). This degree of control levied on politician-agents by citizen-principals may not be as great as often assumed (Hart 2013; Hellwig 2012; Pardos-Prado and Sagarzazu 2016). After all, in order to hold politicians to account, voters must possess a degree of information about the current state of affairs, and how they get their information and from which sources makes them susceptible to elite manipulation.

We next review current research on the economy and the vote in hard times. While the first wave of studies on voter responses to the crisis supported a straightforward reward–punishment argument, recent work—employing a wider array of measures—paints a more nuanced picture of how economic conditions combine with political factors to shape voter decisions during turbulent times. We then advance our 'elite cues' argument, focusing on the role of incumbent parties in shaping public information during and following the collapse of financial markets.

We test our expectations using CSES post-election surveys of twenty-three OECD countries from 1990 to 2016. In line with the conventional economic voting argument, we find that adverse economic conditions during the crisis negatively affect incumbent support. However, the degree to which macro-economic performance influences voters' punishment of incumbent government depends on types of policy efforts made by governing parties. Government's expansionary policies, especially in forms of discretionary spending, mitigate the negative impact of the crisis on incumbent support. By contrast, automatic stabilizers made through taxes and transfers have a weaker and rather negative impact on incumbent support. In addition, we find that when a country experiences slow recovery, incumbent support is in general low regardless of welfare policy. Finally, pro-welfare rhetoric has little impact overall.

6.1. Voting in Hard Times: Blind or Rational Retrospection?

Studies of elections in the rich democracies have long shown that the economy—perhaps more than any other single factor—shapes election outcomes. While economic voting occurs in normal times, during the crisis, as economy becomes a more salient issue, the cost of governing increases too. And as we showed at the end of Chapter 2, analyses of the economy and election outcomes during the Great Recession bear this out. In Figure 2.10, we showed that while economic performance has little impact on incumbent vote during the pre-crisis period, it has a significant and positive impact in the post-crisis period. Bartels (2014), for example, argues that government support in elections following the GFC is driven mainly by economic conditions, with factors associated with policy positions having little to no impact. This purely retrospective view is consistent with what Achen and Bartels (2016) call 'blind' retrospection: voters punish incumbents for bad economy just as they punish incumbents for events wholly outside their control, be they natural disasters, random catastrophes, or outcomes of sporting matches (see also Healy et al. 2010). Regardless of whether governments are in control of an issue and regardless of the policies they make, voters turn against the incumbent whenever their well-being falls below expectations. The blind retrospective model, therefore, predicts massive electoral punishment of the incumbents as a function of the economic decline in hard times.

Nevertheless, the size of the decline does not translate deterministically into a loss of support for the government. As presented in Figure 6.1, the impact of the GFC on incumbent support widely varies across countries. In sixteen of the thirty-three countries, incumbent parties garnered less support in elections following the onset of the crisis in late 2007 than they had in the previous election. For many countries along the European periphery—Iceland, Ireland, Italy, Greece, and Spain—the drop-off was severe. Yet in many countries, incumbents held ground or, in countries like Poland and Slovakia, even gained support during the shock period. By contrast, incumbent party's vote shares were little affected in Australia, Denmark, and Europe's largest economy, Germany. Considering that all but a handful of OECD members experienced sharp declines over this period (see Figure 2.2), the picture shown in Figure 6.1 is, at first glance, puzzling. Variations in the impact of the economy push us to consider how other factors might influence incumbent support. More recent studies of the crisis's institutional and political factors, which have the effect of weakening the extent of economic voting in the context of the Great Recession, find that the magnitude of economic downturn is not the main predictor of incumbent support (Hernández and Kriesi 2016; Talving 2018).

Where the 'blind' variant of the reward–punishment model predicts a straightforward association between economic decline and reduction in governing party vote share, research that qualifies the economy's impact implies a more sophisticated voter. Cross-national analyses of economic voting shows that the impact of the economy is a function of political and institutional

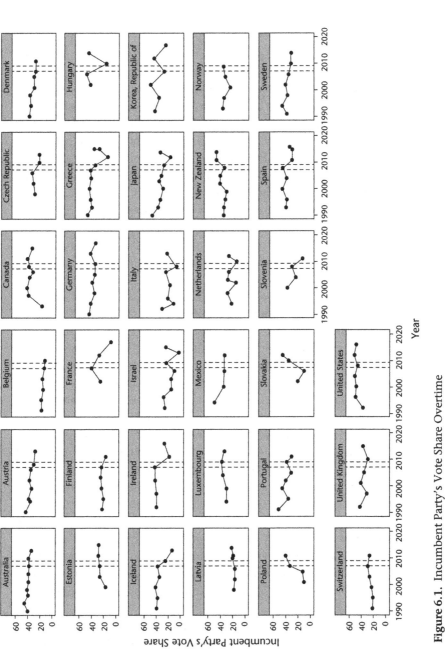

Figure 6.1. Incumbent Party's Vote Share Overtime

Note: Graphs report vote % received in elections for the party of the chief executive. Dashed lines indicate the shock period (2007–9).

Source: various, calculated by authors from national election results.

factors (Powell and Whitten 1993; Hobolt et al. 2013; de Vries and Giger 2014; but see Dassonneville and Lewis-Beck 2017). There also is a growing body of evidence about how voters evaluate economic performance in relative terms, comparing across democratic settings (Kayser and Peress 2012) or over time (Fieldhouse et al. 2020; Kayser and McGrath 2018). Voters use information about economic outcomes to elect competent candidates. However, citizens do not observe the incumbent's competence directly but must rely on observed economic outcomes. The key is to untangle the incumbent's responsibility for macro-economic outcomes from other factors shaping these outcomes, be they technology shocks, trade from abroad, or the actions of other governments. In settings where power is concentrated voters can clearly identify policy responsibility and, thus, engage in economic voting. By contrast, where responsibility is diffused among various actors, the linkage between economic conditions and voting is weak.

According to this concentration of responsibility argument, the existence of multiple levels of institutions and actors shaping economic outcomes impedes voters' ability to identify the sources of economic disasters. This obscurity weakens economic voting. By contrast, other scholars refute the concentration of responsibility argument claiming that voters are capable of distinguishing different levels of economic responsibility (Duch and Stevenson 2008). The magnitude of the economic vote declines not because voters are not capable of identifying sources of responsibility, but because voters recognize that current economic conditions are not the result of government policies. In light of this argument, studies find that the degree to which the domestic economy is driven by external factors can moderate economic voting. Voters are capable of differentiating exogenous shocks to the national economy from economic performance driven by incumbent competency. Consequently, in face of greater economic openness, voters take account of the importance of external influence on domestic economic conditions when making vote decisions (Duch and Stevenson 2010, Hellwig and Samuels 2007, Kayser and Peress 2012).

These different perspectives on retrospective voting structure current debates on economic voting and, in more general terms, promote reflection about prospects for electoral accountability in modern democracies. In what follows, we advance a view of voter responses to the crisis that borrows from both perspectives. We first lay out an argument about how voters respond to incumbent performance during crisis recovery that differs from that of the initial shock. In doing so, we support the notion of a sophisticated voter capable of making complex assignments of responsibility. But we also recognize that popular responses may be shaped by elite cues which may or may not accurately reflect actual outcomes.

6.2. The Shock, the Recovery, and the Policy Response

While most studies focus on the short-term effect of economic shocks in the midst of the crisis, we argue that it is important to consider different stages of the crisis development and recovery. Many economies, particularly in Europe, were heavily affected by the GFC. The large variance across countries exists not only in the magnitude of the economic decline, but also in the rate of recovery. Macro-level economic performance becomes less informative as a basis to assess incumbent competence when the economy is doing poorly everywhere. However, if the country's economy is much slower in recovering and other countries' economies are rebounding, voters are likely to read it as a red light for incumbent competency (Hernández and Kriesi 2016; Lindvall 2014, 2017; see also Kayser and Peress 2012).

In line with these views, we argue that the post-crisis economic recovery is a better predictor of incumbent support than the immediate economic impact of the event. A consideration of the size of the recovery relative to the size of the initial shock provides a more realistic assessment of how citizens observed their government's response to the crisis and, come election time, evaluated them accordingly. After all, policymakers might be forgiven for not righting the ship of state immediately after a global financial crisis. Recognizing the extra-national factors involved, the public may discount the size of the shock when evaluating incumbents and focus blame on non-elected actors (Hellwig et al. 2008). In comparison, the post-crisis economic recovery—observed by voters over a period of months and years from the end of the crisis to Election Day—offers a better record with which to hold policymakers to account.

In addition to economic performance, we assert that voters evaluate competence of incumbents based on their policy efforts and rhetorical promises that signal greater government redistribution. Elites' crisis response may take the form of concrete action, such as regulatory reform or stimulus packages. However, to the extent that institutional and fiscal barriers shape the state's capacity for policy reform (Beramendi et al. 2015), political debate, messaging, and policy promises may be as effective in communicating intent to the electorate. Signals from political elites can shape public economic perceptions and, in turn, voting behaviour (Bisgaard and Slothuus 2018; Mau et al. 2012; Blomberg et al. 2012; Bartels 2002; Carsey and Layman 2006; Margalit 2013). This is especially true during the uncertainty which accompanies the onset of economic crises. In hard times, economic competence emerges as a salient issue in the public mind (Hellwig 2007; Singer 2013). Nonetheless, in many cases, voters require additional sources of information to craft political opinions (Talving 2017).

Cues from political elites are one of these important sources. Individuals rely on political leaders to form opinions about complex political issues without investing much effort (see Bartels 2002; Evans and Andersen 2006; Gomez and Wilson 2003; Wlezien et al. 1997; Tilley and Hobolt 2011). Focusing on incumbent votes and governing parties' behaviour, we emphasize two types of cues through which political elites affect voter decisions. First, governing parties' policy initiatives (or lack thereof) condition the effect of economic performance on voter choice. Economic policy is one of the key predictors of vote choice in hard times. As the salience of economic issues increases, government policies are brought under greater public scrutiny (Talving 2017). Parties in government can signal their attentiveness to voters' economic insecurities using public policy. The large variance in economic growth rates in the post-GFC period (see Figure 2.2) makes policy responses of governments crucial for incumbent support. By providing discretionary stimulus and enhancing redistribution, governing parties can appeal to voters who demand greater social protection in the presence of high economic uncertainty (Mau et al. 2012; Kweon 2018; Blomberg et al. 2012). By creating more favourable economic perceptions, we expect that greater policy effort to offset welfare loss incurred by the crisis will increase support for political incumbents. Conversely, austerity measures will reduce incumbent support.

Second, political elites can employ rhetoric to modulate the magnitude of economic voting (Hart 2013; Pardos-Prado and Sagarzazu 2016). While studies on elite messages and electoral behaviour tend to focus on blame-avoidance and credit-claiming tactics of parties, we further argue that political elites can use rhetoric to signal their competence and policy intentions to voters. Blame avoidance and credit claiming are tactics of responsibility attribution through political rhetoric. Politicians influence citizens' political perception by blaming other actors for bad economic performance or taking credit for favourable economic conditions (Hellwig and Coffey 2011; Lenke and Schmidtke 2017) or blaming others for unpopular reforms like welfare retrenchment (Giger and Nelson 2011; Wenzelburger 2011; Green-Pedersen 2002). While these studies find political rhetoric an effective political instrument for blame avoidance and credit claiming, rhetoric also can be used to communicate one's competence with the electorate. Especially in times of crisis, a government policy response is crucial for voters' decisions as they seek to find a party that can help release the public from economic distress (Hernández and Kriesi 2016). Hence, political elites have an incentive to prime voters on their competence and shape their prospective economic perception through policy pledges. By promising to expand social protection, political parties can soothe citizens' economic anxiety, and assure voters that they will be taken care of by the state when these parties are in power.

6.3. Data and Measures

We test the electoral consequences of the Great Recession using the set of twenty-three OECD democracies from 1996 to 2017 included in Module 1 to 5 of the CSES (CSES 2017). We also incorporate six additional election studies to cover missing cases in the CSES data. The detailed list of countries and years included in the analysis can be found in the Appendix in Chapter 2.[3] This pooled dataset allows us not only to examine conditional effects of incumbent parties' policy efforts and rhetoric on incumbent vote, but to analyze how these conditional effects are further moderated by economic performance of a given country during the crisis and recovery periods.

The dependent variable of interest is incumbent vote. For incumbent vote, respondents who reported voting for the incumbent head of a government party are coded 1 and all others coded 0.[4] Explanatory variables are designed to capture the effects of the Great Recession. We not only examine conditional effects of incumbent parties' policy efforts and rhetoric on incumbent vote, but we analyze how these conditional effects are further moderated by economic performance of a given country during the crisis and recovery periods. As we predict that the effect of economic crisis changes over time, we analyze two periods: the *shock* (2008–9) and *recovery* periods (2010 and onward). To differentiate economic effects during these two periods, we use two dummy variables corresponding to the shock and recovery periods. In order to measure economic performance, we use percentage change in GDP per capita since the previous election. We expect the influence of economic performance to be smaller immediately after the crisis, but to have a long-term impact in the sense that the impact is larger in the recovery period.

We also include measures for the effect of government policies and of political messaging. Government policy effort should measure policies used to stimulate the economy such as tax cuts or expanded spending. In times of crisis, automatic stabilizers kick in, so a spending increase does not indicate an increase in a government's discretionary spending. In order to capture the degree to which incumbent parties used discretionary stimuli, we use the variable, *Austerity*, which measures the cyclically adjusted fiscal balance as a percentage of GDP. A positive value indicates the absence of stimulus indicating austerity, and the extent of stimulus negative. We also use an alternative measure of policy efforts, *Relative redistribution*, by using the reduction in inequality (Gini) after taxes and transfers (Solt 2019). Higher scores indicate

---

[3] Switzerland is excluded in empirical analyses in this chapter because the country has a collective ruling body composed of four parties.

[4] We included non-voters in the 0 category. We reran all analyses excluding non-voters with virtually the same result. See Table A6.1 in the Appendix.

that government policies through taxes and income transfers have effectively improved income redistribution.

Incumbent party's welfare cues are measured using the statements from incumbent chief executive parties delivered in the context of the election campaign. The CSES data are from post-election studies, which facilitated the pairing of party campaign statements with individual-level survey data. We use data from the Comparative Manifestos Project (CMP) to measure the extent to which chief executive parties competing in an election emphasize social welfare concerns in their campaign discourse. As shown in Chapter 1, the measure subtracts a party's score on 'welfare state limitation', 'economic orthodoxy', and 'economic growth: positive' from their emphases on 'welfare state expansion', 'Keynesian demand management', and 'equality: positive'. Higher values indicate that a party is more supportive of welfare expansion.

Models control for several macro- and micro-level factors. We control for sources of economic insecurity such as employment status. Increasing evidence indicates that deepening economic risks have become an important determinant of voting behaviour in deindustrialized societies (Emmenegger et al. 2015; Helgason and Mérola 2017). For employment status, market outsiders (part-time workers, unemployed individuals, and those who are not in the labour market due to disability) are coded as 1, and otherwise as 0. We also include a variable that measures individuals' right–left positions on an 11-point scale, coded such that higher values align with the partisanship of the government.[5] For macro-level factors, we include gross government debt measured as a share of GDP to account for the effect of socio-tropic economic uncertainty on incumbent support.

6.4. Analysis

Since data are structured such that individuals are nested within country-survey years, we estimate models using hierarchical logistic regression models with random intercepts. Multilevel statistical techniques allow us to jointly model individual- and macro-level determinants of incumbent support and to estimate separate variance structures in order to produce unbiased standard errors. Country-survey years specific random intercepts help reduce the danger of omitted variable bias from unobserved country characteristics. We also include country fixed effects to capture unmeasured sources of heterogeneity at the country level.

Model estimates are reported in Table 6.1. The first column presents a baseline model. In line with the economic voting theory, the results indicate

---

[5] That is, the right–left scale is inverted for cases where the incumbent party is left-of-centre.

Table 6.1. Modelling Incumbent Support

	(1)	(2)	(3)	(4)	(5)
Shock period	0.0652	0.120	−0.206	−0.956	−0.345
	(0.167)	(0.207)	(0.314)	(0.975)	(0.324)
Recovery period	−0.0576	−0.166	−0.051	−0.136	−0.229
	(0.147)	(0.169)	(0.204)	(0.576)	(0.281)
ΔGDP per capita	0.028***	0.022**	0.029***	0.029*	0.016
	(0.008)	(0.010)	(0.011)	(0.017)	(0.015)
Austerity	−0.056*	−0.064**	−0.094*	−0.065**	−0.059*
	(0.031)	(0.030)	(0.052)	(0.029)	(0.031)
Relative redistribution	−0.064	−0.060	−0.019	−0.063	−0.046
	(0.048)	(0.049)	(0.049)	(0.047)	(0.051)
Incumbent party's welfare cues	−0.008	−0.012	−0.017*	−0.013	−0.023
	(0.009)	(0.009)	(0.010)	(0.008)	(0.021)
(Ln) Government debt	0.020	−0.027	−0.168	−0.137	−0.123
	(0.221)	(0.217)	(0.226)	(0.213)	(0.224)
Market outsider	−0.109***	−0.109***	−0.109***	−0.109***	−0.109***
	(0.017)	(0.017)	(0.017)	(0.017)	(0.017)
Right–left position	0.001***	0.001***	0.001***	0.001***	0.001***
	(0.000)	(0.000)	(0.000)	(0.000)	(0.000)
Shock × ΔGDP		−0.012	0.013	0.048	−0.025
		(0.017)	(0.022)	(0.043)	(0.032)
Recovery × ΔGDP		0.026*	0.0022	0.199***	0.062*
		(0.014)	(0.020)	(0.072)	(0.034)
Austerity × ΔGDP			0.004		
			(0.003)		
Shock × Austerity			−0.067		
			(0.074)		
Shock × Austerity × ΔGDP			0.011		
			(0.007)		
Recovery × Austerity			0.031		
			(0.059)		
Recovery × Austerity × ΔGDP			−0.011**		
			(0.006)		
Shock × Redistribution				0.031	
				(0.027)	
Redistribution × ΔGDP				−0.000	
				(0.001)	
Shock × Redistribution × ΔGDP				−0.002	
				(0.001)	
Recovery × Redistribution				−0.004	
				(0.015)	
Recovery × Redistribution × ΔGDP				−0.004**	
				(0.002)	
Shock × Welfare cues					0.060**
					(0.030)
Welfare cues × ΔGDP					0.000
					(0.002)
Shock × Welfare cues × ΔGDP					0.004
					(0.004)
Recovery × Welfare cues					0.007
					(0.025)
Recovery × Welfare cues × ΔGDP					−0.003
					(0.003)
Constant	1.429	1.493	0.539	1.932	1.390
	(1.457)	(1.488)	(1.507)	(1.445)	(1.595)

Variance (intercept)	0.204***	0.193***	0.175***	0.165***	0.172***
	(0.031)	(0.030)	(0.0279)	(0.025)	(0.027)
Chi-square	131.54***	140.62***	158.15***	169.75***	161.57***
N individuals	136,144	136,144	136,144	136,144	136,144
N country-surveys	93	93	93	93	93

Note: The dependent variable is scored 1 for voting for the incumbent head of a government party and 0 otherwise. Cells display estimates from multilevel logit regression with random intercepts and country fixed effects. Standard errors are in parentheses. ***$p<0.01$, **$p<0.05$, *$p<0.10$, two-tailed test.

that economic growth increases support for incumbents. In addition, incumbent support declined both in the shock (2008–2009) and during the recovery (2010 and onward). However, the negative impact was larger during the recovery period, implying that the financial crisis has had a long-lasting impact on voting behaviour. Variables related to economic insecurity also influence incumbent support. Market outsiders such as part-time or unemployed workers are less likely to re-elect an incumbent party than those with full-time jobs. Similarly, a high unemployment rate negatively affects voting for incumbents. By contrast, government debt does not have any statistically significant impact. Individuals whose right–left position are aligned with the incumbent, not surprisingly, are more likely to vote for the incumbent.

The remaining models in Table 6.1 examine the joint effects of economic performance and incumbent parties' welfare cues and policy behaviour. Model 2 includes the interaction terms between GDP per capita change and shock/recovery periods. Visualized results are presented in Figure 6.2 for the predicted probabilities of incumbent support during the pre-crisis, crisis, and recovery periods. Consistent with our analyses of incumbent vote shares in Chapter 2, we see that the economy's impact was greater after the crisis than before it. Results also confirm that economic performance will matter more for incumbent support during the recovery period rather than the time immediately after the crisis. During the pre-crisis period, high GDP per capita growth leads to a high probability of incumbent support, indicating that voters hold incumbent elites accountable for their economic performance. Perhaps reflecting heightened levels of uncertainty during the crisis period, economic voting appears to have little impact. Although there is an upward trend, it is moderate in magnitude and the wide confidence intervals mean that incumbent vote probabilities are not significantly different across varying levels of economic growth. By contrast, during the recovery period, we find that increase in predicted probabilities is even larger (over 30 per cent change) than those in the pre-crisis period. These results demonstrate that economic recovery at the later stage of the crisis is more important that economic performance immediately after the crisis. Political consequences of an economic crisis come to realization in the long term rather than in short term.

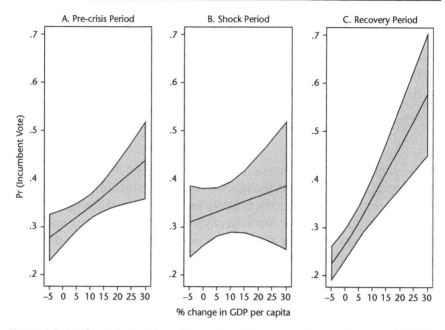

Figure 6.2. Predicted Probability of Incumbent Vote across Varying Degrees of GDP Per Capita Growth

Note: Graphs are based on Model 2 in Table 6.1. Grey areas indicate 90% confidence intervals.

Our top–down elite cue theory predicts that the degree to which economic performance affects support for an incumbent party will be moderated by elite cues and policy efforts. Models 3 and 4 test these claims by examining three-way interactions among shock/recovery dummy, GDP per capita growth, and policy efforts (austerity and relative redistribution) and incumbent parties' welfare cues. The conditional effects of policy behaviour are visualized in Figures 6.3 and 6.4. Figure 6.3 presents the predicted probabilities of incumbent support in cases of high (20) and low GDP per capita growth (−5) across varying degrees of cyclically adjusted fiscal balance (*Austerity*). Recall that a negative value in fiscal balance means greater discretionary spending, and a higher value means stricter austerity.

The periodized results displayed in Figure 6.3 demonstrate the evolution of austerity's mass political effects. Before the onset of the crisis (Figure 6.3A), tight fiscal policies contributed to lower levels of incumbent support, particularly in places with poorly performing economies (low growth). During the shock period, we see a slightly different trend. In strong economies, a diet of austerity can raise incumbent support, ostensibly owing to the greater leeway given to reformers when the economy overall fares well. However, in low-growth cases, austerity measures backfire on incumbent parties, while greater

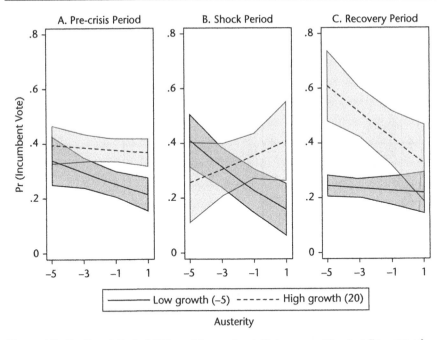

Figure 6.3. Predicted Probabilities of Incumbent Vote across Varying Degrees of Austerity

Note: Graphs are based on Model 3 in Table 6.1. Grey areas indicate 90% confidence intervals.

discretionary spending (aka fiscal stimulus) increases the probability of selecting the incumbent party. Finally, Figure 6.3C shows that, during the recovery period, the governing parties' fiscal policy bears little on incumbent support when economic recovery is slow. This is in contrast to the positive impact of discretionary spending during the shock periods. The implication is that, immediately after the crisis, when economy is hit hard, voters reward government for its expansionary policy while punishing for spending cuts. However, when the economy is slow in recovering from the crisis in the long term, voters punish the incumbent government for the bad economy regardless of its policy efforts. Conversely, in well-performing economies, an expansionary approach has a positive impact on incumbent support. These findings lend support to our claim that policy efforts moderate an impact of economic performance on individuals' voting decisions. Critically, policy efforts differ with respect to the size and pattern of their impact depending on economic conditions during the shock and recovery periods.

We next examine the role of automatic stabilizers present in developed welfare states. Using estimates from Model 4 in Table 6.1, Figure 6.4 displays the predicted probabilities of voting for the incumbent across the range of values for relative redistribution after taxes and transfers. A higher value in

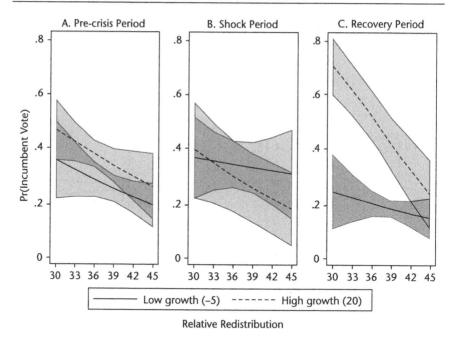

Figure 6.4. Predicted Probabilities of Incumbent Vote across Varying Degrees of Relative Redistribution

Note: The graphs are based on Model 5 in Table 6.1. Grey area indicates 90% confidence intervals.

relative redistribution indicates a higher reduction of income inequality (as captured by the Gini coefficient) attributed to tax and income transfer policies. In all three periods, the state's redistributive efforts lead to *lower* levels of incumbent support. Overall, the negative impact is greater in countries with stronger economies. The magnitude of this effect, however, varies over time. Effects are weakest during the shock period (Figure 6.4B) and strongest during the recovery (6.4C). In post-crisis elections, redistribution serves to blunt the positive gains accrued to incumbents overseeing strong recoveries. By contrast, these automatic stabilizers play a much smaller role for incumbent support in countries with weak recovery. In sum, unlike discretionary spending, automatic stabilizers provided through taxes and transfers have a negative impact on incumbent support. However, their negative impact is smaller when a country suffers from an economic downturn, especially during the recovery period: weak recovery signals bad news for incumbents regardless of welfare policy.

Finally, Model 5 examines conditional effects of incumbent parties' welfare cues. Figure 6.5 presents the visualized results. Overall, the impact of pro-welfare rhetoric appears to be small, particularly as a tool used by governments to curry favour in stagnating economies. During the pre-crisis period,

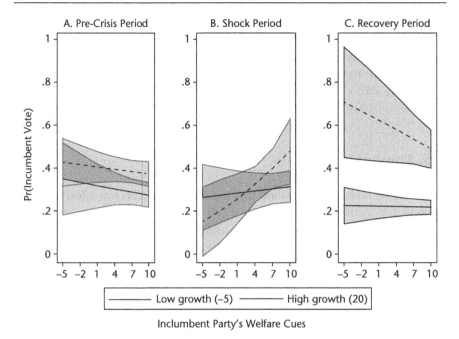

Figure 6.5. Predicted Probabilities of Incumbent Vote across Varying Degrees of Incumbent Party's Welfare Cues

Note: The graphs are based on Model 5 in Table 6.1.Grey area indicates 90% confidence intervals.

incumbent parties' greater emphasis on pro-welfare positions generally brings no change in the probability of supporting the incumbent regardless of the state of the economy. This is true for stagnating economies even after the crisis. For strong economies, incumbent parties' welfare cues have a positive impact during the shock period, but this trend is reversed in the recovery period. We might conclude from these findings that the effect of cues is weak, particularly after the crisis and during the shock period, meaning that, with time, voters get tired of empty promises and are less susceptible to manipulation. As we will see in the next chapter, the impact of elite rhetoric is more pronounced when it comes to the voters' decisions to support particular party types than, as we see here, the decision to punish or reward the incumbent.

Our findings suggest that the effect of the crisis and incumbent parties' policy efforts and welfare cues differ by the stage of the crisis development. The theory of economic voting holds in that we find incumbent parties are rewarded (punished) when the economy is strong (weak). However, the effect of economic performance is strong during the recovery period rather than the shock period, implying that the crisis has a long-term impact. In addition, our findings show that incumbent parties can moderate the crisis effect. However, the degree to which government policy and rhetoric condition the adverse effect of the crisis depends on types of policy efforts as well as the stage of the crisis development. Overall, we find that discretionary spending can effectively mitigate the impact of the crisis in stagnating economies, particularly during the crisis. However, automatic stabilizers and rhetoric have a weaker impact.

6.5. Conclusion

This chapter seeks to understand to what extent the GFC has affected voters' support for incumbent parties and whether government policy efforts and pledges had any moderating effect on mitigating a negative impact of economic downturn. Through analyses of twenty-three OECD countries, we find several interesting results. First and foremost, our results show that voters hold governments to account not just for the size of the crisis itself, but for the robustness of the recovery. These findings call for a need to unpack the effect of the Great Recession (or any financial crisis) and examine it in different periods of crisis shock and recovery. In contrast to many previous studies that argue that the financial crisis did not have much noticeable political impact, this chapter demonstrates that the political consequences of the crisis were long-term, and the size and pattern of the crisis effect change over time.

Second, this chapter shows that economic voting is further aided by government policy, as we observe from the interactive models. The (blind) retrospective voting argument contends that voters punish governing actors, regardless of their responsibility and any policy effort provided in response to a crisis. By contrast, our findings suggest that, while adverse economic conditions during the crisis negatively affect incumbent support, voters can discern cases where government actions may have some reasonable impact on the economy (that is, in shaping the path towards recovery) from those times where policymakers' actions are largely ineffective in the face of global market forces. However, the degree to which government policy and rhetoric condition the adverse effect of the crisis depends on types of policy efforts as well as the stage of the crisis development. Discretionary spending can effectively mitigate the impact of the crisis in stagnating economies during the shock period, while it can have a reverse impact in strong economies during the recovery period. By contrast, automatic stabilizers registered a weaker impact. Lastly, party rhetoric—in the form of (un)favourable messages for social spending—played an amplifying role. Pro-welfare messages increased support when economies fared well but did little to rescue incumbents in hard times.

Overall, our investigation of incumbent support points to a reasonably sophisticated voter—one who can receive signals about the economy and work through the implications of government choices on their own welfare. In emphasizing the role of the economy during the post-crisis recovery stage, rather than the shock period itself, our findings contribute to recent research on the persistence of voter memory and the workings of electoral accountability (e.g. Bechtel and Hainmueller. 2011; Hellwig and Marinova 2015). It is true that voters may punish governments for being in office when things turn bad (see Bartels 2014; Achen and Bartels 2016). But it is equally the case that voters consider how elites respond to adverse conditions, be it in terms of action or rhetoric. Are voters as adept at using information to choose among party types—before, during, and after the GFC? We examine this question in the next chapter.

Appendix

Table 6A1. Reanalysis of Table 6.1 Excluding Non-voters

	(1)	(2)	(3)	(4)	(5)
Shock period	0.054	0.116	−0.213	−0.989	−0.319
	(0.164)	(0.204)	(0.308)	(0.964)	(0.319)
Recovery period	−0.040	−0.138	−0.057	−0.108	−0.157
	(0.145)	(0.166)	(0.201)	(0.570)	(0.277)
ΔGDP per capita	0.027***	0.023**	0.029***	0.029*	0.019
	(0.008)	(0.010)	(0.011)	(0.016)	(0.015)
Austerity	−0.060*	−0.067**	−0.092*	−0.068**	−0.061**
	(0.031)	(0.030)	(0.051)	(0.029)	(0.031)
Relative redistribution	−0.057	−0.051	−0.012	−0.055	−0.036
	(0.047)	(0.048)	(0.048)	(0.047)	(0.050)
Incumbent party's welfare cues	−0.008	−0.012	−0.017*	−0.013	−0.020
	(0.009)	(0.009)	(0.010)	(0.008)	(0.021)
(Ln) Government debt	−0.004	−0.050	−0.206	−0.154	−0.159
	(0.217)	(0.213)	(0.222)	(0.211)	(0.221)
Market outsider	−0.103***	−0.103***	−0.103***	−0.103***	−0.102***
	(0.018)	(0.018)	(0.018)	(0.018)	(0.018)
Right–left position	0.010***	0.010***	0.010***	0.010***	0.010***
	(0.000)	(0.000)	(0.000)	(0.000)	(0.000)
Shock $\times$ ΔGDP		−0.013	0.012	0.048	−0.027
		(0.017)	(0.022)	(0.042)	(0.031)
Recovery $\times$ ΔGDP		0.024*	0.004	0.188***	0.055
		(0.014)	(0.020)	(0.072)	(0.034)
Austerity $\times$ ΔGDP			0.004		
			(0.003)		
Shock $\times$ Austerity			−0.0711		
			(0.0727)		
Shock $\times$ Austerity $\times$ ΔGDP			0.011		
			(0.007)		
Recovery $\times$ Austerity			0.017		
			(0.058)		
Recovery $\times$ Austerity $\times$ ΔGDP			−0.010*		
			(0.005)		

(continued)

155

Table 6A1. Continued

	(1)	(2)	(3)	(4)	(5)
Shock × Redistribution				0.032	
				(0.027)	
Redistribution × ΔGDP				−0.000	
				(0.001)	
Shock × Redistribution × ΔGDP				−0.002	
				(0.001)	
Recovery × Redistribution				−0.003	
				(0.015)	
Recovery × Redistribution × ΔGDP				−0.004**	
				(0.002)	
Shock × Welfare cues					0.057*
					(0.029)
Welfare cues × ΔGDP					0.000
					(0.002)
Shock × Welfare cues × ΔGDP					0.004
					(0.004)
Recovery × Welfare cues					0.002
					(0.024)
Recovery × Welfare cues × ΔGDP					−0.002
					(0.003)
Constant	1.262	1.285	0.439	1.728	1.154
	(1.432)	(1.464)	(1.481)	(1.429)	(1.571)
Variance(intercept)	0.197***	0.187***	0.169***	0.161***	0.167***
	(0.030)	(0.029)	(0.026)	(0.025)	(0.026)
Chi-square	136.45***	145.24***	163.46***	172.84***	166.01***
N country-years	93	93	93	93	93
N individuals	134,094	134,094	134,094	134,094	134,094

Note: The dependent variable is scored 1 for voting for the incumbent head of a government party and 0 otherwise. Cells display estimates from multilevel logit regression with random intercepts and country fixed effects. Standard errors are in parentheses. ***$p < 0.01$, **$p < 0.05$, *$p < 0.1$, two-tailed test.

7

Shaping their own Destiny

Political Parties and Voter Choices Before and After the Crisis

A clarion call heard today among parties and candidates throughout the world is a call for a return to the past. American President's Donald Trump's call to 'Make America Great Again' was but one of many to recapture the glory of days gone by. Election campaigns in places as different as Italy, Poland, and Sweden have featured similar rallying cries. While the references to specific halcyon periods of the past are vague, for many voters this may refer to the times of general peace and prosperity following the great depression and then the Second World War. The 'Thirty Glorious Years' from 1945 to 1975 were indeed a time of unprecedented prosperity and peace among nations. Not coincidentally, politics within nations enjoyed high levels of stability. Extremism of the interwar years was cast aside for the consensus politics of the postwar era. Indeed, the stability of choices on offer from Western party systems was what Lipset and Rokkan (1967) and their collaborators set out to explain. Traditional social cleavages predicted that, save for a critical juncture on the order of the reformation or industrial revolution, the stability of the party system would persist well into the future. But as was apparent by the last quarter of the twentieth century, such predictions would not come to pass. By some combination of changing economies, changing social divides, or changing values, party systems in the established democracies became, once again, beset by party system volatility and polarization.

The twin shocks of the GFC and Great Recession were therefore layered on top of what were already tumultuous political contexts among the OECD countries. Analyses of aggregate-level election outcomes reported in Chapter 2 showed that these crisis events did not cause the shift from electoral stability to volatility—indeed, shifts predate the GFC by a decade or more. The GFC did, however, contribute to further party system change. At first, the

Democracy Under Siege? Parties, Voters, and Elections After the Great Recession. Timothy Hellwig, Yesola Kweon, and Jack Vowles, Oxford University Press (2020). © Timothy Hellwig, Yesola Kweon, and Jack Vowles.
DOI: 10.1093/oso/9780198846208.001.0001

consequences for national party systems resisted generalization: a glance at elections in the wake of the shock, in 2008 and 2009, shows that some party systems became more fragmented, such as in Austria, Greece, and the Netherlands, while others consolidated among a smaller set of competitors: such as Ireland, Italy, and Sweden. However, as concerns shifted from absorbing the shock to the more protracted matter of dealing with the recovery, party system fragmentation and vote volatility increased, particularly among those economies worst hit (see Tables 2.1 and 2.2).

The objective of this chapter is to unpack the mass political response of the shock and recovery by examining the consequences of the GFC and Great Recession on party support in national elections. Chapter 6 did so through the lens of accountability and asked whether and how the economic downfall was associated with support for sitting governments. We showed voters hold governments to account not just for the size of the crisis itself, but for the robustness of the recovery. But what about the effect of the crisis and recovery on the voter's choice over parties, regardless of incumbency status? Did the extraordinary events of 2007–9 affect voter preferences for different sorts of policy responses, as conveyed by parties' ideological position or partisan family? And, per our elite cues argument, to what extent did the policies and rhetoric advanced by vote-seeking parties contribute to voter choice?

As we did in previous chapters for public opinion, participation, and incumbent support, we submit that a more comprehensive test of the GFC's impact on party selection—and, by extension, system volatility—is required. The analysis presented in this chapter is distinct from those that precede it theoretically as well as empirically. Theoretically, we are informed by the supply-side perspective introduced in Chapter 1, which calls for a consideration of how parties manage the crisis, and how such actions in turn influence voter choice in uncertain times. Empirically, we again expand the scope of inquiry to consider the relative influence of policy and rhetoric, and to do so during the shock and the recovery period. Analyses at the aggregate and individual levels reveal that the financial crisis and Great Recession shaped voter decisions. Since 2008, electoral support for the mainstream parties on the centre-left and centre-right has waned, while challenger parties have grown in size. Multivariate analyses of election returns trace some of this shift in party support to the effects to the policies of austerity and to the accumulation of public debt. The implications of the crisis era for support among the political mainstream are less apparent. Nevertheless, we find that elite cues produce a 'crisis effect'. The effect, however, is governed by the policy environment. Voting for the mainstream left declines especially in settings of fiscal austerity. Furthermore, the relative effects of these settings vary with time. Short-term fiscal efforts in the form of stimulus or austerity did much to sway voters during the shock years of 2008 and 2009. With time, however, the electoral impact of these short-term efforts weakened. Over the course of the recovery, party policy rhetoric could prop up support for the left and for challengers during continued hard times.

7.1. Party Responses to the Great Recession

With respect to the study of political parties, the crisis events of the early twentieth century offer a rare lens into how political actors assess and respond to an unexpected event. Indeed, the fall-out of the 2008 financial crisis has captured the attention of researchers on political parties. As discussed in Chapter 5 with respect to turnout and in Chapter 6 for voter assessments of government competence, many treat the crisis as a direct constraint on parties' policy room to maneuvre in democracies. Research on party strategies, however, also emphasizes how parties adapt to the crisis effects, and often in ways at odds with their roles of representing interests. Clements et al. (2018) find that during economic crises governing parties are less responsive to voters, catering instead to the preferences of market elites. This underlines earlier work showing that globalization drives a wedge between voters and their party representatives (Ezrow and Hellwig 2014). Similarly, Traber et al. (2018) pinpoint a gap in issue concerns. They argue that while voters care deeply about the economy in times of crisis, parties charged with leading governments instead downplay the issue—thus leading to a salience gap between political elites and voters. More generally, the rhetoric and reality of economic crisis have contributed to beliefs that parties have '[lost] their structural roots in society, their coherence and their representative function' (Hernández and Kriesi 2016, 207) and have turned 'from maximising competitors into risk averse colluders' (Blyth and Katz 2005, 40). The upshot is that parties' penchant to articulate the interests of their supporters in the electorate may be under stress.

To others, however, the influence of the crisis on parties operates mainly indirectly, by way of its influence on public opinion—the subject of Part II of this book. Chapter 3 showed that parties, by way of their messages during campaigns, can blunt the effects of macro-economic conditions in the economy on feelings of insecurity. And we saw in Chapter 4 how messages from trusted parties can tilt opinion on matters of health and unemployment expenditures. In this respect, research on the GFC and Great Recession is informed by a growing body of work on how one's experience in the global economy can influence policy preferences (e.g. Walter 2010, 2017) and party policy offerings (e.g. Rommel and Walter 2018). Trade shocks have been shown to move voters to the far right or the far left politically, thereby linking economic globalization to political polarization (Autor et al. 2016; Colantone and Stanig 2018). Researchers also find that external shocks contribute to xenophobic beliefs about immigrants, which then translate into support for populist parties (Hays et al. forthcoming).

Yet while the effects of deindustrialization, foreign direct investment, off-shoring, and other components of post-industrial economic change have received substantial support, evidence of a crisis effect per se on voter choice has been mixed. Researchers have examined whether personal hardships incurred by the crisis—in terms of loss of a job or decline in household income—push people to change their choice among competing parties. Examining party preferences from across the Eurozone in 2014, Hobolt and Tilley (2016) report that individuals so affected by the euro crisis were more likely to turn away from governing parties and towards opposition and challenger parties. With respect to the last of these, concerns about immigration and integration pushed them towards challengers on the right. In contrast, Martén (2019) shows from an examination of Swedish data that job loss is associated with more favourable views of the Social Democrats. Margalit (2013) finds that while job loss moves attitudes on welfare spending in the United States, this adverse incurrence has no effects on voting behaviour. And Emmenegger et al.'s study of Dutch voters (2015) finds linkages between labour market dislocations and the vote to be indirect, running through preferences for redistribution. Taking stock of this stream of research on crises and party choice, Margalit (2019, 286) concludes that while economic shocks may affect how voters decide, there remains a great deal of heterogeneity in the direction of the political response and in the magnitude of the effects.

Indeed, among the range of attitudes and behaviours examined in this book, we might expect the GFC's influence on party choice to be the most circumspect. Cleavage-based theories of social change maintain that parties represent particular sides of enduring social conflict—and that, once formed, they persist beyond the cleavage forces that gave rise to them. According to this view, the objective of parties is to aggregate, rather than redirect, the interests of their constituencies. Issue-based arguments are more compatible with rapid electoral change in that they place emphasis on short-term changes in discrete issue positions. This perspective, however, privileges the voter's capacity to make evaluations independent from the views of political elites (e.g. Dalton 1984, 2020; Kayser and Wlezien 2011).

In contrast to the above, our 'elite cues' perspective gives an opening for party response. According to this perspective, parties provide signals to help voters make sense of the world. Parties' chief role is to provide heuristics by simplifying choices of direction. This clarifying role is especially critical in the wake of unanticipated exogenous shocks like the GFC. As we catalogued in Chapter 2, the crisis ushered a whole new set of issue concerns from the rarefied world of policy debates into the public lexicon—e.g. collateralized debt obligations, sovereign debt, and debt restructuring—as well as returned decades-old issues to centre stage—e.g. nationalization and privatization. The multi-layered nature of these issues meant that even the more sophisticated members of the public relied on signals from trusted political elites (Zaller 1992; see also Hellwig and Kweon 2016).

This new—or reissued, as it were—set of concerns gave party elites licence to carve out new issue positions. Consider, for instance, French economic policy under the centre-right Union for a Popular Movement (UMP). Having secured both the presidency and a legislative majority in the previous year, in 2008 the UMP laid out a set of policies and budget characterized by tax reductions and business deregulation. Fallout from the GFC, however, led to an about-face with a return to a more interventionist programme as President Nicolas Sarkozy declared that 'laissez-faire capitalism is over' and denounced the 'dictatorship of the market'—surprising words from a centre-right head of state.[1] In other cases, new issues served as catalyst to develop entirely new parties. In Germany, for example, Alternative für Deutschland came onto the scene in advance of the 2013 Federal elections as a challenger party championing an anti-euro, anti-bailout platform—issues not emphasized by other members of the party system. In Spain, Podemos emerged in 2014 to address a set of issues—in its case, unemployment and economic malaise—made salient by the European debt crisis. The rise of SYRIZA in Greece, from a minor contender to governing party, can be understood in similar fashion as carving out an anti-austerity message which had been ignored by PASOK on the mainstream centre-left and New Democracy on the right.

7.2. Economic Crises and Support for Party Types

We now make a more systemic assessment of the influence of the GFC and Great Recession on party fortunes by charting changes in support among party types. In the wake of the financial crisis, elections throughout the affected regions received the close attention of journalists and scholars alike. Would governments' policy orientations change following the worst economic collapse since the 1930s? And if so, how? Expectations abounded. After many years of neo-liberal economic centre-right policies in many countries, particularly Western Europe, would voters in hard-hit economies tilt leftward and embrace the redistributive and welfare-expanding policies of social democracy? Alternatively, would voters choose competence over policy change and opt for those parties with the strongest reputation for sound

---

[1] *The Economist*, 'Is Sarkozy a Closet Socialist?' (13 Nov. 2008).

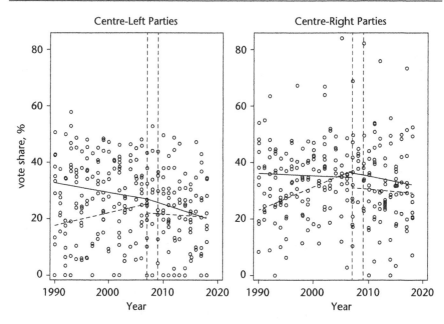

Figure 7.1. Vote % for Centre-Left and Centre-Right Parties

Note: Each dot indicates country-election. Vertical axes indicate vote %s for centre-left (left-hand side) and centre-right (right-hand side) parties in national elections in thirty-four OECD countries. Solid lines are fitted values for established democracies; dashed lines for new democracies. Vertical lines mark the general beginning and end of GFC.

Source: various, calculated by authors from national election results using CMP party families.

economic management? Such an issue ownership account would suggest that parties on the centre-right would best weather the crisis since, in most countries, publics rate these conservative or Christian democratic parties as most competent options on matters of the economy.

Figure 7.1 displays vote shares for centre-left and centre-right parties in national elections held across thirty-four countries from 1990 to 2018.[2] The graph on the left confirms the well-known trend of decline in support for left-of-centre parties across the older established democracies (solid fitted line). Further, rather than turning to the left in times of economic malaise, the downward trajectory continued apace during and after the crisis and recovery

---

[2] Parties are classified using party family designations provided by the Comparative Manifesto Project (Volkens et al. 2015) such that centre-left are social democratic parties (party family code 30) and centre-right combine Christian democratic and conservative parties (codes 50 and 60). Countries included are Australia, Austria, Belgium, Canada, Chile, Czech Republic, Denmark, Estonia, Finland, France, Germany, Greece, Hungary, Iceland, Ireland, Israel, Italy, Japan, South Korea, Latvia, Luxembourg, Mexico, the Netherlands, New Zealand, Norway, Poland, Portugal, Slovakia, Slovenia, Spain, Sweden, Switzerland, the UK, and the USA.

years. Parties on the right of centre, in contrast, generally held fast to their levels of electoral support during and after the crisis, although volatility is greater among newer democracies (dashed line). Interestingly, it appears voters in new democracies turned away from both centre-left and right parties, hinting at their acceptance of anti-establishment parties.

Rather than shifting in left–right policy terms, voters may well have responded to the crisis by turning away from the traditional parties of government in favour of heretofore untested challenger parties. One recent study reports a modest but steady increase in vote shares for populist parties in thirty-two Western democracies, from an average of less than 10 per cent of the vote during the 1990s to 12.4 per cent over the 2000s (Norris and Inglehart 2019).[3] Could economic crisis account for this increase? To see, we examine voter shares separately for mainstream parties and for challenger parties. Following previous research (Spoon and Klüver forthcoming), we define mainstream parties as those belonging to the Christian democrat, conservative, social democrat/socialist, or liberal party families. Challenger parties are diverse in their policy appeals, and include communist, agrarian, green, nationalist, ethnic, and special interest party families.[4] Hence we might associate any systematic differences between the mainstream and challenger groupings less to specific policy appeals (particularly with respect to the left–right economic divide) and more to a protest vote against parties who have long participated in national governments. Figure 7.2 plots support for mainstream and challenger groups. Trends hint at shifts in popular support around the time of the crisis. Prior to 2008 mainstream party strength was relatively stable; suggesting that any loss for certain mainstream parties was made up by others. After 2008, however, the trends suggest widespread mainstream party defection to challengers in old and new democracies alike.

These trends show that the GFC had a noticeable impact on voting behaviour, especially by leading to the decline in support for the centre-left and centre-right and increasing votes for challenger parties. Questions remain, however, whether policy efforts and political rhetoric can moderate the impact of the crisis. Can mainstream parties recover their support with policies that mitigate economic precariousness or through policy pledges that signal parties' concern with citizens' well-being? Informed by the theoretical framework developed in Chapter 1, we next examine the direct and conditional effects of the GFC on party success at the macro- and micro-levels. We first assess the direct impact of the GFC on vote choices. We further examine how stimulus and

---

[3] Norris and Inglehart (2019) classify parties in thirty-two European countries as populist. Parties include authoritarian and libertarian populist types.
[4] We again rely onto the CMP party family classifications to place parties into these party family groupings.

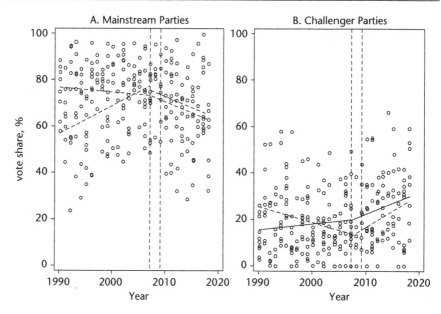

Figure 7.2. Vote % for Mainstream and Challenger Parties

Note: Each dot indicates country-election. Vertical axes indicate vote %s for mainstream (left-hand side) and challenger (right-hand side) parties in national elections in thirty-four OECD countries. Solid lines are fitted values for established democracies; dashed lines for new democracies. Vertical lines mark the general beginning and end of GFC.

Source: Various, calculated by authors from national election results using CMP party families.

discretionary spending as well as pro-welfare rhetoric conditions the GFC's impact on party choice before, during, and after the shock. As we showed in Chapter 6, the effects of these macro-level contexts on voting behaviour are likely to vary by states of crisis development as well as by the economic performance of a country.

7.3. The Economic Crisis and Party Support: Multivariate Analysis

The figures above point to changes in support for different party types over time. The crisis events of 2008–9 appear to be key events in the shift in party loyalties across the OECD. There is evidence in support of a 'crisis effect' on party choice, and one that goes beyond any pre-existing decline in support for traditional parties on the centre-left and centre-right (see Figure 7.2). We might interpret this as evidence that party policies had little bearing on their success in elections before, during, and after the GFC—a view consistent with both the cleavage politics story discussed in Chapter 1 and with the 'blind retrospection' argument described in Chapter 6. Does this mean that the factors driving party choice have changed? Does the set of factors driving party choice differ after the GFC hit compared to what mattered previously? Addressing these questions is key if we are to understand how voters decide in a post-crisis environment. We first re-examine the aggregate party vote shares before turning to more fine-grained analyses of individual voter decisions using the merged survey data introduced in Chapter 5.

7.3.1. Analyses of Aggregate Vote Shares

This section reports results of regressing the vote shares for centre-left, centre-right, mainstream, and challenger party groups (all defined as above) on a set of economic and structural factors. The data are from national elections for choosing the head of government in these thirty-four countries from 1989 to 2016. This gives us 120 elections before the GFC and ninety-eight after. To assess differences in the effects of covariates before and after the crisis, we stratify the sample into pre-crisis and post-crisis elections. Variables include the percentage change in GDP per capita since the previous election, our policy variables, *Austerity* and *Relative redistribution*, and the (logged) level of government debt (natural log). We also control for the electoral system, constitutional design (presidential or not), and age of democracy. Models are estimated using OLS and with standard errors clustered by country with lagged dependent variables on the right-hand side to control for parties' historic levels of support.[5]

Estimates, which appear in Table 7.1, uncover some notable differences contributing to party support pre- versus post-crisis. Parties to the left of centre tend to be adversely affected by strong economies. After (but not before) the crisis, left support suffered in the face of rising debt and, especially, in response to fiscal austerity policies. As we saw in Chapter 5, rising debt also leads to lower turnout, and more so among groups traditionally disposed to the left. This suggests that social democrats were more likely to be hurt than helped by the downturn. Yet if there is little aggregate-level support for a post-crisis turn to the left, there also is scant evidence of a rightward shift. Votes for centre-right parties were unswayed by policy factors. Neither debt nor austerity drove down their support, though we do observe a positive influence of economic growth for right-leaning parties in the post-crisis elections. The right also benefited from operating in more residual welfare states, as shown by the negatively signed coefficient on *Relative redistribution*. These findings are consistent with research indicating that the effects of the GFC and sovereign debt

---

[5] Estimates using seemingly unrelated regression are qualitatively identical to those reported here.

Table 7.1. Modelling Vote Percentages for Party Groups, Pre- and Post-GFC

	Centre-Left		Centre-Right		Mainstream		Challenger	
	Pre	Post	Pre	Post	Pre	Post	Pre	Post
	(1A)	(1B)	(2A)	(2B)	(3A)	(3B)	(4A)	(4B)
ΔGDP per capita	-0.154**	0.072	-0.016	0.288**	-0.242	0.159	0.043	-0.155
	(0.075)	(0.143)	(0.145)	(0.111)	(0.184)	(0.204)	(0.136)	(0.132)
Austerity	-0.438*	-0.848**	-0.250	-0.483	-0.185	-0.820**	0.170	0.460**
	(0.234)	(0.388)	(0.358)	(0.398)	(0.253)	(0.354)	(0.207)	(0.218)
Relative redistribution	0.149	0.158	-0.035	-0.393**	0.156*	-0.050	-0.144*	0.182
	(0.094)	(0.114)	(0.137)	(0.151)	(0.090)	(0.153)	(0.086)	(0.125)
(Ln) Government debt	-2.127	-4.312***	-0.755	-1.812	-1.100	-4.776**	0.996	2.958**
	(1.366)	(1.265)	(1.576)	(1.988)	(0.966)	(1.845)	(0.957)	(1.117)
New democracy	-4.896*	-3.309*	-2.350	-8.132***	0.915	-4.837***	-1.436	3.898*
	(2.962)	(1.871)	(4.047)	(2.672)	(2.688)	(2.215)	(2.192)	(2.133)
PR system	-4.798	-0.744	-2.342	0.621	-5.529***	-0.032	6.009***	0.006
	(2.975)	(2.495)	(2.277)	(1.956)	(1.744)	(2.508)	(1.634)	(1.977)
President system	-1.458	9.084**	5.191	-4.962	0.491	2.417	1.469	1.317
	(3.305)	(4.395)	(3.837)	(3.968)	(2.088)	(5.485)	(2.159)	(3.746)
Lagged vote share	0.686***	0.694***	0.584***	0.627***	0.671***	0.747***	0.787***	0.895***
	(0.098)	(0.091)	(0.155)	(0.077)	(0.064)	(0.116)	(0.060)	(0.096)
Constant	15.862**	16.018***	19.446**	31.652***	27.663***	33.655***	2.023	-12.554**
	(7.339)	(5.002)	(9.529)	(10.400)	(7.450)	(11.118)	(4.721)	(6.126)
R^2	0.655	0.758	0.427	0.648	0.586	0.611	0.786	0.789
N	120	98	120	98	120	98	120	98

Note: Cells report coefficients from ordinary least squares regression with robust standard errors clustered by country in parentheses. ***$p < 0.01$, **$p < .0.05$, *$p < 0.1$, two tailed test.

crises on the choice among parties were, at most, modest (Bartels 2014; LeDuc and Pammett 2013; Margalit 2019; but see Hobolt and Tilley 2016). Indeed, to the extent that a party's identity as either centre-left or centre-right conveys information about its solutions for or management of economic crisis, then we might conclude that policy orientations mattered little to voters facing tough times.

A comparison of mainstream and challenger parties, displayed in the last four columns of Table 7.1, tells a different story. Before the crisis, vote shares for mainstream and challengers were unrelated to economic factors, with only institutional differences registering an effect.[6] But post-crisis, austerity policies and, especially, government debt figure strongly in the shift away from the mainstream and towards challengers.[7] The results indicate that it is not poor economic performance but how governments manage the crisis that moves voter support. Fiscal austerity and high government debt turn voters away from the mainstream parties, giving rise to anti-establishment parties. We return to this point in the individual-level analyses reported in the next section.

7.3.2. Analyses of Individual Party Choice

Analyses of aggregated vote shares data show how crisis policies shifted support for different policy packages, as conveyed by party groups. To better isolate the mass politics impact of elite policy and pronouncements before, during, and after the GFC, we leverage the pooled individual-level dataset of twenty-four OECD democracies from 1996 to 2017 included in Module 1 to 5 of the CSES (CSES 2017). As in the previous two chapters, we also incorporate six additional election studies to cover missing cases in the CSES data. The detailed list of countries and years included in the analysis can be found in the appendix for Chapter 2.

The choice of dependent variable requires us to examine support for political party types across diverse party systems. Analyses of popular support cross-nationally have addressed this issue in different ways. Studies of party support across European democracies—typically employing survey data from the European Social Survey or European Election Study programmes—tend to gather parties into four (e.g. Rovny and Rovny 2017), five (e.g. Hobolt and Tilley 2016; Rommel and Walter 2017), or six (Häusermann and Kriesi 2015) groups. The inclusion of non-European OECD members in our CSES-based

---

[6] Specifically, proportional electoral rules reduce mainstream party support by nearly 6 per cent while increasing support for challengers at an equal amount.

[7] We also isolated those parties on the far right by omitting the centrist agrarian and typically left-leaning green parties from the challenger group. Analyses of this more ideologically homogeneous set of parties were no different from what we report for challengers in general.

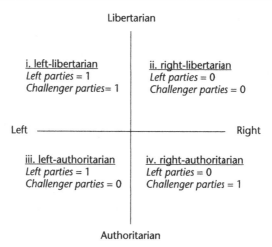

Figure 7.3. Linking *Left parties* and *Challenger parties* Variables to Two-Dimensional Space of Political Competition in Advanced Economies

sample amplifies differences across nations. Given these considerations, and informed by the macro-level analyses above, we examine how the crisis influenced voting for two broad party groupings: *Left parties* and *Challenger parties*. *Left parties* is scored 1 for parties belonging to social democratic, communist, and green party families, as per CMP classifications, and 0 for liberal, Christian democratic, conservative, agrarian, nationalist, ethnic, and special interest parties. *Challenger parties* is scored 1 for communist, agrarian, green, nationalist, ethnic, and special interest party families and 0 for members of social democratic, liberal, Christian democratic, and conservative parties.[8] Non-voters, our concern in Chapter 5, are excluded from the analysis.[9]

The strategy of collapsing heterogeneous party systems into a pair of dichotomous indicators with overlapping membership allows us to capture the broad contours of the two key policy divisions characterizing most advanced capitalist democracies. Figure 7.3 provides a schematic representation of the expected positions of different party groups in terms of two dimensions of contestation. The horizontal axis pertains to the economic divide, with parties favouring redistribution, social spending, and government intervention on the left and parties championing free markets and deregulation to the right. The vertical dimension captures the cultural divide. Students of party systems have assigned a wide range of labels to this 'second dimension' of party

---

[8] Three of our country cases, Chile, South Korea, and the USA, did not have any non-trivial challenger parties and accordingly are dropped from the analyses.

[9] We replicate our baseline specifications from Table 7.2 including non-voters and report results in Table A7.1 in the chapter appendix.

competition. These include cosmopolitan-authoritarian (Norris and Inglehart 2019), green-alternative-libertarian—traditional-authoritarian-nationalist, or GAL-TAN (Marks et al. 2002), and integration-demarcation (Kriesi et al. 2008). Generally speaking, however, this cross-cutting cultural divide encompasses positions on a wide range of issues pertaining to culturally liberal or universalist values on the one end to the opposing defence of traditional (or authoritarian) values and forms of society. The intersection of the two dimensions produces four ideological types: (i) left-libertarian, (ii) right-libertarian, (iii) left-authoritarian, and (iv) right-authoritarian.

Explanatory variables are similar to those in the previous two chapters. We again analyze two periods: the *shock* (2008–9) and *recovery* periods (2010 and onward). In order to measure economic performance, we use percentage change in GDP per capita since the previous election as before. We again include *Austerity*, or the cyclically adjusted fiscal balance as a percentage of GDP, *Relative redistribution*, or the reduction in inequality (Gini) after taxes and transfers (Solt 2019), as measures of policy effort. As a measure of elite cues, we follow previous chapters by employing party statements on welfare concerns. *Party welfare cues* averages the election platform measures across all parties in the election included in *Left parties* or *Challenger parties*. Finally, controls include *New democracy*, *Government debt*, *Market outsider*, *Female*, *Age* (as the natural log), *Education*, and *Household income*, all as previously described.

7.3.3. Analysis

Since our data are structured such that individuals are nested within countries, we estimate models using hierarchical logistic regression with random intercepts for each survey and with country-level fixed effects (see discussion in Chapters 5 and 6). Table 7.2 reports results of our baseline specifications, examining the influence of economic and political factors on left versus right parties (Model 1) and challenger versus mainstream party support (Model 2). Estimates reported in the top two rows point to some evidence of period effects. Coefficients reported in the first column suggest voters were less apt to select the left after the crisis relative to the pre-crisis elections. Policies of austerity were disadvantageous for the left. Model 2 results hint that the gains were reaped not by the centre-right but by parties challenging politics as usual, as indicated by positively signed coefficients on both period indicators. That said, estimates reported in these baseline specifications provide little support for strong period-related effects. Rather, the message from these baseline specifications is consistent with existing research pointing to weak and/or transitory effects of economic decline on party choice.

Table 7.2. Baseline Models for Voting for Left-of-Centre and Challenger Parties

	(1)	(2)	(1)	(2)
	Left vs.	Challenger vs.	Left vs.	Challenger vs.
	Right	Mainstream	Right	Mainstream
Shock period	0.017	0.251	0.139	0.069
	(0.237)	(0.257)	0.256	0.271
Recovery period	−0.356*	0.063	−0.226	0.169
	(0.191)	(0.195)	0.206	0.204
ΔGDP per capita	−0.002	−0.000	−0.014	−0.015
	(0.011)	(0.013)	0.012	0.013
Austerity	−0.074*	−0.038	−0.082	−0.024
	(0.040)	(0.036)	0.044	0.037
Relative redistribution	0.021	0.014	−0.039	−0.025
	(0.065)	(0.069)	0.070	0.071
Party welfare cues	1.328	0.678	1.230	−1.658
	(1.439)	(1.706)	1.698	1.951
(Ln) Government debt	−0.017	0.033	−0.012	−0.135
	(0.304)	(0.313)	0.313	0.319
Female	0.105***	−0.113***	0.125***	−0.102***
	(0.012)	(0.016)	0.013	0.017
(Ln) Age	−0.073***	−0.442***	−0.097***	−0.437***
	(0.016)	(0.021)	0.018	0.022
Education	0.063***	0.050***	0.092***	0.047***
	(0.006)	(0.008)	0.007	0.009
Household income	−0.064***	−0.089***	−0.069***	−0.088***
	(0.005)	(0.006)	0.005	0.006
Market outsider	0.139***	0.070***	0.142***	0.065**
	(0.017)	(0.022)	0.018	0.023
Working class			0.171***	0.034
			0.049	0.048
Shock period × Working class			−0.008	0.038
			0.121	0.131
Recovery period × Working class			−0.099	0.075
			0.088	0.086
Constant	−0.626	−0.636	−0.626	−0.636
	(1.979)	(2.093)	(1.979)	(2.093)
Variance (intercept)	0.442***	0.347***	0.425***	0.316***
	(0.074)	(0.064)	0.077	0.061
Variance (Working class)			0.101***	0.068***
			0.020	0.017
Chi-square	596.550***	681.280***	596.550***	732.361***
N countries	24	21	23	20
N country-surveys	102	84	90	77
N individuals	129,517	106,093	111,447	94,072

Note: For Model 1 the dependent variable is scored 1 for voting for a party on the left of centre and 0 for other parties, and for Model 2 it is scored 1 for voting for a challenger party and 0 for other parties. Non-voters omitted from the analysis. Cells display estimates from multilevel logit regression with random intercepts and slopes with standard errors in parentheses. Country fixed effects were also included.
***$p < 0.01$, **$p < 0.05$, *$p < 0.1$, two-tailed test.

If, at first blush, the crisis played little role in party choice across this sample, then where should we look to explain party choice? As discussed in our opening chapter, cleavage-based arguments tie party support not to short-term shocks but to more durable social divisions, and there is evidence that such alignments have been changing over time (Kitschelt and Rehm 2015). On this front, our models show those with higher incomes favouring the right and mainstream; market outsiders are more apt than insiders to vote for challengers and for parties on the left. While these findings are consistent with what we would expect, Models 1 and 2 do not assess whether the impact of cleavages—in this case, social class—differs across the pre-crisis, crisis, and post-crisis periods. Defined simply as the divide between those whose incomes come from non-manual or from manual labour, recent findings from the UK, Germany, and France show that vote choice for labour and social democratic parties no longer has any relation to this traditional class dimension (Dalton 2020, 163). While class voting in these terms (Alford 1962) has been in decline over the long term in most of the developed democracies, we test the possi- bility that the GFC has had the effect of 'launching the final blow'. We therefore re-estimate models conditioning the shock and recovery period indicators on a variable for social class, *Working class*, coded 1 for working class and 0 otherwise. Here we define working class are those who work in manual or 'blue collar' occupations, plus those who perform manual work in the service sector: principally in protective services, and restaurant and bar staff. Where respondents declared no occupation, that of their partners was used, if available.[10] Figure 7.4 uses model estimates to display the effect of class on party choice by way of marginal effects. But what about the crisis? The graph on the left shows that, on average, members of the working class remain marginally more likely to support parties on the left than those on the right. This effect weakens slightly but remains within confidence intervals during the shock and recovery periods. Figure 7.4B shows that social class, thus measured, has little impact on supporting challengers in all the three periods, although the movement, if any, is in the right direction. These results lend some support to claims that the GFC may have continued or even accelerated the reshaping of class-based voting. However, the effects are weak, confidence intervals overlap considerably and vary widely across our cases.[11]

---

[10] It should be acknowledged that CSES occupational data are of uneven quality, and significant numbers of country cases drop out because of missing data. Nor does the full IMD data base provide sufficient information for the use of the Oesch categories used in Chapter 4's Module 4-based analysis.

[11] These findings are slightly stronger if one removes income from the model. We assessed the effect of other proxies for class, including income and education, but none exerted statistically significant differences across our periods.

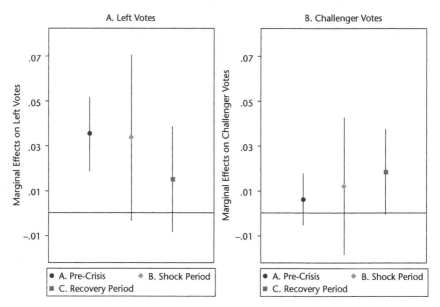

Figure 7.4. Marginal Effects of Being a Manual Worker on the Probability of Voting Left-Wing or Challenger Parties

Note: The graphs report the marginal effect (first difference) of voting for a left party (graph A) or challenger party (graph b) with 90% CIs produced from estimates in Models 3 and 4 in Table 7.2.

To identify shifts in party support over the crisis years, we follow the theoretical framework advanced in this book and examine the conditional effects of party policies and rhetoric (i.e. Figure 1.6). The baseline effects examined in Table 7.2 gloss over differences in how politics and economics jointly shape voting behaviour, and whether the effects vary over time. We therefore examine the effects of variables of interest on party support before, during, and after the GFC. For each dependent variable we first condition coefficients on ΔGDP per capita by GFC Shock and Recovery. We then further condition parameter effects with interactions with *Austerity*, *Relative redistribution*, and *Party welfare cues*. To facilitate substantive interpretation, we examine predicted vote choice probabilities via post-estimation calculations. Interested readers may consult parameter estimates provided in the chapter appendix.

How did the performance of the economy influence the voters' choices? Did the impact of economic conditions on the vote function differently before, during, after the GFC? The previous chapter showed, as theories of retrospective voting would predict, that voters are more likely to support political incumbents when the economy has improved. This connection, however, varied systematically over the three periods considered here: it was modest in elections before and during the crisis period, and then strongest during the

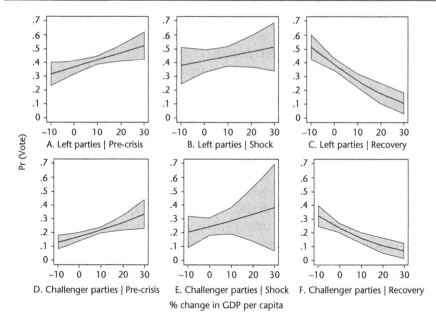

Figure 7.5. Predicted Vote Probabilities for Left vs Right and Challenger vs Mainstream Parties across % Change GDP Per Capita

Note: Graphs A, B, and C are based on Table A7.2 Model 1. Graphs D, E, and F are based on Table A7.3 Model 1. Grey areas indicate 90% confidence intervals.

recovery. Do we observe similar shifts in the salience of economic conditions with respect to party choice? To answer this question, Figure 7.5 displays predicted probabilities of voting for a left party versus a right party (top row, graphs A, B, and C) and for a challenger versus a mainstream party (bottom row, graphs D, E, F) for elections occurring before, during, and after the GFC.

Graphs reveal considerable heterogeneity across periods. For elections prior to the onset of the financial crisis, the direct effects of the economy are modest but meaningful. Per capita growth increases support for both left and challenger parties in elections between 1996 and 2007 in growing economies. This positive impact continues during the crisis years, though the certainty of the estimates declines owing to fewer data points. With respect to support for the left, this relationship may reflect the pro-cyclical relationship between economic performance and support for more expansionary social policies (Durr 1993): if times are good, a vote for the left is warranted; but if the economy suffers, voters opt for the parties believed to be more competent managers (e.g. Lindvall 2017). With respect to challenger parties, this association might reflect a greater capacity of voters to take a risk on a non-proven option which appeals on non-economic grounds.

The recovery is different. The steep downward slope in Figure 7.5C shows that in poorly performing economies left parties fared well, about as expected compared to earlier periods (7.5A and B). However, for those economies that successfully rebounded from the crisis, support for the left declined. For instance, Ireland's strong recovery was associated with a precipitous fall in support for the Labour Party, which saw its vote share decline from nearly 20 per cent in the 2011 election to less than 7 per cent in 2016. Or consider Poland, where a strong recovery contributed to the country's rightward shift between 2011 and 2015, with losses for the centrist Civic Platform being matched by gains to the right-wing Law and Justice Party. Voter support for political challengers also increased in stagnating economies during the post-crisis period. The difference in the correlates of support for challengers across time periods is telling: prior to the GFC, an improving economy aided these non-mainstream, or 'niche' parties. But after the crisis set in, challenger party appeal increased as voters sought answers for the economic malaise that the traditional 'mainstream' parties could not deliver. It is during this period, from 2010 onward, that we see upstart parties making gains in polities with slow-to-recover economies. This includes most notably SYRIZA and Golden Dawn in Greece and Podemos in Spain. In addition to these two Mediterranean cases, the rise of the True Finns in the 2011 Finnish election and of the Freedom Party in the 2015 Dutch election are also consistent with our findings that challengers fared well in economies, like those of Finland and the Netherlands, with anaemic post-crisis performance (see Figure 2.4).

In sum, by examining how the influence of election-to-election economic change differs over different periods, we find that the crisis did reshape voter considerations by moving away from centre-right parties to take a chance on the left or, alternatively, unproven challengers. This effect, however, was more likely to be realized over time.

But what might parties do to make the best of hard times? Following our supply-side approach, we consider both policy response and policy rhetoric as possible intervening factors.[12] Figure 7.6 charts support for left and challenger parties and takes the short-term fiscal measures into account. Consider the prospects of lower than average growth, displayed in the graphs by the solid lines. As above, a poor economy helped the left and hurt the right in terms of voter support during elections in the post-crisis recovery period. Figure 7.6 shows, however, that the size of this 'tough times advantage' for the left was reduced in countries going through fiscal tightening, or austerity. Further,

---

[12] We also investigated the conditioning effects of automatic stabilizers (*Relative redistribution*) but found that these long-term policy orientations had little bearing on party choice within countries as estimated in our fixed effects modelling.

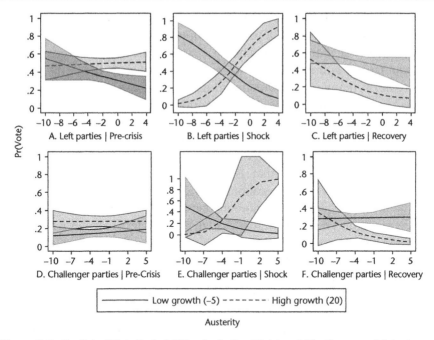

Figure 7.6. Predicted Vote Probabilities for Left vs Right and Challenger vs Mainstream Parties across Degrees of Austerity

Note: Graphs A, B, and C are based on Table A7.2 Model 2. Graphs D, E, and F are based on Table A7.3 Model 2. Horizontal axes report the range of in-sample values for *Austerity*. Solid lines report predicted probability of voting for the party when ΔGDP/capita is low (−5%); dashed lines report predicted probability of voting for the party when ΔGDP/capita is high (+20%). Shaded areas display 90% confidence intervals.

this effect not only characterized the recovery period (Figure 7.6C) but also the pre-crisis and, especially, shock years (Figure 7.6A and B). The neo-liberal response to tighten discretionary spending during a downturn hurts the left's chances in future elections. We also find that austerity, in and of itself, did little to bolster the probability of selecting challenger parties.[13] Collectively, findings with respect to short-term fiscal levers demonstrate how austerity can be used by parties on the centre-right to shore up support. Examples of resilient centre-right parties adopting this strategy include New Democracy in Greece in 2012, the German Christian Democrats in 2013, and the British Conservatives in 2015.

---

[13] A partial exception is the (rare) case where austerity was paired with a rebounding economy during the shock period (Figure 7.6E). The lack of data on challenger party support during this time frame means we must take these results as suggestive rather than definitive.

Next, we examine whether the messages parties convey during election campaigns sway voter decisions. In elections leading up to and during the GFC, voters were more likely to choose a party on the left when the economy was doing well and more likely to opt for an option to the right-of-centre when the economy was underperforming, all else equal (Figure 7.5). And with respect to mainstream versus challenger options, a robust economy aided the latter while perilous performance increased the probability of choosing a mainstream option. One explanation for these results is that voters acted in pro-cyclical terms. When things were going well, they supported parties on the left and challengers—that is, those parties who might expand the welfare state. But when the economy slowed down, the median voter opted for the more competent and more market-friendly orientation of parties on the centre-right. The crisis led to a change in the voter's calculus wherein the left fared better in poor economies.

But just as Chapter 6 showed how a consideration of elite cues provided the scope conditions under which the economic voter operates, we find here that the influence of economic conditions on party choice in general is dependent on elite messages. Figure 7.7 reports results in terms of predicted probabilities as pro-welfare cues range from weak to strong along the x-axes. When the economy was doing well, left parties improved their electoral chances by signalling their support for more generous welfare protections. But in poorly performing environments, such signals had the opposite effect. In struggling economies it instead is the case that the more the left talks up welfare protections, the less likely they are to receive the voter's support (Figures 7.7A and 7.7B). This result underlines the pro-cyclical argument that voters are more amenable to the left, and to its pro-welfare messages, in good times. But as we saw in Figure 7.3, this calculus reverses during the recovery and the left and challengers hold an advantage in poor times as more and more people opt for policy relief despite possible tax increases or—more likely—higher deficits. And Figures 7.7C and 7.7F reveal that 'bad times' effect is augmented when these parties signal a willingness to discuss expansionary social policies.

Made possible by the breadth of post-election surveys assembled by the CSES, these analyses show how the crisis and the supply-side reactions during different time periods combine to influence voters' decisions. The resulting picture is complex and, given the many electoral contexts included in our sample, varies in ways we are unable to capture. Nonetheless, by considering the factors shaping electoral choice across both of these divides we can approximate the voter's decision to select one of four party groups, corresponding roughly to the four quadrants in the two-dimensional Figure 7.3: mainstream left (iii), mainstream right (ii), challenger left (i), challenger right (iv). For instance, if the parameter estimate for a given

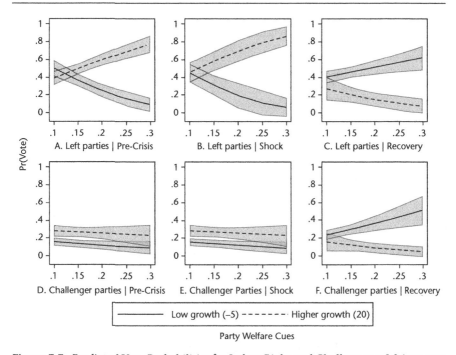

Figure 7.7. Predicted Vote Probabilities for Left vs Right and Challenger vs Mainstream Parties across Degrees of Party Welfare Cues

Note: Graphs A, B, and C are based on Table A7.2 Model 4. Graphs D, E, and F are based on Table A7.3 Model 4. Horizontal axes report the range of in-sample values for Party welfare cues. Solid lines report predicted probability of voting for the party when ΔGDP/capita is low (−5%); dashed lines report predicted probability of voting for the party when ΔGDP/capita is high (+20%). Shaded areas display 90% confidence intervals.

covariate carries a positive sign in a model of *Left parties* but negative for a model of *Challenger parties* (see e.g. *Female* in Table 7.2), then we may infer that its overall impact increases the probability of voting for a mainstream (non-challenger) left parties and decreases the probability of choosing a challenger party on the right.

Proceeding thus, we summarize the effects of a range of different conditions on party choice in Table 7.3. These summaries reported in table cells yield three main conclusions:

1. 'Supply-side' factors—policy responses and policy rhetoric—shape how the crisis is reflected in voter choices for different party types.

2. The influence of these factors varies with time. Government decisions to adopt austerity proved harmful for the support for the mainstream left. This effect, however, was strongest initially, during the shock period, and then weakened during the recovery years. The temporal effects of

Table 7.3. The Great Recession and Party Vote: Who Wins? Who Loses?

Condition	Pre-Crisis Period	Shock Period	Recovery Period
% change GDP per capita	Strong economy benefits left challengers; Poor economy benefits mainstream right	Economy has no effect	Strong economy benefits mainstream right, costs left and challengers
Austerity	Austerity in poor economy costs mainstream left and benefits mainstream right	Austerity in poor economy hurts left; helps right	Austerity harms vote for left, especially during robust recoveries
Stimulus	Stimulus in poor economy helps mainstream left and hurts mainstream right	Stimulus in poor economy helps left; hurts right	Weak evidence that stimulus helps left
Pro-welfare message	Benefits left during good times; helps mainstream right during bad times	Benefits left during good times; helps mainstream right during bad times	Helps left and challengers during bad times

Note: Cells report authors' summary of influence of conditions labelled in first column on the choice to vote for different party types (left or right, mainstream or challenger) during the pre-crisis, shock, and recovery periods.

rhetoric are even starker: in bad times, touting pro-welfare messages initially played into the hands of the mainstream right, as voters sought stability, but then shifted to favour the left during the recovery.

3. While the crisis helped challengers overall, the conditioning effects of supply-side factors matter more for left versus right decisions than for mainstream versus challengers. Longer term trends displayed in Figures 7.1 and 7.2 provide the headline stories that the crisis contributed to the rise of challenger parties and weakening of the political mainstream—trends which continued during the recovery years. But elite cues provide an important nuance which has received little attention. A consideration of policy change and policy rhetoric illustrates how parties on the left and right could improve their chances with voters despite external shocks.

7.4. Conclusion

Economic downturns have the power to shift voter choices and reshape party systems. Such was the case after the First World War. The stock market crash of 1929 and ensuing Great Depression helped remake national party systems in the Western democracies. Voters turned away from the extremism of the interwar years in favour of building cross-class alliances in support of the rebuilding effort through a centrist pragmatism. Relatedly, the wake of the

Great Depression was a breakthrough for liberal and social democratic parties which pledged to use the market for socially equitable purposes. Today, in the first quarter of the twenty-first century, things are different. One of the more puzzling outcomes of the Great Recession was the modesty of its imprint on voter choices and party systems. Despite the enormity of the crisis, the conventional wisdom is that the crisis did very little to change how citizens evaluate their choices at the polls.

An objective of this book is to push against this received wisdom. Theoretically, we are informed by a supply-side perspective which grants political elites a high degree of agency to shape public perceptions and choices. Empirically, our inquiry benefits from the accumulation of data on elections, parties, and voters before, during, and after the GFC. As a result, we find that the unprecedented economic decline did shape electoral choices in terms of left versus right and mainstream versus challenger. Uncovering these effects, however, requires us to take both temporal and supply-side factors into account. Regarding time, we engage with debates about whether economic downturns 'swing' voters to the right or the left. Lindvall (2014, 2017) shows that initially downturns push voters toward parties on the centre-right. With time, however, recessions lead to gains for the left. The reason for such dynamics, according to Lindvall, stems from how the duration of the recession affects groups in society. Short downturns tend to affect only marginal groups. The median voter in advanced societies accordingly embraces parties on the right out of concerns that a vote for the left will result in higher taxes and greater redistribution towards marginal groups. However, with time the effects of a stagnant economy are felt by larger and larger shares of society. Concerns about taxes pale in comparison to calls for improved social protections.

In line with Lindvall, our analyses of elections during the Great Recession years of 2008–16 show that support for the left increases in poorly performing economies during the aftermath of the crisis (i.e. the recovery period). We also find some evidence showing that the right gains immediately following the shock. However, as shown in Figure 7.3B, evidence supporting this 'swing-to-the-right' hypothesis is contingent on a policy of fiscal tightening, or austerity. By considering policy efforts like fiscal austerity/stimulus as well as the rhetoric of competing parties, findings from this chapter support a general argument that mass responses to the Great Recession were structured by political elites. The next chapter extracts our key take-aways and explores the broader meaning for support for democratic politics.

Appendix

Table 7.A1. Replication of Table 7.2 with Non-Voters Included

	(1)	(2)
	Left vs.Right	Challenger vs. Mainstream
Shock period	−0.015	0.202
	(0.226)	(0.246)
Recovery period	−0.362**	0.040
	(0.182)	(0.185)
ΔGDP per capita	−0.004	−0.003
	(0.011)	(0.012)
Austerity	−0.079**	−0.047
	(0.038)	(0.034)
Relative redistribution	0.007	0.008
	(0.062)	(0.066)
Party welfare cues	1.025	0.716
	(1.367)	(1.624)
(Ln) Government debt	−0.036	−0.045
	(0.288)	(0.313)
Female	0.094***	−0.109***
	(0.011)	(0.016)
(Ln) Age	0.192***	−0.168***
	(0.015)	(0.020)
Education	0.107***	0.107***
	(0.006)	(0.008)
Household income	−0.021***	−0.045***
	(0.004)	(0.006)
Market outsider	0.081***	0.034*
	(0.015)	(0.021)
Constant	−1.379	−1.543
	(1.879)	(1.994)
Variance(intercept)	0.398***	0.347***
	(0.067)	(0.064)
Chi-square	679.580***	439.510***
N country-surveys	102	84
N individuals	151,333	123,966

Note: For Model 1 the dependent variable is scored 1 for voting for a party on the left of centre and 0 otherwise, and for Model 2 it is scored 1 for voting for a challenger party and 0 otherwise. Cells display estimates from multilevel logit regression with random intercepts and country fixed effects with standard errors in parentheses. ***$p < 0.01$, **$p < 0.05$, *$p < 0.10$, two-tailed test.

Table 7.A2. Models of Vote for Left Parties

	(1)	(2)	(3)	(4)
Shock period	0.179	−0.187	−0.233	−0.091
	(0.291)	(0.421)	(1.094)	(0.695)
Recovery period	0.053	0.067	0.976	−1.571***
	(0.213)	(0.255)	(0.729)	(0.538)
ΔGDP per capita	0.025	0.039***	0.033	−0.114***
	(0.014)	(0.015)	(0.025)	(0.036)
Austerity	−0.063*	−0.093	−0.047	−0.064*
	(0.038)	(0.065)	(0.038)	(0.034)
Relative redistribution	0.036	0.088	0.007	0.061
	(0.063)	(0.060)	(0.064)	(0.060)
Party welfare cues	1.130	1.019	1.188	−8.314***
	(1.358)	(1.287)	(1.340)	(2.821)
(Ln) Government debt	0.026	−0.286	−0.015	0.144
	(0.286)	(0.289)	(0.297)	(0.270)
Female	0.105***	0.105***	0.105***	0.105***
	(0.012)	(0.012)	(0.012)	(0.012)
(Ln) Age	−0.073***	−0.073***	−0.073***	−0.073***
	(0.016)	(0.016)	(0.016)	(0.016)
Education	0.064***	0.064***	0.064***	0.064***
	(0.006)	(0.006)	(0.006)	(0.006)
Household income	−0.064***	−0.065***	−0.065***	−0.064***
	(0.005)	(0.005)	(0.005)	(0.005)
Market outsider	0.139***	0.139***	0.139***	0.139***
	(0.017)	(0.017)	(0.017)	(0.017)
GFC shock × ΔGDP/capita	−0.008	0.056*	0.022	0.010
	(0.023)	(0.031)	(0.055)	(0.045)
Recovery × ΔGDP/capita	−0.086***	−0.130***	−0.057	0.140*
	(0.021)	(0.037)	(0.058)	(0.059)
GFC shock × Austerity		−0.066		
		(0.096)		
ΔGDP/capita × Austerity		0.005		
		(0.004)		
GFC shock × ΔGDP/capita × Austerity		0.029***		
		(0.010)		
Recovery × Austerity		−0.017		
		(0.071)		
Recovery × Austerity		−0.015*		
		(0.008)		
GFC shock × Redistribution			0.012	
			(0.031)	
ΔGDP/capita × Redistribution			−0.001	
			(0.001)	
GFC shock × ΔGDP/capita × Redistribution			−0.001	
			(0.002)	
Recovery × Redistribution			−0.027	
			(0.020)	
Recovery × ΔGDP/capita × Redistribution			−0.001	
			(0.002)	
GFC shock × Welfare cues				−0.430
				(5.332)
ΔGDP/capita × Welfare cues				0.922***
				(0.226)
GFC shock × ΔGDP/capita × Party cues				0.128
				(0.315)

(continued)

Table 7.A2. Continued

	(1)	(2)	(3)	(4)
Recovery × Welfare cues				10.793***
				(3.265)
Recovery × ΔGDP/capita × Welfare cues				−1.463***
				(0.364)
Constant	−1.438	−2.286	−0.335	−1.172
	(1.937)	(1.852)	(1.977)	(1.795)
Variance(intercept)	0.388***	0.335***	0.368***	0.312***
	(0.064)	(0.055)	(0.060)	(0.050)
Chi-squared	622.171	649.111	628.394	658.467
N country-surveys	102	102	102	102
N individuals	129,517	129,517	129,517	129,517

Note: The dependent variable is scored 1 for voting for a challenger party and 0 for other parties. Non-voters omitted from the analysis. Cells display estimates from multilevel logit regression with random intercepts with standard errors in parentheses. ***$p < 0.01$, **$p < 0.05$, *$p < 0.1$, two-tailed test.

Table 7.A3. Models of Vote for Challenger Parties

	Model 1	Model 2	Model 3	Model 4
Shock period	0.520*	−0.061	0.036	0.545
	(0.284)	(0.552)	(1.964)	(0.558)
Recovery period	0.457**	0.328	−0.305	−0.458
	(0.216)	(0.280)	(1.285)	(0.395)
ΔGDP per capita	0.035**	0.032	−0.129	0.027
	(0.016)	(0.022)	(0.116)	(0.029)
Austerity	−0.020	0.033	0.010	−0.008
	(0.034)	(0.070)	(0.036)	(0.032)
Relative redistribution	0.020	0.053	−0.004	0.023
	(0.067)	(0.070)	(0.085)	(0.069)
Party welfare cues	−0.184	−0.156	−0.743	−3.267
	(1.649)	(1.688)	(1.800)	(2.364)
(Ln) Government debt	0.238	0.202	0.202	0.087
	(0.306)	(0.313)	(0.314)	(0.294)
Female	−0.113***	−0.113***	−0.113***	−0.113***
	(0.016)	(0.016)	(0.016)	(0.016)
(Ln) Age	−0.442***	−0.442***	−0.442***	−0.442***
	(0.021)	(0.021)	(0.021)	(0.021)
Education	0.050***	0.051***	0.051***	0.050***
	(0.008)	(0.008)	(0.008)	(0.008)
Household income	−0.089***	−0.089***	−0.089***	−0.089***
	(0.006)	(0.006)	(0.006)	(0.006)
Market outsider	0.070***	0.070***	0.070***	0.070***
	(0.022)	(0.022)	(0.022)	(0.022)
GFC shock × ΔGDP/capita	−0.009	0.146	−0.236	−0.074
	(0.037)	(0.181)	(0.369)	(0.121)
Recovery × ΔGDP/capita	−0.086***	−0.118***	0.229	0.007
	(0.023)	(0.037)	(0.214)	(0.054)
GFC shock × Austerity		−0.107		
		(0.100)		
ΔGDP/capita × Austerity		−0.002		
		(0.004)		
GFC shock × ΔGDP/capita × Austerity		0.042		
		(0.048)		

Recovery × Austerity	−0.077			
	(0.075)			
Recovery × ΔGDP/capita × Austerity	−0.009			
	(0.009)			
GFC shock × Redistribution		0.011		
		(0.052)		
ΔGDP/capita × Redistribution		0.004		
		(0.003)		
GFC shock × ΔGDP/capita × Redistribution		0.006		
		(0.009)		
Recovery × Redistribution		0.022		
		(0.034)		
Recovery × ΔGDP/capita × Redistribution		−0.008		
		(0.005)		
GFC shock × Welfare cues				−1.274
				(4.832)
ΔGDP/capita × Welfare cues				0.079
				(0.184)
GFC shock × ΔGDP/capita × Welfare cues				0.633
				(1.806)
Recovery × Welfare cues				7.544***
				(2.730)
Recovery × ΔGDP/capita × Welfare cues				−0.658**
				(0.328)
Constant	−1.523	−2.480	−0.511	−0.865
	(2.030)	(2.145)	(2.668)	(2.006)
Variance(intercept)	0.305***	0.295***	0.287***	0.262***
	(0.055)	(0.053)	(0.052)	0.047)
Chi-squared	822.677	828.541	833.700	849.770
N country-surveys	84	84	84	84
N individuals	106,093	106,093	106,093	106,093

Note: The dependent variable is scored 1 for voting for a challenger party and 0 for other parties. Non-voters omitted from the analysis. Cells display estimates from multilevel logit regression with random intercepts with standard errors in parentheses. ***$p < 0.01$, **$p < 0.05$, *$p < 0.1$, two-tailed test.

8

Mass Politics in a Post-Crisis World

Whither Democracy?

This book is motivated by a quest to understand whether and how economic crises affect how people understand politics, evaluate events, and act accordingly. It details how the largest economic slowdown in the industrialized economies since the 1930s influenced citizens and their elected representatives. How did 'the crisis', in its many forms, matter? And when did its mass political effects take hold? We address these questions by making a holistic consideration of mass politics. Previous monographs on the crisis and electorates either lack a comprehensive analysis—choosing to examine only parts of the landscape that comprise 'mass politics', lacking a consideration of the temporal dimension, or both. Perhaps not coincidentally, with some exceptions previous studies have concluded that mass politics during the crisis functioned more or less as we might expect. That is, the influence of economic factors on mass opinion and behaviour in 'crisis times' was not fundamentally different from 'normal times', only stronger.

A decade on, this book has revisited the question of popular responses to the economic crises. Advancing a supply-side or 'elite cues' approach, it highlights the influence of political parties and the governments they comprise on how mass public opinions and behaviour were influenced by the calamitous events between 2007 and 2010, and by their aftermath. Our examination of how the GFC and Great Recession affected citizen responses was made possible by a rich array of post-election surveys from countries around the OECD. Citizen responses include feelings of material insecurity, policy demands, political participation, economic voting and support for incumbents, external political efficacy, satisfaction with democracy, and the choice among party offerings. Our results paint a complex picture. In some cases, such as popular preferences for spending on health care, the depth and persistence of the crisis made little difference. For other outcomes, such as the impact of economic conditions on

Democracy Under Siege? Parties, Voters, and Elections After the Great Recession. Timothy Hellwig, Yesola Kweon, and Jack Vowles, Oxford University Press (2020). © Timothy Hellwig, Yesola Kweon, and Jack Vowles.
DOI: 10.1093/oso/9780198846208.001.0001

voting for the incumbent, the crisis served as an amplifier of already present dynamics. For many others, 'crisis effects' were indirect, filtered through austerity policies, debt levels, and political discourse. Furthermore, these interactive relationships vary in magnitude—and even direction—across the pre-crisis, crisis, and post-crisis periods. While the picture is complex, we have shown in this book that elections and party politics, and not market forces alone, contributed to the crisis impact.

In this final chapter we revisit our findings in three parts. We first consider how lessons from this book contribute to and challenge two research traditions in political science: the political economy of the welfare state and the study of electoral continuity and change. Second, we step back from day-to-day issues and election debates to consider the larger matter of the crisis and its impact on representative democracy. And third, we extract some lessons from the 1990s through the 2010s to speculate about the future of mass politics. To what extent does the period examined represent a departure from 'normal times'? And how do insights from this study help predict alternative paths for the years ahead?

8.1. The Welfare State, Electoral Change, and the Global Financial Crisis

As noted in Chapter 1, this book contributes to a line of research that combines insights from what grew up as two distinct areas of inquiry within the study of politics: the comparative political economy of the welfare state, on the one hand, and the study of electoral change in established democracies, on the other. This synthesis is reflected most clearly in our theoretical framework. As depicted in Figure 1.6, our scope of inquiry is laid out in two parts. The first posits a connection between a shock deemed external to the domestic political system—the global financial crisis—and then posits some effects on policymakers' actions and strategies. The second contends that these policy responses in turn condition how mass publics react to the crisis.

8.1.1. *Responding to External Shocks: Lessons for the Study of the Welfare State*

The comparative welfare state literature has long focused on how domestic and transnational factors come together to explain policy outcomes. For instance, contributors to Flora and Heidenheimer (1981) weighed the effects of different institutional and economic contexts to understand why the origins of policy precursors to the postwar welfare state vary starkly in timing and issue area across nations. Gourevitch (1984) showed how differences in social coalitions helped to explain why some governments countered the Great Depression with wide-ranging reforms while others did not. And Katzenstein (1978) and his collaborators systematically assessed how welfare states differed in their foreign policy responses to then-unforeseen shocks originating in global energy markets. This emphasis on how domestic factors mediate international shocks has continued apace.

Since the 1990s, the question of adapting to economic change has been at the heart of research on the political economy of the welfare state. Some argue that broad changes associated with post-industrial globally integrated national economies have left governments with little policy room to manoeuvre. This line of reasoning predicts a convergence of policy outcomes in an increasingly globalized world and, pushed to its limits, foretells a welfare state in crisis (e.g. Albrow 1997). Others build on earlier work on the welfare state and emphasize the influence of how interests are organized, the shape of public and private section connections, and the way political institutions create incentives for cooperation or competition as important mediators between structural economic change and policy outcomes (Beramendi et al. 2015; Iversen 2005; Iversen and Soskice 2015). Reality, of course, may lie between these perspectives, such that globalization's effects on outcomes are contingent on policy domain (e.g. Burgoon 2001).

The merits of each side of this debate notwithstanding, research on the political economy of the welfare state usually stops short of claiming to assess the behaviour of political parties or the views and behaviours of the electorate at large (cf. Häusermann et al. 2013). Yet a separate but related body of work on the mass politics of globalization cautions against drawing similar conclusions with respect to the effect of external shocks on parties and voters as one does for policy outcomes (Hellwig 2014; Vowles and Xezonakis 2016). By examining how an external shock—the global financial crisis and its aftermath—works through policy outcomes and party strategies to affect citizens, this book takes insights from welfare state scholarship and extends them into mass politics.

While the depth and especially the persistence of the economic downturn was certainly unwelcome, our results point to a silver lining: electoral politics matters. Our elite cues approach reveals that the crisis, as gauged by timing of elections and per capita growth rates, affected mass politics. These effects, however, were usually filtered through parties' policy and rhetorical responses. We find, for instance, that stimulus and discretionary spending can moderate the adverse impact of the crisis on subjective security and policy demands. This could be good news for weathering future crises because governments can enhance consumer confidence and keep national economies afloat. Needless to say, such optimism requires that governments are able to increase public spending. Continued high debt levels in many OECD members may limit opportunities for deficit spending. Rhetoric also works according to our story, particularly in cases of policy preferences (Chapter 4) and policy-based voting (Chapter 7), especially in the short term.

With respect to the actions and rhetoric of elites, our findings suggest that that while there may be little governments acting alone can do to avert future financial crises, they can take steps to blunt their adverse effects. Viewed through the lens of the welfare state, our findings suggest a renewed scope for government activity. To an extent, this conclusion is consistent with research on the welfare state going back at least as far as work by Cameron (1978), Ruggie (1982), and Katzenstein (1985) on the connections between world markets and domestic politics. As these and later studies (Garrett 1998; Swank 2002) argue, integration into world markets leads governments to erect social policy regimes to compensate those most affected by external competition. But more recent studies of how voters and their party representatives react to globalization, deindustrialization, and economic displacement in general paints a very different picture (Autor et al. 2016; Rommel and Walter 2017; for a review, see Hellwig forthcoming).

With the perspective provided by hindsight, a narrative has been constructed to make sense of the longer term political impact of the financial crisis of 2008–9. Today, the GFC is typically interpreted as a beginning point in a cascading set of events that gave rise to an anti-liberal, anti-democratic zeitgeist overtaking the West. The GFC and, especially, the sovereign debt crisis exposed raw divisions between the richer and poorer members of the European Union. As this reasoning continues, by 2015 the economic anxiety sparked by the crash in financial markets was amplified by cultural concerns about the rise of immigrants seeking refuge from civil war and violence in Syria and Afghanistan. Fears of a loss of economic and political control led to surprising outcomes of elections in 2016 and 2017, including Britain's decision to leave the EU and the election of anti-establishment and isolationist Donald Trump as President of the United States. More broadly, authoritarian populist and far-right politicians achieved newfound success. Examples are France and the Netherlands in 2017 and Italy and Sweden in 2018. The mass politics story suggests that citizens have disturbingly low faith in their elected representatives. And, to an extent, this is what our findings reveal. We show that the GFC contributed to feelings of economic anxiety, to voting against incumbents, greater support for challenger parties, and, as realized in terms of increasing public debt, to lower turnout and greater party system volatility.

On the other hand, we find no evidence that the GFC adversely affected public support for policy spending on health care and support for the unemployed either directly in terms of the size of the shock and indirectly channelled through feelings of insecurity. Publics also adjusted their behaviour in response to the crisis. For instance, while neo-liberal fiscal policies adversely affected political participation before the crisis, the relationship between austerity and turnout went away post-crisis. Ballooning public debt contributed to lower turnout levels throughout the time covered by our data. Even the most straightforward of expectations—that the crisis turned voters away from political incumbents and mainstream parties in general—received only partial support in our data. For incumbent support, government policies mattered. Fiscal stimulus and more encompassing redistributive policies blunted the adverse effects of economic decline for governing party survival. Mainstream parties fared better, even in prolonged economic recoveries, in contexts of fiscal expansion and when they championed the protective features of the welfare state.

Taken together, findings reported in this book provide a space for domestic political influence even in the face of external shocks the size of which had not been seen in a generation. We have taken a longer term perspective and considered the crisis's impact across a wider range of non-Eurozone, non-European cases in the OECD. Our analysis and case selection leads to a more optimistic set of findings with respect to government policy capacity than previous studies suggested (Bermeo and Bartels 2014; Beramendi et al. 2015).

8.1.2. *The Public Reacts: Lessons for the Study of Electoral Change*

With the passage of time, the tumultuous events of 2008 and 2009 recede into the past and enable us to better assess their electoral effects. We have the opportunity to weigh in on questions of electoral change. Did the GFC serve as catalyst for dealignment or realignment? Previous experiences of electoral change provide precedents. The 1930s set the scene for the New Deal realignment in the United States which led to a Democratic Party majority in Congress for decades to come. The New Deal realignment may be traced to the expansion and changing orientation of the electorate in terms of the entry of large numbers of blue-collar workers, Catholics, and African Americans in the Democratic Party coalition (Key 1959). Labour and social democratic parties became major and, in some cases, dominant parties in many other Western democracies following similar pathways. In the early decades of the twentieth century, expansion of the franchise interacted with growing social and occupational networks to create clear ties between constituencies in the electorate and political parties. In Western democracies, these voter–party alignments persisted for decades, as catalogued by Lipset and Rokkan's (1967) seminal work.

Social changes of the late 1960s gave rise to renewed consideration of electoral change as electoral volatility increased in many countries during 1970s, particularly in north-western Europe (Dalton et al. 1984, 10). A host of factors, but generally traced to rising affluence, labour force restructuring, urbanization, and greater educational attainment, drove a wedge between voter demands and elite responses. As Dalton et al. (1984, 8) asserted, 'A major factor in the destabilization of democratic party systems was the initial inability or unwillingness of the major established parties to respond fully to the new demands placed upon them.' Partisan dealignment and/or decay, as the case may be, continued apace in many post-industrial societies in the waning decades of the twentieth century, particularly with respect to the weakening of ties to social democratic and labour parties on the left. By century's turn, many scholars maintained that social divisions in Western democracies had evolved to such an extent that an alternative libertarian/authoritarian cleavage rivalled the importance of the left/right divide (Kitschelt 1994; Kriesi et al. 2008). Indeed, most new entrants to national party systems, or 'challenger parties', are defined far more by their position on this cultural divide than by their stance on taxes, spending, and the regulation of the market (see Figure 7.3). Between 1946 and the end of the 1970s, parties defined primarily in terms of positions along this cultural axis attained, on average, just over 5 per cent of the vote in national elections; since the 1980s that proportion has doubled in size (Norris and Inglehart 2019, 9).

Enter the GFC. As noted above, a narrative has emerged placing the GFC at the beginning of a 'wave' of developments washing over the Western democracies. This wave includes the refugee crisis, Brexit, and (re)assertion of national interests over what many see as the failed promise of postwar liberal institutionalism. But did the crisis trigger electoral change? To a certain extent, the answer is yes. We showed in Chapter 2 that electoral volatility has increased. Our analyses in Part II (Chapters 3 and 4) reveal that pressures of the crisis led to greater insecurity and a call for renewed policy responses, particularly for those most affected by the downturn. And analyses reported in Part III indicate that elites mattered in ways not apparent in recent history. For instance, in Chapter 5 we showed that the accumulation of public debt bore strongly on people's decision to participate or not in national elections. Much of the connection between debt and turnout ran through perceptions of government policy autonomy. While confirming previous research on the negative connection between economic decline and incumbent support, Chapter 6 showed that the degree to which macro-economic performance influences voters' punishment of incumbent government depends on governing parties' policy behaviour and rhetorical messages—and did so especially during the recovery period. The crisis also facilitated the turn away from the mainstream parties and towards political newcomers, as we show in Chapter 7. We also show that during the crisis and recovery period, the traditional pattern of manual/non-manual class voting may have further weakened and, indeed, it had disappeared in several countries by the end of our period.

Collectively, these findings suggest that over the last decade public political engagement has changed. Shifts in the foundations of electoral behaviour, however, are due less to a realignment of issue conflicts or changing voter priorities, as studies of previous party dealignments maintain (Key 1959; Dalton et al. 1984; Franklin et al. 1992). Instead they have much to do with the supply side. Our study thus adds to a small but growing body of work on mass politics in post-industrial society that emphasizes how electorally salient social divisions can be politically constructed (Elff 2009; Evans and Tilley 2017; Jansen et al. 2013). This line of research maintains that social cleavages are less resistant to change than typically believed. Party policies, politicians' rhetoric, and the social composition of political elites have changed, but the appeals parties make still garner voters' attention. As a gauge of electoral success, pragmatism often prevails over principle. As we suggested in Chapter 2, parties can champion different policies over time. Opportunities for veering from expectations *increase* following unanticipated exogenous shocks like the GFC. As a result, political elites have considerable agency to shape public perceptions and behaviour.

8.2. From More Specific to More Diffuse: The GFC and Satisfaction with Democracy

In focusing on public opinion and political behaviour, this book has been concerned with fundamental features of citizen politics in representative democracies. We also made a decision to emphasize those parts of mass politics which, we know from previous research, are most susceptible to influence by exogenous shocks. But this means we have left aside what some would argue is an even more basic requirement for an effective democracy: a general sense of acceptance with how the system works. On the one hand, we have reason to think that satisfaction with the basic functions of democracy in these OECD countries should be resistant to economic shocks, no matter how severe. After all, scholars have long voiced concern about the consistency and stability of popular support for democracy, particularly with respect to the capacity of democracy as an appropriate system of government in modern societies (Habermas 1973; Crozier et al. 1975; Pharr and Putnam 2000). Yet democracy has nonetheless continued to prevail in the countries of the developed world.

But as today's very real concerns with 'democratic backsliding' reveal, support for and satisfaction with democracy remain susceptible to erosion. Studies commonly find a connection between economic conditions and satisfaction with how democracy works (Clarke et al. 1993; Wike et al. 2019). With respect to the GFC, early research linking the crisis to satisfaction with democracy from four country cases found effects conditioned on timing and election outcomes (Tillman 2016). Other early research finds that, compared to the period 1996 to 2006, satisfaction with democracy dropped in a selection of countries at elections from 2007 to 2009 (Thomas 2016). Other work shows that economic perceptions mattered to satisfaction with national democracy during the economic crisis (Armingeon and Guthmann 2013). Consistently negative effects have been observed in the more adversely affected countries during the recovery period (Cordero and Simón 2016).

In light of these findings, we close this book with a look at relationship between the GFC and its aftermath and satisfaction with the workings of democracy. While a comprehensive analysis must be left for future research, we focus on extending our basic argument to look at system support. Do the findings we report with respect to the effect of economic crisis on feelings of security, support for political incumbents, and so on, extend to satisfaction with the democratic system in general?

We draw on the pooled individual-level data from the CSES modules 1–5 described in Chapter 2 as the CSES has asked this question consistently since the mid-1990s (see Thomas 2016).[1] While this satisfaction with democracy measure has been criticized for being vague with respect to the object of measurement (Canache et al. 2001), this survey item nonetheless provides a more diffuse indicator of system support than those pertaining to the government of the day.[2] This makes it informative relative to the more 'specific' outcomes, in the sense of Easton's (1965) framework, examined in previous chapters. Moreover, earlier work has shown the satisfaction with democracy item to be one of the key factors affecting people's normative commitment to democracy (Chu et al. 2008).

Following previous studies (e.g. Thomas 2016), responses are recoded into a dichotomous variable that captures citizens' satisfaction—those who are very satisfied and satisfied—and dissatisfaction—those who are dissatisfied and very dissatisfied—with democracy. Figure 8.1 reports country-level responses for elections included in our pooled dataset. We observe some evidence of a decline—in Australia, Canada, Chile, and especially Portugal and Ireland. Yet for just as many countries assessments of how well democracy works held steady from times previous or even increased.[3] This aggregate picture is thus edifying: despite mass demonstrations reported in the media, most people in most countries seemed to weather the crisis without it affecting their basic views on how well their democracy works. At the same time, the picture highlights

---

[1] The specific question wording is 'On the whole, are you very satisfied, fairly satisfied, not very satisfied, or not at all satisfied with the way democracy works in [COUNTRY]?'

[2] Canache et al. (2001) also criticize the measure for lacking a referent to other systems of governance.

[3] Note, however, that the figure does not include one important outlier, Greece. The 2015 Greek election survey reported only 5 per cent of respondents as (somewhat/very) satisfied with how democracy works in their country.

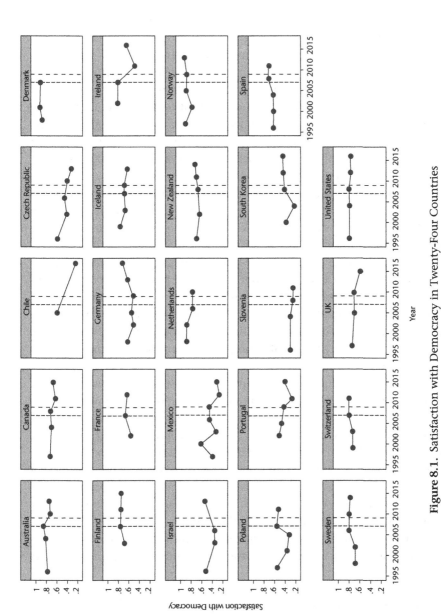

Figure 8.1. Satisfaction with Democracy in Twenty-Four Countries

Note: Vertical axes report share satisfied. Dashed vertical lines report period of GFC.

Source: CSES modules 1–5, as described in text.

large country-level differences, some of which may be due to how they weathered the crisis or differences in the elite response.

Accordingly, in Table 8.1 we report results of regressing individual satisfaction with democracy on a set of survey- and individual-level covariates. These include our period indicators for the shock and recovery, *GDP per capita*, *Austerity*, *Incumbent welfare cues*, and *Government debt*, all as previously described. To these we add a measure of party polarization (Dalton 2008) to control for previous work showing it to depress democratic satisfaction

Table 8.1. Modelling Satisfaction with Democracy

	(1)	(2)
GFC shock period	−0.081	−0.171
	(0.123)	(0.148)
Recovery period	0.079	−0.086
	(0.117)	(0.141)
ΔGDP per capita	0.011*	0.003
	(0.006)	(0.007)
Austerity	0.027	0.025
	(0.023)	(0.023)
Welfare cues	−0.015**	−0.016**
	(0.007)	(0.007)
Polarization	−0.157**	−0.097
	(0.074)	(0.079)
(Ln) Government debt	−0.326**	−0.276*
	(0.154)	(0.153)
Ideology extremism	0.008**	0.008**
	(0.004)	(0.004)
Female	−0.049***	−0.049***
	(0.013)	(0.013)
(Ln) Age	−0.048***	−0.048***
	(0.018)	(0.018)
Education	0.093***	0.093***
	(0.007)	(0.007)
Income	0.133***	0.133***
	(0.005)	(0.005)
Market outsider	−0.130***	−0.130***
	(0.018)	(0.018)
Shock period × ΔGDP per capita		0.007
		(0.012)
Recovery period × ΔGDP per capita		0.040*
		(0.020)
Constant	2.428***	2.187***
	(0.498)	(0.503)
Variance (intercept)	0.094***	0.090***
	(0.015)	(0.014)
Chi-squared	1980.508	2010.443
N of individuals	120140	120140
N of country-surveys	85	85

Note: Cells display estimates from multilevel logit regression with random intercepts and country fixed effects. Standard errors in parentheses. ***$p<0.01$, **$p<0.05$, *$p<0.10$, two-tailed test.

(Ezrow and Xezonakis 2011). We also control at the individual level for gender, age, education, household income, and market status. Lastly, we add a measure of ideological extremism, such that higher values connote more extreme positions.[4]

Consistent with Figure 8.1, regression estimates show no direct effects with respect to the shock or recovery period. Publics in these OECD countries were as satisfied—or dissatisfied, as the case may be—with how democracy worked after the crisis as they were before. Women, the less educated, those with lower income levels, market outsiders are all less satisfied, all else equal. Politics also matters. Those with moderate views in terms of right–left ideology tend to be less satisfied. Elite polarization also drives down democratic sentiment, a finding that should give us pause in as much as the crisis served as a catalyst for growing policy divisions.

We also find that attitudes towards the political system are influenced to the magnitude of the crisis. Satisfaction is positively tied to per capita GDP growth. The impact of the economy on democratic (dis)affection, however, varies with respect to the crisis period. Figure 8.2 draws on estimates from the interactive specification reported in Table 8.1, Model 2, to show the positive effect of growth on satisfaction—or perhaps better said, a negative effect on dissatisfaction is concentrated entirely in the recovery period. During the pre-crisis and crisis periods, the well-established economy–satisfaction connection is absent, only to appear in sharp relief during the years following. Predicted probabilities indicate that in the years following the crisis, the relationship between economic conditions and one's sense of how well the political system works in the OECD has increased. Debt accumulation also matters for citizen satisfaction with their democracies. As charted in Figure 8.3, in countries with debt shares over 100 per cent of GDP (e.g. Portugal), citizens are about 15 per cent less likely to be satisfied with how their country's democracy works compared to those with debt levels less than 10 per cent of GDP (e.g. Estonia).[5]

As in earlier chapters, we examine whether the impact of economic factors, like growth and debt, and political factors, like welfare cues and polarization, on democratic attitudes vary with respect to period effects. As we did for other outcomes, we further examine the impact of growth on citizen satisfaction with democracy in their country. We do so by conditioning the coefficient on *GDP per capita* by *Austerity*, *Welfare cues*, and *Polarization* (see Table A8.1 in the Appendix). Each of these factors conditions the slope on *GDP per capita*.

---

[4] The variable is measured by subtracting five from the 0–10 right–left scale and then normalizing the score by squaring and taking the square root.
[5] We assessed the stability of this effect and found that it stayed quite stable before, during, and after the crisis. Needless to say, levels of sovereign debt were nearly everywhere higher after than before the GFC.

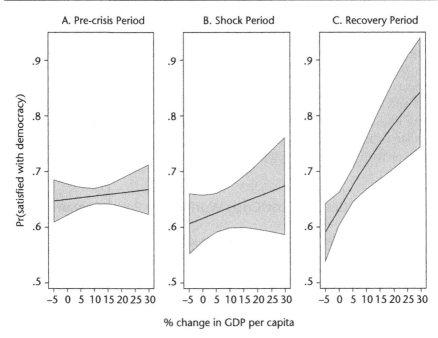

Figure 8.2. Per Capita Growth since Previous Election and Satisfaction with Democracy

Source: Table 8.1 Model 2. Shaded areas represent 90% confidence intervals.

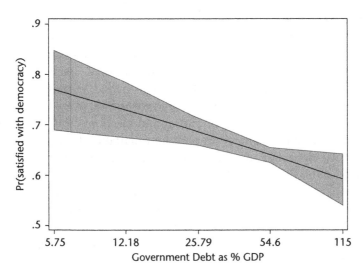

Figure 8.3. Government Debt and Satisfaction with Democracy

Source: Table 8.1 Model 1. Shaded areas represent 90% confidence intervals.

The positive influence of per capita growth on democratic satisfaction increases with fiscal stimulus policies, with free market messages, and with party system polarization. Taken together, analyses of the post-election surveys from the 1990s to the 2010s tell us that mass opinion about how democracy works is sensitive to shorter term factors both economic (growth rates and debt levels) and political (policies, party positions, and elite cues). These findings add to present-day concerns about the weak foundation of popular beliefs in the promise of democracy, even in the world's oldest democracies (Levitsky and Ziblatt 2018).

8.3. Mass Politics in a Post-Crisis World: Two Paths Forward

On 14 August 2019, the Dow Jones Industrial Average dropped over 800 points, or 3.05 per cent, the fourth worst percentage drop of all time. Turbulence in US markets was matched elsewhere. This spate of market volatility ignited fears that, after a modest but prolonged period of expansion following the Great Recession, the world economy may be heading for another downturn. And many worry that the safeguards put in place after the recession were too weak or short-lasting to sufficiently rein in market forces, particularly forces of globalization, financialization, and the ultra-flexible gig economy. Indeed, just as in crises past (Galbraith 1954; Kindleberger 1978), economists provided sound accounts of what went wrong (e.g. Reinhart and Rogoff 2010). Yet despite these warnings, mass publics—the subject of this book—by and large have been quick to assign crisis periods like the GFC to the past and return to normal times.

But what are 'normal times'? For those who came to age during the latter part of the twentieth century in the relatively affluent democracies of Western Europe, North America, Japan, and Oceania, 'normal' likely refers to the decades following the Second World War. This period, marked by war's end at the beginning and the OPEC oil embargo at the end, was a time of general peace and prosperity. In terms of parties and elections, this was a time of stability as governments altered in partisan orientation between the centre-left and centre-right. But, as noted previously, this period of 'normal politics' soon frayed about the edges. The 1980s or, in some countries, 1990s brought an end to the postwar mixed economy consensus. With the fall of the Berlin Wall, formerly communist countries transitioned with lesser or greater friction to capitalist democracies. Taking the place of the postwar consensus was a new neo-liberal consensus. This consensus, shared by left and right, believed the capacity of states to intervene in markets to enhance social welfare was limited if not counterproductive. Mainstream politicians spoke of managing economic changes, realized variously as deindustrialization, outsourcing of production, globalization of services, financialization, and labour market dualism. It is perhaps inevitable that this playbook led to a backlash and a re-embracing of nationalism, populism, and political extremism. Some parties adapted to this new reality, others saw their support dwindle.

So where does that leave us after the global financial crisis and the Great Recession? Broadly speaking, we submit there are two possible equilibria, or paths, for mass politics in the post-crisis world. The first acknowledges that there is no going back, no return to the *trente glorieuses* or to some kind of new class compromise engineered by national welfare states. According to this view the upper-middle income economies of the OECD have returned to a period of normalcy ex-ante. The era of the postwar welfare state was the deviation rather than the norm. As succinctly put by Schäfer and Streeck (2013, 1):

> For almost three decades, OECD countries have—in fits and starts—run deficits and accumulated debt. Rising interest payments and welfare-state maturation have meant that an ever smaller part of government revenue is available today for discretionary spending and social investment. Whichever party comes into office will find its hands tied by past decisions. The financial and fiscal crisis... has only exacerbated the long-shrinking of the room governments have to maneuvre.

This first path, then, characterizes the financial crisis as a final but key catalyst in a return to the normalcy of pre-1945 capitalism and an era in which policymakers did little to respond to the demands of their citizen-principals.[6]

A second path for mass politics in a post- or, perhaps more accurately, *between*-crisis world is what we would describe as a partial return to the second half of the twentieth century. We emphasize *partial* return because the story of the crisis (contributed) to a change in elite politics which is still unfolding. Connections between the political parties' ideologies and the issue preferences of their constituencies have become weaker and party systems have fragmented. The analyses reported here do not suggest a reversal to these trends. The responses to the crisis by parties and the governments they form varies considerably but is predicted less by their long-standing ideologies than by need to act decisively. Yet the crisis response did bring with it a return to notions of government capacity. The neo-liberal narrative that came on the scene in the 1980s and gained traction during the 1990s—that there is little governments can do in the face of global capitalism—has shifted with

---

[6] It is worth noting that the term 'normalcy' in English entered the popular lexicon in the USA with Warren G. Harding's successful 1920 campaign for president. To Harding, a 'return to normalcy' implied a return to a time before the First World War—an era which today's observers would hardly equate with effective representative democracy for all.

the GFC. Public intervention in national economies and in industries thought to be off-limits reappeared in national conversations. In short, as emphasized in research into the politics of advanced capitalism (Beramendi et al. 2015), policy capacity remains a variable across the OECD, rather than a constant.

Findings from this study of mass politics speak to both paths. To a degree, our findings are consistent with the first 'return to the nineteenth century' pathway. Perceptions of a lack of political efficacy, we find, reduce the likelihood of participating in elections. For those who do participate, we find a connection between adverse economic conditions and support for non-mainstream parties, and this connection has strengthened in the post-crisis era.[7] And debt accumulation—a tell-tale sign of welfare state maturation, according to Schäfer and Streeck (2013)—does in fact lead to lower levels of satisfaction with a nation's democracy.

On balance, however, our analyses support the second pathway. What governments do makes a difference. Fiscal stimulus and discretionary spending can moderate the adverse impact of the crisis on subjective security and policy demands. Parties can also condition public opinion and behaviour through their rhetoric, albeit more in the short term than in the long term, and depending on the state of more fundamental variables like the magnitude and persistence of the economic downturn. On the one hand, this could be good news for the future crisis because governments can enhance consumer confidence in the economy. Unfortunately, most advanced economies have even higher deficits and more public debt after the GFC than they had before it, which reduces the room for public spending. Indeed, a consistent finding across our chapters pertains to the importance of sovereign debt. Debt shapes mass politics in many ways, ranging from voter participation to satisfaction with how democracy works. And compared to other factors, debt's effects are less conditional on our two conditioning factors of interest, time-period and elite cues. More optimistically, some countries have managed to keep debt down and consequently do have the option to engage in more stimulus. This, paired with persistently low interest rates for government borrowing, makes a case for debt-funded stimulus.

We end, then, with an ounce of optimism. Despite its deleterious effects, the financial crisis and the Great Recession may have made elections and party politics relevant once again. The room to manoeuvre is not as narrow as some believe it to be, at least with respect to the options that are possible. We hope future work builds on, questions, and refines this conclusion. After all, the next crisis may be more imminent than we think.

---

[7] In fact, according to Figure 7.4, before the crisis strong economic growth was positively tied to the probability of selecting a challenger party.

Appendix

Table 8.A1. Modelling Satisfaction with Democracy, Interactive Models

	(1)	(2)	(3)
Shock period	−0.232	−0.198	−0.214
	(0.225)	(0.219)	(0.664)
Recovery period	−0.077	0.008	−1.868***
	(0.164)	(0.168)	(0.542)
ΔGDP per capita	−0.010	0.013	−0.051***
	(0.008)	(0.009)	(0.018)
Austerity	0.093**	0.031	0.017
	(0.037)	(0.024)	(0.023)
Welfare cues	−0.016**	0.002	−0.018***
	(0.008)	(0.013)	(0.007)
Polarization	−0.065	−0.054	−0.275***
	(0.074)	(0.083)	(0.095)
(Ln) Government debt	−0.116	−0.273*	−0.142
	(0.153)	(0.150)	(0.150)
Ideology extremism	0.008**	0.008**	0.008**
	(0.004)	(0.004)	(0.004)
Female	−0.049***	−0.049***	−0.049***
	(0.013)	(0.013)	(0.013)
(Ln) Age	−0.049***	−0.049***	−0.048***
	(0.018)	(0.018)	(0.018)
Education	0.093***	0.093***	0.093***
	(0.007)	(0.007)	(0.007)
Household income	0.133***	0.133***	0.133***
	(0.005)	(0.005)	(0.005)
Market outsider	−0.130***	−0.130***	−0.130***
	(0.018)	(0.018)	(0.018)
GFC Shock × ΔGDP per capita	−0.029	−0.011	0.037
	(0.033)	(0.022)	(0.087)
Recovery × ΔGDP per/capita	0.019	0.042	0.181*
	(0.033)	(0.031)	(0.099)
ΔGDP per capita × Austerity	−0.006***		
	(0.002)		
GFC shock × Austerity	−0.046		
	(0.052)		
Recovery × Austerity	−0.018		
	(0.044)		
GFC shock × ΔGDP per capita × Austerity	−0.012		
	(0.012)		
Recovery × ΔGDP per capita × Austerity	−0.002		
	(0.006)		
ΔGDP per capita × Welfare cues		−0.002*	
		(0.001)	
GFC shock × Welfare cues		0.002	
		(0.021)	
Recovery × Welfare cues		−0.016	
		(0.018)	
GFC shock × ΔGDP per capita × Welfare cues		0.004	
		(0.004)	
Recovery × ΔGDP per capita × Welfare cues		−0.001	
		(0.005)	

(*continued*)

Table 8.A1. Continued

	(1)	(2)	(3)
ΔGDP per capita × Polarization			0.016**
			(0.005)
GFC shock × Polarization			0.024
			(0.187)
Recovery × Polarization			0.496***
			(0.143)
GFC shock × ΔGDP per capita × Polarization			−0.010
			(0.027)
Recovery × ΔGDP per capita × Polarization			−0.036
			(0.031)
Constant	1.740***	1.991***	2.400***
	(0.500)	(0.523)	(0.489)
Variance (intercept)	0.077***	0.082***	0.075***
	(0.012)	(0.013)	(0.012)
Chi-square	2117.110	2075.002	2135.289
N of individuals	120140	120140	120140
N of country-surveys	85	85	85

Note: Cells display estimates from multilevel logit regression with random intercepts and country fixed effects. Standard errors in parentheses. ***$p<0.01$, **$p<0.05$, *$p<0.10$, two-tailed test.

Bibliography

Achen, Christopher H., and Larry M. Bartels. 2016. *Democracy for Realists*. Princeton: Princeton University Press.

Adams, James, and Zeynep Somer-Topcu. 2009. 'Policy Adjustment by Parties in Response to Rival Parties' Policy Shifts: Spatial Theory and the Dynamics of Party Competition in Twenty-Five Post-War Democracies.' *British Journal of Political Science* 39(4), 825–46.

Albrow, Martin. 1997. *The Global Age*. Palo Alto, CA: Stanford University Press.

Alesina, A., and P. Giuliano. 2011. 'Preferences for Redistribution.' In J. Benhabib, A. Bisin, and M. O. Jackson, eds, *Handbook of Social Economics*, 1A. 93–132. Amsterdam: North-Holland.

Alford, Robert R. 1962. 'A Suggested Index of the Association of Social Class and Voting.' *Public Opinion Quarterly* 26(3), 417–25.

Alcañiz, Isabella, and Timothy Hellwig. 2011. 'Who's to Blame? The Distribution of Responsibility in Developing Democracies.' *British Journal of Political Science* 41(2), 389–411.

Alt, J. E., A. Jensen, H. A, Larreguy, D. D. Lassen, and J. Marshall. 2017. 'Contagious Political Concerns: Identifying Unemployment Shock Information Transmission Using the Danish Population Network.' Paper presented at the Annual Meeting of the American Political Science Association, San Francisco, 31 Aug.–3 Sept.

Anderson, C. J. 2007. 'The End of Economic Voting? Contingency Dilemmas and the Limits of Democratic Accountability.' *Annual Review of Political Science* 10, 271–96.

Anderson, C. J., and J. D. Hecht. 2012. 'Voting When the Economy Goes Bad, Everyone is in Charge, and No One is to Blame: The Case of the 2009 German Election.' *Electoral Studies* 31(1), 5–19.

Anderson, C. J., and J. D. Hecht. 2014. 'Crisis of Confidence? The Dynamics of Economic Opinions During the Great Recession.' In N. Bermeo and L. Bartels, eds, *Mass Politics in Tough Times*, 40–71. New York: Oxford University Press.

Anderson, C. J., and J. Pontusson. 2007. 'Workers, Worries, and Welfare States: Social Protection and Job Insecurity in 15 OECD Countries.' *European Journal of Political Research* 46(2), 211–35.

Anderson, C. J., A. Blais, S. Bowler, T. Donovan, and O. Listhaug. 2007. *Losers' Consent: Elections and Democratic Legitimacy*. Oxford: Oxford University Press.

Ansell, Ben. 2014. 'The Political Economy of Ownership: Housing Markets and the Welfare State.' *American Political Science Review* 108(2), 383–402.

Armingeon, Klaus, and Kai Guthmann. 2013. 'Democracy in Crisis? The Declining Support for National Democracy in European Countries, 2007–2011.' *European Journal of Political Research* 53(3), 423–42.

Autor, David, David Dorn, Gordon H. Hanson, and Kaveh Majlesi 2016. 'Importing Political Polarization: The Electoral Consequences of Rising Trade Exposure', MIT Working Paper, <https://economics.mit.edu/files/11499>, accessed June 2018.

Barnes, Lucy, and Ann Wren. 2012. 'The Liberal Model in the Crisis: Continuity and Change in Great Britain and Ireland.' In Nancy Bermeo and Jonas Pontusson, eds, *Coping with Crisis: Government Reactions to the Great Recession*, 286–324. New York: Russell Sage.

Barnes, Samuel H., Max Kaase, et al. 1979. *Political Action: Mass Participation in Five Western Democracies*. Beverly Hills, CA: Sage.

Bartels, Larry. 2002. 'Beyond the Running Tally: Partisan Bias in Political Perceptions.' *Political Behavior* 24(2), 117–50.

Bartels, Larry M. 2014. 'Ideology and Retrospection in Electoral Responses to the Great Recession.' In N. Bermeo and L. M. Bartels, eds, *Mass Politics in Tough Times: Opinions, Votes, and Protest in the Great Recession*, 185–223. New York: Oxford University Press.

Bartolini, Stefano, and Peter Mair. 1990. *Identity, Competition, and Electoral Availability. The Stabilization of the European Electorate, 1885-1985*. Cambridge, Cambridge University Press.

Bechtel, Michael M., and Jens Hainmueller. 2011. 'How Lasting is Voter Gratitude? An Analysis of the Short- and Long-Term Electoral Returns of Beneficial Policy.' *American Journal of Political Science* 55(4), 852–68.

Beramendi, Pablo, Silja Häusermann, Herbert Kitschelt, and Hanspeter Kriesi, eds. 2015. *The Politics of Advanced Capitalism*. New York: Cambridge University Press.

Berkmen, S. Pelin, Gaston Gelos, Robert Rennhack, and James P. Walsh. 2012. 'The Global Financial Crisis: Explaining Cross-Country Differences in the Output Impact.' *Journal of International Money and Finance* 31(1), 42–59.

Bermeo, Nancy, and Larry M. Bartels. 2014. 'Mass Politics in Tough Times.' In N. Bermeo and L. M. Bartels, eds, *Mass Politics in Tough Times: Opinions, Votes, and Protest in the Great Recession*, 1–39. New York: Oxford University Press.

Bermeo, Nancy, and Jonas Pontusson, eds. 2012. *Coping with Crisis: Government Reactions to the Great Recession*. New York: Russel Sage Foundation.

Bezemer, Dirk J. 2010. 'Understanding Financial Crisis through Accounting Models.' *Accounting, Organizations and Society* 35, 676–88.

Bisgaard, Martin, and Rune Slothuus. 2018. 'Partisan Elites as Culprits? How Party Cues Shape Partisan Perceptual Gaps.' *American Journal of Political Science* 62(2), 456–69.

Blomberg, Helena, Johanna Kallio, Olli Kangas, Christian Kroll, and Mikko Niemelä. 2012. 'Attitudes among High-Risk Groups.' In Stefan Svallfors, ed., *Contested Welfare States: Welfare Attitudes in Europe and Beyond*. Stanford, CA: Stanford University Press.

Blyth, Mark, and Richard S. Katz. 2005. 'From Catch-All Politics to Cartelisation: The Political Economy of the Cartel Party.' *West European Politics* 28(1), 33–60.

Bohle, Dorothee, and Béla Greskovits. 2012. *Capitalist Diversity in Europe's Periphery*. Ithaca, NY: Cornell University Press.

Bornschier, Simon. 2010. *Cleavage Politics and the Populist Right: The New Cultural Conflict in Western Europe*. Philadelphia: Temple University Press.

Burgoon, Brian. 2001. 'Globalization and Welfare Compensation: Disentangling the Ties that Bind.' *International Organization* 55(3), 509–51.

Burgoon, Brian, and Fabian Dekker. 2010. 'Flexible Employment, Economic Insecurity and Social Policy Preferences in Europe.' *Journal of European Social Policy* 20(2), 126–41.

Burnham, W. D. 1987. 'The Turnout Problem.' In A. J. Reichley, ed., *Elections American Style*, 97–133. Washington, DC: Brookings Institution.

Cameron, David A. 1978. 'The Expansion of the Public Economy: A Comparative Analysis.' *American Political Science Review* 72(4), 1243–61.

Cameron, David A. 2012. 'European Fiscal Responses to the Great Recession.' In Nancy Bermeo and Jonas Pontusson, eds, *Coping with Crisis: Government Responses to the Great Recession*. New York: Russell Sage Foundation.

Campbell, Angus, Philip E. Converse, Warren E. Miller, and Donald E. Stokes. 1960. *The American Voter*. Ann Arbor: University of Michigan Survey Research Center.

Canache, Damarys, Jeffery J. Mondak, and Mitchell A. Seligson. 2001. 'Meaning and Measurement in Cross-National Research on Satisfaction with Democracy.' *Public Opinion Quarterly* 65: 506–28.

Caramani, Daniele. 2004. *The Nationalization of Politics*. New York: Cambridge University Press.

Carsey, Thomas, and Geoffrey Layman. 2006. 'Changing Sides or Changing Minds? Party Identification and Policy Preferences in the American Electorate.' *American Journal of Political Science* 50, 464–77.

Chaiken, Shelley, and Allison Ledgerwood, 2012. A theory of heuristic and systematic information processing. In P. A. M. Van Lange, A. W. Kruglanski, & E. T. Higgins (Eds.), *Handbook of Theories of Social Psychology*. Thousand Oaks, CA: Sage, 246–66.

Chiaramonte, Alessandro, and Vincenzo Emanuele. 2015. 'Party System Volatility, Regeneration and DeInstitutionalization in Western Europe (1945–2015) Party Politics.' <http://ppq.sagepub.com/content/early/2015/08/24/1354068815601330>. abstract; doi:10.1177/1354068815601330).

Cho, Hyekyung. 2012. 'Korea's Experience with Global Financial Crisis.' North South Institute. <http://www.nsi-ins.ca/wp-content/uploads/2012/09/2012-How-to-prevent-the-next-crisis-Korea.pdf>.

Chu, Yun-han, Michael Bratton, Marta Lagos, Sandeep Shastri, and Mark Tessler. 2008. 'Public Opinion and Democratic Legitimacy.' *Journal of Democracy* 19(2), 74–87.

Chung, Heejung, and Wim van Oorschot. 2011. 'Institutions versus Market Forces: Explaining the Employment Insecurity of European Individuals During the (Beginning of the) Financial Crisis.' *Journal of European Social Policy* 21(4), 287–301.

Clarke, Harold D., Nitish Dutt, and Allan Kornberg. 1993. 'The Political Economy of Attitudes toward Polity and Society in Western European Democracies.' *Journal of Politics* 33(4), 998–1021.

Clarke, Harold D., David Sanders, Marianne C. Stewart, and Paul Whiteley. 2009. *Performance Politics and the British Voter*. Cambridge: Cambridge University Press.

Clements, Clarke, Kyriaki Nanou, and José Real-Dato. 2018. 'Economic Crisis and Party Responsiveness on the Left–Right Dimension in the European Union.' *Party Politics* 24(1), 52–64.

Clift, Ben. 2015. 'The UK Macroeconomic Policy Debate and the British Growth Crisis: Debt and Deficit Discourse in the Great Recession.' In Jeremy Green, Colin Hay and Peter Taylor-Gooby, eds, *The British Growth Crisis*, 151–73. Basingstoke: Palgrave Macmillan.

Colantone, Italo, and Piero Stanig. 2018. 'Global Competition and Brexit.' *American Political Science Review* 112(2), 201–18.

Comparative Study of Electoral Systems (www.cses.org). CSES MODULE 1 FULL RELEASE [dataset]. 15 Dec. 2015 version. doi:10.7804/cses.module1.2015-12-15

Comparative Study of Electoral Systems (www.cses.org). CSES MODULE 2 FULL RELEASE [dataset]. December 15, 2015 version. doi:10.7804/cses.module2.2015-12-15

Comparative Study of Electoral Systems (www.cses.org). CSES MODULE 3 FULL RELEASE [dataset]. December 15, 2015 version. doi:10.7804/cses.module3.2015-12–15

Comparative Study of Electoral Systems (www.cses.org). CSES MODULE 4 ADVANCE RELEASE [dataset and documentation]. April 2017 version. doi:10.7804/cses.module4.2018-05-29

Comparative Study of Electoral Systems (www.cses.org). CSES MODULE 4 FOURTH ADVANCE RELEASE [dataset]. April 11, 2017 version. doi:10.7804/cses.module4.2017-04-11

Comparative Study of Electoral Systems (www.cses.org). CSES MODULE 4 FULL RELEASE [dataset and documentation]. May 29, 2018 version. doi:10.7804/cses.module4.2018-05-29

Comparative Study of Electoral Systems (www.cses.org). CSES INTEGRATED MODULE DATASET (IMD) [dataset and documentation]. December 4, 2018 version. doi:10.7804/cses.imd.2018-12-04.

Cordero, Guillermo, and Pablo Simón. 2016. 'Economic Crisis and Support for Democracy in Europe.' *West European Politics* 39(2), 305–25.

Crouch, Colin. 2004. *Post-Democracy*. Oxford: Polity Press.

Crowley, Stephen. 2006. 'East European Labor, the Varieties of Capitalism, and the Expansion of the EU.' <http://councilforeuropeanstudies.org/files/Papers/Crowley.pdf>.

Crozier, M., Samuel P. Huntington, and J. Watanuki, J. 1975. *The Crisis of Democracy: Report on the Governability of Democracies to the Trilateral Commission*. New York: New York University Press.

Cusack, Thomas, Torben Iversen, and Philipp Rehm. 2006. 'Risks at Work: The Demand and Supply Sides of Government Redistribution.' *Oxford Review of Economic Policy* 22(3), 365–89.

Dalton, Russell J. 1984. 'Cognitive Mobilization and Partisan Dealignment in Advanced Industrial Democracies.' *Journal of Politics* 46 (Feb.), 264–84.

Dalton, Russell J. 2008. 'The Quantity and the Quality of Party Systems: Party System Polarization, its Measurement and its Consequences.' *Comparative Political Studies* 41, 899–920.

Dalton, Russell J. 2020. *Citizen Politics: Public Opinion and Political Parties in Advanced Industrial Democracies*, 7th ed. Thousand Oaks, CA: CQ Press.

Dalton, Russell J., and Christopher J. Anderson, eds. 2011. *Citizens, Context, and Choice: How Context Shapes Citizens' Electoral Choices*. Oxford: Oxford University Press.

Dalton, Russell J., David M. Farrell, and Ian McAllister. 2011. *Political Parties and Democratic Linkage*. Oxford: Oxford University Press.

Dalton, Russell J., Scott Flanagan, and Paul Beck, eds. 1984. *Electoral Change in Advanced Industrial Democracies*. Princeton: Princeton University Press.

Dancygier, Rafaela, and Michael Donnelly. 2014. 'Attitudes toward Migration in Good Times and Bad.' In N. Bermeo and L. Bartels, eds, *Mass Politics in Tough Times*, 148–84. New York: Oxford University Press.

Dassonneville, Ruth, and Michael S. Lewis-Beck. 2014. 'The Economic Voter and Economic Crisis.' *Acta Politica* 49(4), 369–71.

Dassonneville, Ruth, and Michael S. Lewis-Beck. 2017. 'Rules, Institutions and the Economic Vote: Clarifying Clarity of Responsibility.' *West European Politics* 40(3), 621–44.

Dassonneville, Ruth. 2015. 'Stability and Change in Voting Behaviour. Macro and Micro Determinants of Electoral Volatility.' Ph.D. thesis, University of Leuven.

De Vries, Catherine, and Nathalie Giger. 2014. 'Holding Governments Accountable? Individual Heterogeneity in Performance Voting.' *European Journal of Political Research* 53(2), 346–62.

Devore, Marc R. 2015. 'Defying Convergence: Globalisation and Varieties of Defence-Industrial Capitalism.' *New Political Economy* 20(4), 569–93.

Downs, Anthony. 1957. *An Economic Theory of Democracy*. New York: Harper.

Duch, Raymond D., and Randy Stevenson. 2008. *The Economic Vote: How Political and Economic Institutions Condition Election Results*. New York: Cambridge University Press.

Duch, Raymond D., and Randy Stevenson. 2010. 'The Global Economy, Competency and the Economic Vote.' *Journal of Politics* 72(1), 105–23.

Durr, Robert H. 1993. 'What Moves Policy Sentiment?' *American Political Science Review* 87(1), 158–70.

Elff, Martin. 2009. 'Social Divisions, Party Positions and Electoral Behavior.' *Electoral Studies* 28, 297–308.

Emanuele, Vincenzo. 2015. *Dataset of Electoral Volatility and its Internal Components in Western Europe (1945–2015)*, Rome: Italian Center for Electoral Studies.

Emmenegger, Patrick. 2009. 'Specificity versus Replaceability: The Relationship between Skills and Preferences for Job Security Regulations.' *Socio-Economic Review* 7(3), 407–30.

Emmenegger, Patrick, Paul Marx, and Dominik Schraff. 2015. 'Labour Market Disadvantage, Political Orientation and Voting: How Adverse Labour Market Experiences Translate into Electoral Behaviour.' *Socio-Economic Review* 13(2), 189–213.

Erikson, Robert, John H. Goldthorpe, and Lucienne Portocarero. 1979. 'Intergenerational Class Mobility in Three Western European Societies.' *British Journal of Sociology* 30(4), 415–41.

Esping-Andersen, Gøsta. 1990. *The Three Worlds of Welfare Capitalism*. Princeton: Princeton University Press.

Easton, David. 1965. *A Systems Analysis of Political Life*. New York: John Wiley.

Evans, Geoffrey, and Robert Andersen. 2006. 'The Political Conditioning of Economic Perceptions.' *Journal of Politics* 68(1), 194–207.

Evans, Geoffrey, and James Tilley. 2017. *The New Politics of Class*. Oxford: Oxford University Press.

Ezrow, Lawrence. 2010. *Linking Citizens and Parties: How Electoral Systems Matter for Political Representation*. Oxford: Oxford University Press.

Ezrow, Lawrence, and Timothy Hellwig. 2014. 'Responding to Voters or Responding to Markets? Political Parties and Public Opinion in an Era of Globalization.' *International Studies Quarterly* 58(4), 816–27.

Ezrow, Lawrence, and Georgios Xezonakis. 2011. 'Citizen Satisfaction with Democracy and Parties' Policy Offerings.' *Comparative Political Studies* 44(9): 1152–78.

Fearon, James D. 1999. 'Electoral Accountability and the Control of Politicians: Selecting Good Types versus Sanctioning Poor Performance.' In Bernard Manin, Adam Przeworski, and Susan Stokes, eds, *Democracy, Accountability, and Representation*, 55–97. Cambridge: Cambridge University Press.

Feenstra, Robert C., Robert Inklaar, and Marcel P. Timmer. 2015. 'The Next Generation of the Penn World Table' *American Economic Review* 105(10), 3150–82. http://www.ggdc.net/pwt.

Fieldhouse, Edward, Jane Green, Geoffrey Evans, Jonathan Mellon, Christopher Prosser, Hermann Schmitt, and Cees van der Eijk. 2020. *Electoral Shocks: The Volatile Voter in a Turbulent World*. New York: Oxford University Press.

Fischer, Stanley. 2008. 'Impact of the Global Financial Crisis on Israel's Economy.' Address to the General Assembly of the Association of Publicly Traded Companies, Jerusalem, 8 Dec. <http://www.bis.org/review/r081219c.pdf>

Flora, Peter, and Arnold J. Heidenheimer. 1981. *The Development of Welfare States in Europe and America*. New Brunswick, NJ: Transaction Books.

Fraile, Marta, and Sergi Pardos-Prado. 2014. 'Correspondence between the Objective and Subjective Economies: The Role of Personal Economic Circumstances.' *Political Studies* 62(4), 895–912.

Framing the Economy Network and Advisory Group. 2018. *Framing the Economy: How to Win the Case for a Better System*. London: New Economy Organisers' Network, the New Economics Foundation, the Frameworks Institute and the Public Interest Research Centre. <http://neweconomics.org/wp-content/uploads/2018/02/Framing-the-Economy-NEON-NEF-FrameWorks-PIRC.pdf>

Franklin, Mark N. 2004. *Voter Turnout and the Dynamics of Electoral Competition in Established Democracies since 1945*. Cambridge: Cambridge University Press.

Franklin, Mark N., Tom Mackie, and Henry Valen, eds. 1992. *Electoral Change: Responses to Evolving Social and Attitudinal Structures in Western Countries*. New York: Cambridge University Press.

Galbraith, John Kenneth. 1954. *The Great Crash 1929*. New York: Houghton Mifflin.

Gallagher, Michael. 2017. Election indices dataset at <http://www.tcd.ie/Political_Science/staff/michael_gallagher/ElSystems/index.php>

Garrett, Geoffrey. 1998. *Partisan Politics in the Global Economy*. New York: Cambridge Uni-versity Press.

Gerber, Alan. S., and Gregory A. Huber. 2010. 'Partisanship, Political Control and Economic Assessments.' *American Journal of Political Science* 54(1), 153–73.

Giger, Nathalie, and Moira Nelson. 2011. 'The Electoral Consequences of Welfare State Retrenchment: Blame Avoidance or Credit Claiming in the Era of Permanent Austerity?' *European Journal of Political Research* 50(1), 1–23.

Gingrich, Jane, and Ben Ansell. 2012. 'Preferences in Context Micro Preferences, Macro Contexts, and the Demand for Social Policy.' *Comparative Political Studies* 45(12), 1624–54.

Gingrich, Jane, and Silja Häusermann. 2015. 'The Decline of the Working-Class Vote, the Reconfiguration of the Welfare Support Coalition and Consequences for the Welfare State.' *Journal of European Social Policy* 25(1), 50–75.

Goldthorpe, John H., ed. 1984. *Order and Conflict in Contemporary Capitalism*. Oxford: Clarendon Press.

Goldthorpe, John H. 2000. *On Sociology: Numbers, Narratives, and the Integration of Research and Theory*. Oxford: Oxford University Press.

Gomez, Brad T., and J. Matthew Wilson. 2003. 'Causal Attribution and Economic Voting in American Congressional Elections.' *Political Research Quarterly* 56(3), 271–82.

Gourevitch, Peter A. 1986. *Politics in Hard Times*. Ithaca, NY: Cornell University Press.

Green, Jane, and Will Jennings. 2017. *The Politics of Competence: Parties, Public Opinion, and Voters*. Cambridge: Cambridge University Press.

Green-Pedersen, Christoffer. 2002. *The Politics of Justification: Party Competition and Welfare-State Retrenchment in Denmark and the Netherlands from 1982 to 1998*. Amsterdam: Amsterdam University Press.

Habermas, Jurgen. 1973. *Legitimation Crisis*. Boston: Beacon Press.

Hacker, J. S., P. Rehm, and M. Schlesinger. 2013. 'The Insecure American: Economic Experiences, Financial Worries, and Policy Attitudes.' *Perspectives on Politics* 11, 23–49.

Hacker, Jacob S. 2006. *The Great Risk Shift: The Assault on American Jobs, Families Health Care, and Retirement and How you Can Fight Back*. New York: Oxford University Press.

Hacker, Jacob S., Gregory A. Huber, Austin Nichols, Philipp Rehm, and Stuart Craig. 2011. *Economic Insecurity and the Great Recession: Findings form the Economic Security Index*. New York: Rockefeller Foundation.

Hall, Peter A., and David Soskice, eds. 2001. *Varieties of Capitalism: The Institutional Foundations of Comparative Advantage*. New York: Oxford University Press.

Halpin, P. 2016. 'Irish 2015 GDP Growth Raised to 26 Percent on Asset Reclassification.' *Reuters*, 16 July <http://uk.reuters.com/article/uk-ireland-economy-idUKKCN0ZS0ZC>.

Hannon, P. 2016. 'Developed-Country Economic Growth Slows Sharply, OECD Says.' *Wall Street Journal*, 19 Feb. <http://www.wsj.com/articles/developed-country-economic-growth-slows-sharply-1455879603>.

Hart, Austin. 2013. 'Can Candidates Activate or Deactivate the Economic Vote? Evidence from Two Mexican Elections.' *Journal of Politics* 75(4), 1051–63.

207

Häusermann, Silja, and Hanspeter Kriesi. 2015. 'What do Voters Want? Dimensions and Configurations in Individual-Level Preferences and Party Choice.' In Pablo Beramendi, Silja Häusermann, Herbert Kitschelt, and Hanspeter Kriesi, eds, *The Politics of Advanced Capitalism*, 202–30. New York: Cambridge University Press.

Häusermann, Silja, Thomas Kurer, and Hanna Schwander. 2015. 'High-Skilled Outsiders? Labor Market Vulnerability, Education, and Welfare State Preferences.' *Socio-Economic Review* 13(2), 235–58.

Häusermann, Silja, Thomas Kurer, and Bruno Wuest. 2017. 'Participation in Hard Times: How Constrained Government Depresses Turnout among the Highly Educated.' *West European Politics* 41(2), 448–71.

Häusermann, Silja, Georg Picot, and Dominik Geering. 2013. 'Review Article: Rethinking Party Politics and the Welfare State—Recent Advances in the Literature.' *British Journal of Political Science* 43(1), 221–40.

Hays, Jude C. 2009. *Globalization and the Politics of Embedded Liberalism*. Oxford: Oxford University Press.

Hays, Jude C., Jae-Jae Spoon, and Junghyun Lim. Forthcoming. 'Ideology and Trade: The Path to Right-Wing Populism in Europe.' *Electoral Studies*.

Healy, Andrew J., Neil Malhotra, and Cecilia Hyunjung Mo. 2010. 'Irrelevant Events Affect Voters' Evaluations of Government Performance.' *Proceedings of the National Academy of Sciences* 107(29), 12804–9, DOI: 10.1073/pnas.1007420107.

Heath, Oliver. 2013. 'Policy Representation, Social Representation, and Class Voting in Britain.' *British Journal of Political Science* 45, 173–93.

Heath, Oliver. 2018. 'Policy Alienation, Social Alienation and Working-Class Abstention in Britain, 1964–2010.' *British Journal of Political Science* 48, 1053–73.

Helgason, Agnar Freyr, and Vittorio Mérola. 2017. 'Employment Insecurity, Incumbent Partisanship, and Voting Behavior in Comparative Perspective.' *Comparative Political Studies* 50(11), 1489–1523.

Hellwig, Timothy. 2007. 'Globalization and Perceptions of Policy Maker Competence: Evidence from France.' *Political Research Quarterly* 60(1), 146–58.

Hellwig, Timothy. 2012. 'Constructing Accountability: Party Position Taking and Economic Voting.' *Comparative Political Studies* 45(1), 91–118.

Hellwig, Timothy. 2014. *Globalization and Mass Politics: Retaining the Room to Maneuver*. New York: Cambridge University Press.

Hellwig, Timothy. Forthcoming. 'Globalization, Electoral Change, and Representation.' In Robert Rohrschneider and Jacques Thomassen, eds, *Oxford Handbook of Political Representation in Liberal Democracies*. Oxford: Oxford University Press.

Hellwig, Timothy, and Eva Coffey. 2011. 'Public Opinion, Party Messages, and Responsibility for the Financial Crisis in Britain.' *Electoral Studies* 30, 417–26.

Hellwig, Timothy, and Ian McAllister. 2019. 'Party Positions, Asset Ownership, and Economic Voting.' *Political Studies* 67(4), 912–31.

Hellwig, Timothy, and Dani M. Marinova. 2015. 'More Misinformed than Myopic: Economic Retrospections and the Voter's Time Horizon.' *Political Behavior* 37(4), 865–87.

Hellwig, Timothy, and David Samuels. 2007. 'Voting in Open Economies: The Electoral Consequences of Globalization.' *Comparative Political Studies* 40(3), 283–306.

Hellwig, Timothy, and Yesola Kweon. 2016. 'Taking Cues on Multidimensional Issues: The Case of Attitudes toward Immigration.' *West European Politics* 39(4), 710–30.

Hellwig, Timothy, Eve M. Ringsmuth, and John R. Freeman. 2008. 'The American Public and the Room to Maneuver: Responsibility Attributions and Policy Efficacy in an Era of Globalization.' *International Studies Quarterly* 52(4), 855–80.

Hernández, Enrique, and Hanspeter Kriesi. 2016. 'The Electoral Consequences of the Financial and Economic Crisis in Europe.' *European Journal of Political Research* 55(2), 203–24.

Hobolt, Sara B., and James Tilley. 2016. 'Fleeing the Centre: The Rise of Challenger Parties in the Aftermath of the Euro Crisis.' *West European Politics* 39(5): 971–91.

Hobolt, Sara, James Tilley, and Susan Banducci. 2013. 'Clarity of Responsibility: How Government Cohesion Conditions Performance Voting.' *European Journal of Political Research* 52(2), 164–87.

Hooghe, Liesbet, and Gary Marks. 2017. 'Cleavage Theory Meets Europe's Crises: Lipset, Rokkan, and the Transnational Cleavage.' *Journal of European Public Policy* 25(1), 109–35.

Huber, Evelyne, and John D. Stephens. 2001. *Development and Crisis of the Welfare State.* Chicago: University of Chicago Press.

Huber, Evelyne, and John D. Stephens. 2015. 'Postindustrial Social Policy.' In Pablo Beramendi et al., eds, *The Politics of Advanced Capitalism*, 259–81. New York: Cambridge University Press.

Huebscher, Evelyne, Thomas Sattler, and Markus Wagner. 2018. 'Voter Responses to Fiscal Austerity.' 30 Oct. Available at SSRN: <https://ssrn.com/abstract=3289341>

Humpage, Louise. 2015. *Policy Change, Public Attitudes and Social Citizenship: Does Neoliberalism Matter?* Bristol: Policy Press.

Huntington, Samuel H. 1968. *Political Order in Changing Societies.* New Haven: Yale University Press.

Hutter, Swen, and Hanspeter Kriesi, eds. 2019. *European Party Politics in Times of Crisis.* Cambridge: Cambridge University Press.

Inglehart, Ronald. 1984. 'Changing Cleavage Alignments in Western Democracies.' In R. Dalton, S. Flanagan, and P. Beck, eds, *Electoral Change in Advanced Industrial Democracies*, 25–69. Princeton: Princeton University Press.

Inglehart, Ronald. 1990. *Culture Shift in Advanced Industrial Society.* Princeton: Princeton University Press.

International Institute for Democracy and Electoral Assistance. 2019. 'Voter Turnout Database.' https://www.idea.int/data-tools/data/voter-turnout.

International Monetary Fund. 2019. *Fiscal Monitor*, Apr. Washington, DC: IMF.

ISSP Research Group. 2008. International Social Survey Programme: Role of Government IV—ISSP 2006. GESIS Data Archive, Cologne. ZA4700 Data file Version 1.0.0.

Iversen, Torben. 2005. *Capitalism, Democracy, and Welfare.* New York: Cambridge University Press.

Iversen, Torben. 2006. 'Individual-Level Measures of Skill-Specificity.' Harvard University <http://www.people.fas.harvard.edu/~iversen/SkillSpecificity.htm>.

Iversen, Torben, and Thomas Cusack. 2000. 'The Causes of Welfare State Expansion: Deindustrialization or Globalization?" *World Politics* 52(3), 313–49.

Iversen, Torben, and David Soskice. 2001. 'An Asset Theory of Social Policy Preferences.' *American Political Science Review* 95(4), 875–911.

Iversen, Torben, and David Soskice. 2012. 'Modern Capitalism and the Advanced Nation State: Understanding the Causes of the Crisis.' In Nancy Bermeo and Jonas Pontusson, eds, *Coping with Crisis: Government Responses to the Great Recession*, 35–64. New York: Russell Sage Foundation.

Iversen, Torben, and David Soskice. 2015. 'Democratic Limits to Redistribution: Inclusionary versus Exclusionary Coalitions in the Knowledge Economy.' *World Politics* 67 (Apr.), 185–225.

Jackman, Robert W. 1987. 'Political Institutions and Voter Turnout in the Industrial Democracies.' *American Political Science Review* 81(2), 405–24.

Jansen, Giedo, Geoffrey Evans, and Nan Dirk de Graaf. 2013. 'Class Voting and Left–Right Party Positions.' *Social Science Research* 42(2), 376–400.

Johns, Rob, and A.-K. Kölln. Forthcoming. 'Moderation and Competence: How a Party's Ideological Position Shapes its Valence Reputation.' *American Journal of Political Science*.

Kam, Cindy D. 2005. 'Who Toes the Party Line? Cues, Values, and Individual Differences.' *Political Behavior* 27(2), 163–82.

Karp, Jeffrey A., and Caitlin Milazzo. 2016. 'Globalization and Voter Turnout in Times of Crisis.' In Jack Vowles and Georgios Xezonakis, eds, *Globalization and Domestic Politics: Parties, Public Opinion, and Elections*, 190–208. Oxford: Oxford University Press.

Kasara, K., and P. Suryanarayan. 2015. 'When do the Rich Vote Less than the Poor and Why? Explaining Turnout Inequality across the World.' *American Journal of Political Science* 59(3), 613–27.

Katzenstein, Peter J., ed. 1978. *Between Power and Plenty*. Madison, WI: University of Wisconsin Press.

Katzenstein, Peter J. 1985. *Small States in World Markets*. Ithaca, NY: Cornell University Press.

Kayser, Mark A. 2014. 'The Elusive Economic Vote.' In Lawrence LeDuc, Richard G. Niemi and Pippa Norris, eds, *Comparing Democracies 4: Elections and Voting in a Changing World.*, 112–32. Thousand Oaks, CA: Sage.

Kayser, Mark A., and Liam F. McGrath. 2018. 'The Long Shadow of Opposition: Electoral Benchmarking Against Previous Governments.' Working paper, Hertie School of Governance.

Kayser, Mark A., and Michael Peress. 2012. 'Benchmarking across Borders: Electoral Accountability and the Necessity of Comparison.' *American Political Science Review* 106(3), 661–84.

Kayser, Mark A., and Christopher Wlezien. 2011. 'Performance Pressure: Patterns of Partisanship and the Economic Vote.' *European Journal of Political Research* 50(3), 365–94.

Key, V. O., Jr. 1949. *Southern Politics in State and Nation*. Knoxville, TN: University of Tennessee Press.

Key, V. O., Jr. 1959. 'Secular Realignment and the Party System.' *Journal of Politics* 21: 198–210.

Kindleberger, Charles P. 1978. *Manias, Panics, and Crashes.* Hoboken, NJ: Wiley.

King, Desmond, and David Rueda. 2008. 'Cheap Labor: The New Politics of "Bread and Roses" in Industrial Democracies.' *Perspectives on Politics* 6(2), 279–97.

Kiran, Jiyan. 2018. 'Expanding the Framework of the Varieties of Capitalism: Turkey as a Hierarchical Market Economy.' *Journal of Eurasian Studies* 9(1), 42–51.

Kitschelt, Herbert. 1994. *The Transformation of European Social Democracy.* New York: Cambridge University Press.

Kitschelt, Herbert, and Anthony McGann. 1995. *The Radical Right in Western Europe.* Ann Arbor, MI: University of Michigan Press.

Kitschelt, Herbert, and Philipp Rehm. 2014. 'Occupations as a Site of Political Preference Formation.' *Comparative Political Studies* 47(12), 1670–1706.

Kitschelt, Herbert, and Philipp Rehm. 2015. 'Party Alignments: Change and Continuity.' In Pablo Beramendi, Silja Hausermann, Herbert Kitschelt, and Hanpeter Kriesi, eds, *The Politics of Advanced Capitalism*, 179–201. New York: Cambridge University Press.

Kitschelt, Herbert, Peter Lange, Gary Marks, and John D. Stephens, eds. 1999. *Continuity and Change in Contemporary Capitalism.* New York: Cambridge University Press.

Kriesi, Hanspeter. 2014. 'The Political Consequences of the Economic Crisis in Europe: Electoral Punishment and Popular Protest.' In N. Bermeo and L. M. Bartels, eds, *Mass Politics in Tough Times: Opinions, Votes, and Protest in the Great Recession*, 297–333. New York: Oxford University Press.

Kriesi, Hanspeter, Edgar Grande, et al. 2008. *West European Politics in the Age of Globalization.* Cambridge: Cambridge University Press.

Kriesi, Hanspeter, Edgar Grande, et al. 2012. *Political Conflict in Western Europe.* Cambridge: Cambridge University Press.

Kweon, Yesola. 2018. 'Types of Labor Market Policy and the Electoral Behavior of Insecure Workers.' *Electoral Studies* 55, 1–10.

Laakso, Markku, and Rein Taagepera, 1979. 'Effective Number of Parties: A Measure with Application to West Europe.' *Comparative Political Studies* 12(1), 3–27.

Ladner, Matthew, and Christopher Wlezien. 2007. 'Partisan Preferences, Electoral Prospects, and Economic Expectations.' *Comparative Political Studies* 40(5), 571–96.

Laver, Michael J., and Ian Budge. 1992. 'Measuring Policy Distances and Modelling Coalition Formation.' In Ian Budge and Michael J. Laver, eds, *Party Policy and Government Coalitions*, 15–40. London: Palgrave Macmillan.

LeDuc, Lawrence, and Richard G. Niemi. 2014. 'Voting Behavior: Choice and Context.' In Lawrence LeDuc, Richard G. Niemi, and Pippa Norris, eds, *Comparing Democracies 4*, 133–49. London: Sage.

LeDuc, Lawrence, and Jon H. Pammett. 2013. 'The Fate of Governing Parties in Times of Crisis.' *Electoral Studies* 32, 494–9.

Leighley, J. E., and Nagler, J. 2013. *Who Votes Now? Demographics, Issues, Inequality, and Turnout in the United States.* Princeton: Princeton University Press.

Lenke, Falk, and Henning Schmidtke. 2017. 'Making Sense of the Great Recession: Responsibility Attributions in Tough Times.' In S. Schneider, H. Schmidtke, S. Haunss, and J. Gronau, eds, *Capitalism and its Legitimacy in Times of Crisis*, 95–121. London: Palgrave Macmillan.

Levitsky, Steven, and Daniel Ziblatt. 2018. *How Democracies Die*. New York: Crown.

Lewis-Beck, Michael S., and Marina Costa Lobo. 2017. 'The Economic Vote: Ordinary vs. Extraordinary Times.' In K. Arzheimer, J. Evans, and M.S. Lewis-Beck, eds, *The Sage Handbook of Electoral Behaviour*, 606–29. London: Sage.

Lewis-Beck, Michael S., Richard Nadeau, and Martial Foucault. 2013. 'The Compleat Economic Voter: New Theory and British Evidence.' *British Journal of Political Science* 43(2), 241–61.

Lijphart, Arend. 1979. 'Religious vs. Linguistic vs. Class Voting: The Crucial Experiment of Comparing Belgium, Canada, South Africa and Switzerland.' *American Political Science Review* 73(2), 442–58.

Lindvall, Johannes. 2014. 'The Electoral Consequences of Two Great Crises.' *European Journal of Political Research* 53(4), 747–65.

Lindvall, Johannes. 2017. 'Economic Downturns and Political Competition since the 1970s.' *Journal of Politics* 79(4), 1302–14.

Lipset, Seymour Martin, and Stein Rokkan. 1967. 'Cleavage Structures, Party Systems, and Voter Alignments.' In S. M. Lipset and S. Rokkan, eds, *Party systems and Voter Alignments: Cross-National Perspectives*, 1–67. New York: Free Press.

Lobo, Marina Costa, and Michael S. Lewis-Beck. 2012. 'The Integration Hypothesis: How the European Union Shapes Economic Voting.' *Electoral Studies* 31(3), 522–8.

Lübke, Christiane, and Marcel Erlinghagen. 2014. 'Self-Perceived Job Insecurity across Europe over Time: Does Changing Context Matter?' *Journal of European Social Policy* 24(4), 319–36.

Luxembourg Income Study. 2019. *LIS Inequality and Poverty Key Figures*. <https://www.lisdatacenter.org>, accessed July 2019.

Magalhães, Pedro. 2014. 'Introduction: Financial Crisis, Austerity and Electoral Politics.' *Journal of Elections, Public Opinion and Parties* 24(2), 125–33.

Mainwaring, Scott, Carlos Gervasoni, and Annabella España-Najera. 2017. 'Extra- and Within-System Electoral Volatility.' *Party Politics* 23(6), 623–35.

Mair, Peter. 2013. *Ruling the Void: The Hollowing of Western Democracy*. London: Verso.

Margalit, Yotam. 2013. 'Explaining Social Policy Preferences: Evidence from the Great Recession.' *American Political Science Review* 107(1), 80–103.

Margalit, Yotam. 2019. 'Political Responses to Economic Shocks.' *Annual Review of Political Science* 22, 277–95.

Marks, Gary, Liesbet Hooghe, and Carole J. Wilson. 2002. 'Does Left/Right Structure Party Positions on European Integration?' *Comparative Political Studies* 35(8), 965–89.

Marshall, John, and Stephen J. Fisher. 2015. 'Compensation or Constraint? How Different Dimensions of Economic Globalization Affect Government Spending and Electoral Turnout.' *British Journal of Political Science* 45(2), 353–89.

Martén, L. 2019. 'Demand for Redistribution: Individuals' Response to Economic Shocks.' *Scandinavian Journal of Economics* 121(1), 225–42.

Marx, Karl, and Friedrich Engels. 1848. *The Communist Manifesto*. Petersfield: Harriman House, 2010.

Mau, Steffen, Jam Mewes, and Nadine M. Schöneck. 2012. 'What Determines Subjective Socio-Economic Insecurity? Context and Class in Comparative Perspective.' *Socio-Economic Review* 10, 655–82.

Meyer, Thomas. 2013. *Constraints on Party Policy Change.* Colchester: ECPR Press.

Moene, Karl Ove, and Michael Wallerstein. 2001. 'Inequality, Social Insurance, and Redistribution.' *American Political Science Review* 95, 859–74.

Näswall, Katharina, and Hans De Witte. 2003. 'Who Feels Insecure in Europe? Predicting Job Insecurity from Background Variables.' *Economic and Industrial Democracy* 24(2), 189–215.

Naumann E., Buss C, Bähr J. 2015. 'How Unemployment Experience Affects Support for the Welfare State: A Real Panel Approach.' *European Sociological Review* 32, 81–92.

Nickell, S. 1981. 'Biases in Dynamic Models with Fixed Effects.' *Econometrica* 49, 1417–26.

Nieuwbeerta, Paul, and Wout Ultee. 1999. 'Class Voting in Western Industrialized Democracies, 1945–1990: Systematizing and Testing Explanations', *European Journal of Political Research* 35(1), 123–60.

Nölke, Andreas, and Arjan Vliegenthart, 2009. 'Enlarging the Varieties of Capitalism: The Emergence of Dependent Market Economies in East Central Europe.' *World Politics* 61(4), 670–702.

Norris, Pippa, and Ronald Inglehart. 2019. *Cultural Backlash: Trump, Brexit, and Authoritarian Populism.* New York: Cambridge University Press.

OECD. 2005. 'GDP and GNI.' *OECD Observer No. 246/247.* <http://oecdobserver.org/news/archivestory.php/aid/1507/GDP_and_GNI.html>.

OECD. 2013. 'Factbook Country Statistical Profiles: Household Income and Wealth, Households and NPISHs Debt.' <http://stats.oecd.org/index.aspx?queryid=39309>.

OECD. 2014. 'OECD Economic Surveys: Finland.' <http://www.oecd.org/eco/surveys/Overview_Finland_2014.pdf>.

OECD. 2016. 'Income Inequality Update.' Paris: OECD. <http://www.oecd.org/social/income-distribution-database.htm>.

OECD. 2017. 'Quarterly National Accounts, Gross Domestic Product Expenditure Approach: Per Head, US$, Constant Prices, Fixed PPPs.' <http://stats.oecd.org/index.aspx?queryid=66948>.

OECD. 2019. 'Public Social Spending is High in Many OECD Countries.' Paris: OECD. <http://www.oecd.org/social/expenditure.htm>.

Oesch, Daniel. 2006. *Redrawing the Class Map. Stratification and Institutions in Britain, Germany, Sweden and Switzerland.* Basingstoke: Palgrave Macmillan.

Oesch, Daniel. 2008. 'The Changing Shape of Class Voting: An Individual-Level Analysis of Party Support in Britain, Germany and Switzerland.' *European Societies* 10(3), 329–55.

Oesch, Daniel. 2012. 'The Class Basis of the Cleavage between the New Left and the Radical Right: An Analysis for Austria, Denmark, Norway and Switzerland.' In J. Rydren, ed., *Class Politics and the Radical Right*, 31–51. London: Routledge.

Oesch, Daniel. 2015. 'Occupational Structure and Labor Market Change in Western Europe since 1990.' In Pablo Beramendi et al., eds, *The Politics of Advanced Capitalism*, 112–32. New York: Cambridge University Press.

Offe, Claus. 2013. 'Participatory Inequality in the Austerity State: A Supply-Side Approach.' In Armin Schäfer and Wolfgang Streeck, eds, *Politics in the Age of Austerity*, 196–218. Cambridge: Polity Press.

Pardos-Prado, Sergi, and Carla Xena. 2019. 'Skill Specificity and Attitudes toward Immigration.' *American Journal of Political Science* 63(2), 286–304.

Pardos-Prado, Sergi, and Iñaki Sagarzazu. 2016. 'The Political Conditioning of Subjective Economic Evaluations: The Role of Party Discourse.' *British Journal of Political Science* 46(4), 799–823.

Pharr, Susan J., and Robert D. Putnam, eds. 2000. *Disaffected Democracies: What's Troubling the Trilateral Countries?* Princeton: Princeton University Press.

Pierson, Paul. 1994. *Dismantling the Welfare State?* Cambridge: Cambridge University Press.

Plümper, T., and V. Troeger. 2007. 'Efficient Estimation of Time-Invariant and Rarely Changing Variables in Panel Data Analysis with Unit Effects.' *Political Analysis* 15, 124–39.

Pontusson, Jonas, and Damien Raess. 2012. 'How (and Why) is This Time Different? The Politics of Economic Crisis in Western Europe and the US.' *Annual Review of Political Science* 15, 13–33.

Popkin, Samuel, and Michael Dimock. 1998. 'Political Knowledge and Citizen Competence.' In S. Elkin and K. Soltan, eds, *Citizen Competence and Democratic Institutions*, 117–46. Philadelphia, PA: University of Pennsylvania Press.

Powell, G. Bingham, and Guy D. Whitten. 1993. 'A Cross-National Analyses of Economic Voting: Taking Account of the Political Context.' *American Journal of Political Science* 37(2), 391–414.

Pozsar, Zoltan, Tobias Adrian, Adam Ashcraft, and Hayley Boesky. 2013. 'Shadow Banking.' *FRBNY Economic Policy Review* (1 Dec.). Federal Reserve Bank of New York.

Przeworski, Adam. 1985. *Capitalism and Social Democracy.* Cambridge: Cambridge University Press.

Radcliff, Benjamin 1992. 'The Welfare State, Turnout, and the Economy: A Comparative Analysis.' *American Political Science Review* 86(2), 444–54.

Rehm, Philipp. 2009. 'Risks and Redistribution: An Individual-Level Analysis.' *Comparative Political Studies* 42, 855–81.

Rehm, Philipp. 2016. *Risk Inequality and Welfare States: Social Policy Preferences, Development, and Dynamics.* New York: Cambridge University Press.

Rehm, Philipp, Jacob S. Hacker, and Mark Schlesinger. 2012. 'Insecure Alliances: Risk, Inequality, and Support for the Welfare State.' *American Political Science Review* 106(2), 386–406.

Reinhart, Carmen M., and Kenneth S. Rogoff. 2009. *This Time is Different: Eight Centuries of Financial Folly.* Princeton: Princeton University Press.

Reinhart, Carmen M., and Kenneth S. Rogoff. 2010. 'Growth in a Time of Debt.' NBER Working Paper No. 15639. <https://www.nber.org/papers/w15639.pdf>.

Rokkan, S. 1999. *State Formation, Nation-Building and Mass Politics in Europe.* Oxford: Oxford University Press.

Rommel, Tobias, and Stefanie Walter. 2018. 'The Electoral Consequences of Offshoring: How the Globalization of Production Shapes Party Preferences in Multi-Party Systems.' *Comparative Political Studies* 51(5), 621–58.

Ronald, Richard, Christian Lennartz, and Justin Kadi. 2017. 'What Ever Happened to Asset-Based Welfare? Shifting Approaches to Housing Wealth and Welfare Security.' *Policy and Politics* 45(2), 173–93.

Rovny, Allison E., and Jan Rovny. 2017. 'Outsiders at the Ballot Box: Operationalizations and Political Consequences of the Insider-Outsider Dualism.' *Socio-Economic Review* 15(1), 161–85.

Rudel, Thomas K., and Linda Hooper. 2005. 'Is the Pace of Social Change Accelerating? Latecomers, Common Languages, and Rapid Historical Declines in Fertility.' *International Journal of Comparative Sociology* 46(4), 275–96.

Rueda, David. 2007. *Social Democracy Inside Out: Partisanship, and Labor Market Policy in Industrialized Democracies*. Oxford: Oxford University Press.

Ruggie, John Gerald. 1982. 'International Regimes, Transactions, and Change: Embedded Liberalism in the Postwar Economic Order.' *International Organization* 36(2), 379–415.

Sanders, David, and Gabor Tóka. 2013. 'Is Anyone Listening? Mass and Elite Opinion Cueing in the EU.' *Electoral Studies* 32(1), 13–25.

Schäfer, Armin, and Wolfgang Streeck. 2013. *Politics in the Age of Austerity*. London: Polity Press.

Scheve, Kenneth, and Matthew J. Slaughter. 2004. 'Economic Insecurity and the Globalization of Production.' *American Journal of Political Science* 48(4), 662–74.

Schmidt, Vivien A. 2016. 'Varieties of Capitalism: A Distinct French Model?' In Robert Elgie, Amy Mazur, Emiliano Grossmanan, and Andrew Appleton, eds, *Oxford Handbook of French Politics*, 607–35. Oxford: Oxford University Press.

Schneider, Ben Ross. 2009. 'Hierarchical Market Economies and Varieties of Capitalism in Latin America.' *Journal of Latin American Studies* 41(3), 553–75.

Schumpeter, Joseph A. 1994 [1942]. *Capitalism, Socialism and Democracy*. London: Routledge.

Schwartz, Herman, and Leonard Seabrooke. 2008. 'Varieties of Residential Capitalism in the International Political Economy: Old Welfare States and the New Politics of Housing.' *Comparative European Politics* 6, 237–61.

Seki, Katsunori, and Laron K. Williams. 2014. 'Updating the Party Government Dataset.' *Electoral Studies* (June), 270–9.

Singer, Matthew M. 2013. 'The Global Economic Crisis and Domestic Political Agendas.' *Electoral Studies* 32(3), 404–10.

Social Security Administration. 2016a. *Social Security Programs throughout the World: Europe 2016*. Washington, DC: Social Security Administration.

Social Security Administration. 2016b. *Social Security Programs throughout the World: Asia and the Pacific 2016*. Washington, DC: Social Security Administration.

Social Security Administration. 2017. *Social Security Programs throughout the World: The Americas 2017*. Washington, DC: Social Security Administration.

Solt, Frederick. 2008. 'Economic Inequality and Democratic Political Engagement.' *American Journal of Political Science* 52(1), 48–60.

Solt, Frederick. 2016. 'The Standardized World Income Inequality Database.' *Social Science Quarterly* 97(5), 1267–81. SWIID Version 6.2, March 2018 (2018-03-23).

Solt, Frederick. 2019. 'Measuring Income Inequality across Countries and Over Time: The Standardized World Income Inequality Database.' SWIID Version 8.1, May 2019.

Soroka, Stuart, and Christopher Wlezien. 2010. *Degrees of Democracy: Politics, Public Opinion, and Policy*. New York: Cambridge University Press.

Spoon, Jae-Jae, and Heike Klüver. Forthcoming. 'Party Convergence and Vote Switching: Explaining Mainstream Party Decline across Europe.' *European Journal of Political Research.*

Steiner, Nils D. 2010. 'Economic Globalization and Voter Turnout in Established Democracies.' *Electoral Studies* 29, 444–59.

Steiner, Nils D., and Christian W. Martin. 2012. 'Economic Integration, Party Polarisation and Electoral Turnout.' *West European Politics* 5(2), 238–65.

Stevenson, Randolph T. 2001. 'The Economy and Policy Mood: A Fundamental Dynamic of Democratic Politics?' *American Journal of Political Science* 45(3), 620–33.

Stock, J. H., and M. W. Watson. 2003. 'Has the Business Cycle Changed and Why?' *NBER Macroeconomics Annual* 17, 159–230.

Stockemer, D., and L. Scruggs. 2012. 'Income Inequality, Development and Electoral Turnout: New Evidence on a Burgeoning Debate.' *Electoral Studies* 31, 764–73.

Streeck, Wolfgang. 2014. *Buying Time: The Delayed Crisis of Democratic Capitalism.* London: Verso Books.

Summers, P. M. 2005. 'What Caused the Great Moderation? Some Cross-Country Evidence.' *Federal Reserve Bank of Kansas City Economic Review* 3, 5–32.

Swank, Duane. 2002. *Global Capital, Political Institutions, and Policy Change in Developed Welfare States.* New York: Cambridge University Press.

Talving, Liisa. 2017. 'The Electoral Consequences of Austerity: Economic Policy Voting in Europe in Times of Crisis.' *West European Politics* 40(3), 560–83.

Talving, Liisa. 2018. 'Economic Voting in Europe: Did the Crisis Matter?' *Comparative European Politics* 16, 695–723.

Tavits, Margit, and Joshua D. Potter. 2015. 'The Effect of Inequality and Social Identity on Party Strategies.' *American Journal of Political Science* 59(3), 744–58.

Thomas, Kathrin. 2016. 'Democratic Support and Globalization.' In Jack Vowles and Georgios Xezonakis, eds, *Globalisation and Domestic Politics*, 209–34. Oxford, Oxford University Press.

Thomassen, Jacques, ed. 2014. *Elections and Democracy: Representation and Accountability.* Oxford: Oxford University Press.

Tilley, James, and Sara B. Hobolt. 2011. 'Is the Government to Blame? An Experimental Test of How Partisanship Shapes Perceptions of Performance and Responsibility.' *Journal of Politics* 73(2), 316–30.

Tillman, Erik R. 2016. 'Has the Global Financial Crisis Changed Citizen Behaviour? A Four Country Study.' In Jack Vowles and Georgios Xezonakis, eds, *Globalisation and Domestic Politics*, 113–32. Oxford, Oxford University Press.

Tooze, Adam. 2018. *Crashed: How a Decade of Financial Crises Changed the World.* London: Viking.

Traber, Denise, Nathalie Giger, and Silja Häusermann. 2018. 'How Economic Crises Affect Political Representation: Declining Party-Voter Congruence in Times of Constrained Government.' *West European Politics* 41(5), 1100–24.

Verba, S., K. L. Schlozman, and H. Brady. 1995. *Voice and Equality: Civic Voluntarism in American Politics.* Cambridge, MA: Harvard University Press.

Volkens, Andrea, Werner Krause, Pola Lehmann, Theres Matthieß, Nicolas Merz, Sven Regel, and Bernhard Weßels. 2019. *The Manifesto Data Collection. Manifesto Project (MRG/CMP/MARPOR)*. Berlin: Wissenschaftszentrum Berlin für Sozialforschung (WZB). https://doi.org/10.25522/manifesto.mpds.2019b

Vowles, Jack. 2016. 'Globalization, Government Debt, Government Agency, and Political Efficacy: A Cross-National Comparison.' In Jack Vowles and Georgios Xezonakis, eds, *Globalization and Domestic Politics: Parties, Public Opinion, and Elections*, 155–71. Oxford: Oxford University Press.

Vowles, Jack. 2018. 'The Big Picture: Turnout at the Macro-Level.' In J. Fisher, M. Cantijoch, E. Fieldhouse, M. Franklin, R. Gibson, and C. Wlezien, eds, *The Routledge Handbook of Elections, Voting Behavior and Public Opinion*, 57–68. Oxford: Routledge.

Vowles, Jack, and Georgios Xezonakis, eds. 2016. *Globalisation and Domestic Politics: Parties, Public Opinion, and Elections*. Oxford: Oxford University Press.

Walker, Carl. 2011. 'Personal Debt, Cognitive Delinquency and Techniques of Governmentality: Neoliberal Constructions of Financial Inadequacy in the UK.' *Journal of Community and Applied Psychology* 22(6), 533–8.

Walter, Stefanie. 2010. 'Globalization and the Welfare State: Testing the Microfoundations of the Compensation Hypothesis.' *International Studies Quarterly* 54(2), 403–26.

Walter, Stefanie. 2017. 'Globalization and the Demand-Side of Politics: How Globalization Shapes Labor Market Risk Perceptions and Policy Preferences.' *Political Science Research and Methods* 5(1), 55–80.

Wenzelburger, Georg. 2011. 'Political Strategies and Fiscal Retrenchment: Evidence from Four Countries.' *West European Politics* 34(6): 1151–84.

Wiggan, Jay. 2012. 'Telling Stories of 21st Century Welfare: The UK Coalition Government and the Neo-Liberal Discourse of Worklessness and Dependency.' *Critical Social Policy* 32(3), 383–405.

Wike, Richard, Laura Silver, and Alexandra Castillo. 2019. *Many across the Globe are Dissatisfied with how Democracy is Working*. Washington, DC: Pew Research Center.

Williamson, John. 1990. 'What Washington Means by Policy Reform', in J. Williamson, ed., *Latin American Adjustment: How Much has Happened?*, 7–20. Washington, DC: Institute for International Economics.

Wlezien, Christopher, Mark Franklin, and Daniel Twiggs. 1997. 'Economic Perceptions and Vote Choice: Disentangling the Endogeneity.' *Political Behavior* 19(1), 7–17.

World Bank. 2018a. 'Health Expenditure, Public, (% of GDP).' <https://data.worldbank.org/indicator/SH.XPD.PUBL.ZS> (accessed Apr. 2018).

World Bank. 2018b. 'Unemployment, Total (% Of Total Labor Force).' <https://data.worldbank.org/indicator/SL.UEM.TOTL.NE.ZS> (accessed Apr. 2018).

Zaller, John R. 1992. *The Nature and Origins of Mass Opinion*. Cambridge: Cambridge University Press.

Index